THE WIGAN BRANCH RAILWAY

By
Dennis Sweeney

TRIANGLE
PUBLISHING

Copyright © D.J.Sweeney 2008
First published 2008 by Triangle Publishing.
British Library Cataloguing in Publication Data.
Sweeney D.J.
The Wigan Branch Railway.
ISBN 978 0 9550030 35
Printed in Great Britain by The Amadeus Press Ltd, Cleckheaton.
Artwork by Alan Palmer.
Written, compiled and edited by D.J.Sweeney.
Cover design by Scene, Print & Design Ltd, Leigh.
Designed and Published by
Triangle Publishing,
509, Wigan Road,
Leigh, Lancs.
WN7 5HN.
Tel. 01942/677919. www.trianglepublishing.co.uk

All rights reserved. No part of this publication may be reproduced in any shape or form or by any means electrical, digital, mechanical, photographic, photocopied or stored in any retrieval system without prior written permission of the Author and/or Triangle Publishing.

Cover Photo: The former Wigan Branch Railway metals still, occasionally, play host to the steam locomotive. On 29th August 2005, ex-LMS 4-6-2 'Pacific' No.6201 *Princess Elizabeth*, approaches Golborne Junction on the Up Slow with a return charter from Blackpool.
Author.

CONTENTS

	Page
Introduction	4
Acknowledgements	5

CHAPTER I

The Wigan Branch Railway	7
Parkside	8
Golborne Junction	27
Golborne Station	37
Bamfurlong	61
Springs Branch Junctions	75
Wigan, Chapel Lane	91
Wigan North Western	93

CHAPTER II

The New Springs Branch	125
Central Wagon Company and Thompson's Yard	140
Kirkless	151
Springs Branch Sheds	162

CHAPTER III

The Platt Bridge Junction Railway and The Bamfurlong Junctions Railway	187
Bibilography & Abbreviations	200

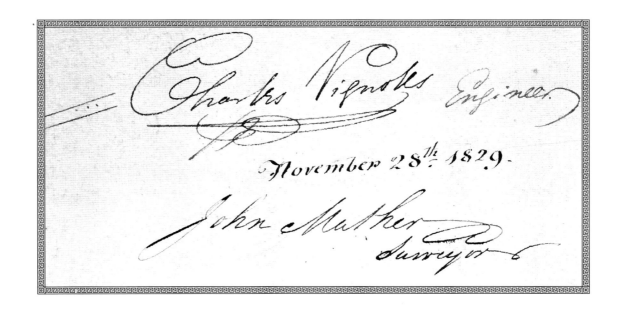

INTRODUCTION

At the ripe old age of almost 92, my Grandfather had died in 1967 with, it is pleasing to say, his faculties intact. When I considered the changes that he had seen in his lifetime I began to wonder if anyone, other than his generation, would experience such a profound transformation, in all walks of life, ever again!

At the time of his birth, the railways were still in the ascendancy and the industrial revolution in full swing. Man had yet to take the first faltering wings toward controlled flight; the age of the internal combustion engine had still to make its impact and the Union Flag of Empire covered the globe. Britain's influence, both militarily and commercial was unsurpassed, supported by a Navy that ruled the waves. Telephonic communications arrived in the nineteenth century, of which the railways were quick to utilise, to be greatly expanded upon in the twentieth.

The bloody conflict of World War I, in which so many young men from the four corners of the globe suffered a merciless slaughter, shook the very foundations of society and social order, the repercussions of which are still with us today. Advances in medicine, economic upheaval and social changes were punctuated by a second World conflict, followed by orbiting satellites, manned space flight and the gradual decline of Britain as a major power.

Yet, much of what was familiar to my Grandfather as, say a young man in his twenties or thirties, was still in evidence when I was a schoolboy. After W.W.II the rebuilding of Britain, allied with the motorway construction of later years, had still to be implemented in a period of Post-War austerity that continued for some years after the cessation of hostilities in 1945.

Since the 1960s however, we have seen a downward spiral in the industrial manufacturing base of Great Britain, another transport revolution which is still being implemented despite the evils of pollution and chronic congestion, and a decline in the moral and social convictions of the population as a whole.

We are, today, better clothed, better fed, all the education we could want and endowed with a health service (for all its faults) that my Grandfather could only have dreamed of in his youth when the infant mortality rate brought grief to almost every household. He would be amazed at some of today's technology; he would also be appalled at some aspects of today's society.

I mention these things because it is all a far cry from 1875, when the social structure had hardly changed in centuries and the daily burden of toil for the working classes could break the hardest of men.

Hardly changed that is, except in the field of transport, for although the arrival of the canals in the eighteenth century offered the industrialist the means of increased payloads, the drawback being that it was still a comparatively slow mode of transport and at times subject to climatic extremes.

The railways were to change all that. Whilst the initial impetus for construction of the railways was at the behest of industry, the railway companies were quick to realise that the opportunity of providing accommodation for the lower orders of society was a means of increasing their profits. There were of course vociferous critics of this policy, the landed gentry frowned upon the very idea of encouraging their subordinates to travel.

By 1832, Manchester, Liverpool, Warrington, Bolton and Wigan were all connected by mainline, public railways. Nowhere on the globe at such an early stage in the development of railways could this be equalled, let alone surpassed and in this area of the North-West, an important base of England's economic expansion, industry quickly grew to meet the demands and challenges that commerce required.

Nowhere is this more apparent than Wigan, often the butt of music hall comedians and vividly portrayed in all its work-a-day grime in George Orwell's *The Road to Wigan Pier*.

Wigan bestrode rich seams of coal, often at shallow depth, its 'Cannel Coal' prized for the manufacture of coke and gas. Every industry in the land needed coal or its by-products and the manifestation of this demand was a proliferation in mining activity.

Many of the mines were on a small scale employing fewer than twenty miners whilst others were much larger concerns. Mining activity itself fuelled the founding and expansion of industry within the area; iron works, blast furnaces, rolling mills, wagon works, engineering and factorys. The list is almost endless, all eager to set up their works close to a ready supply of coal and, if possible, railway connections.

All this went hand in hand with the expansion of the railways and Ince, to the South-East of Wigan, was a maize of industrial and mainline railways, each criss-crossing the other. Per square acre, Ince probably had more railway than any comparable parish in the country.

Little of this now remains. The mines have long since gone from Wigan and much of the heavy engineering industry associated with it. The railways suffered the same fate and even the Springs Branch, from its junction with the main line, now extends for little more than 100 yards.

One can, however, with a mite of diligence, trace where once railway and industrial activity took place and in doing so obtain an insight into the way our Grandfathers and their Fathers toiled in another age.

Within the text, the operating Railway Company is given during the date as and when referred to, given in past tense, or a more general term as in 'Wigan branch' or West Coast Mail Line (WCML) etc.

Likewise the colliery or other industrial companies are similarly quoted as in some instances many changes of ownership occurred, often having similar names as in Richard Evans & Sons or Turner & Evans, or The Ince Hall Coal Company or similar.

Also, certain informative facts are repeated at the appropriate place within the text as an aid to the reader and I hope I have succeeded in relating these facts in a fashion making it easily readable.

All scales and dimensions are given in Imperial Measure.

Dennis Sweeney,
Leigh,
2008.

ACKNOWLEDGEMENTS

Once again I am indebted to former Signalman Bill Paxford's extensive knowledge of signalling matters recounted from his experiences with the London Midland & Scottish Railway and British Railways at the various locations covered in these volumes.

Peter Hampson and Tony Oldfield have provided valuable information relating to early signalling installations, gained from innumerable visits to the Public Records Office at Kew.

Former railwayman Jim Carter has provided photographs that few can equal in quality. Eddie Bellass, Dr J.G. Blears, John Sloane, Alan Hart, Gerry Bent, Ian Isherwood, Tom Sutch and G. Mellor have also provided important contributions.

On a note of personal sadness I must pay tribute to my dear friend W.D.Cooper, late of Garstang, Lancashire, who passed away in December 1998. Those of you who have read my previous publications *A Lancashire Triangle Parts One & Two* will know that Wilfred provided many illustrations for inclusion and his enthusiasm to help with this present work was equally forthcoming. He was a railway enthusiast right to the very end and his efforts through the camera lens have left us with some splendid visions of the steam railway and its environment from the 1930s right up to the passing of steam workings on British Railways in 1968.

Alan Palmer, whose skills as a Commercial Artist have been seen in the artwork for Triangle Publications over the years, regrettably passed away earlier this year. He was also a fine modelmaker, having a passion for local buses. It is hoped his scratch-built collection will be on display at the Manchester Museum of Transport to which it has been donated.

I must also pay tribute to the late Harry Townley who provided information relating to the early activities of various mining companies, their colliery railways and their arrangements with the London & North Western Railway and its former constituent companies covered in this volume. Harry, together with his associates, Jim Peden, Frank Smith and Alex Appleton, researched and produced a number of works covering the industrial railways of the Wigan, Manchester, St. Helens and Widnes coalfields and their work is unlikely ever to be surpassed.

Due thanks are accorded to Alan Davies, formerly at Leigh Archives, who has searched out the relevant Ordnance Survey data, and to staff at Preston Records Office whose help is greatly appreciated.

John Hall, formerly of Wigan, who now resides in Canada, has provided much useful information from the *Railway and Travel Monthly* editions of the early twentieth century. I express my sincere thanks to these and to all contributors who have provided material for inclusion.

Finally, I must thank Brian Kaye for his dedication and enthusiasm in compiling the Train Movement Tables.

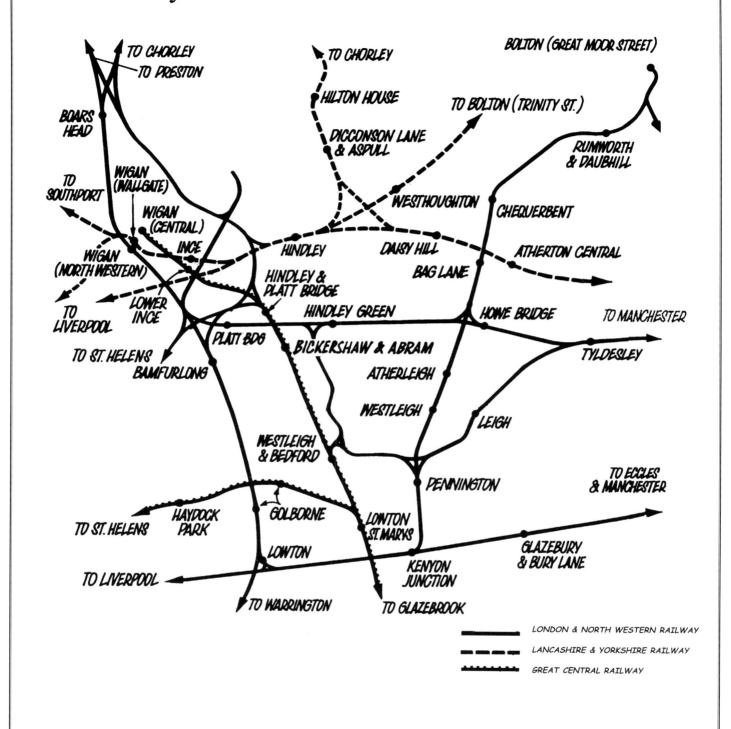

I. THE WIGAN BRANCH RAILWAY

Plate 1. With the gasworks and Wigan No.1 ARP box in the background, 'Britannia' Class No.70004 *William Shakespeare* departs the environs of Wigan North Western in 1965 with an express parcels train for Crewe.   *Alex Mann.*

PARKSIDE

Parkside was one of the original stations on the Liverpool & Manchester Railway, and also the scene of a fatal accident on opening day, 15th September 1830, when William Huskisson M.P., an ardent supporter of the Liverpool & Manchester Railway's Bill during its difficult passage through parliament, was run over by George Stephenson's celebrated locomotive *Rocket*. A memorial was erected at the site giving testimony to the fact and, in 2001 after years of neglect, was restored to something like its former glory. Witnesses to this unfortunate incident were a number of Wigan Branch Railway Board Members who were amongst those assembled in a temporary viewing stand.

The Wigan Branch Railway, for which preliminary surveys had been completed in 1829, was to meet with the Liverpool & Manchester Railway at Parkside. Promoted by a number of Wigan coal proprietors, one of whom, Ralph Thickness became its first Chairman, the Wigan Branch Railway was eventually to become an integral part of the West Coast Main Line (WCML) to Scotland.

The Wigan Branch Railway Bill was read for the third and final time in the House of Commons on 6th May 1830, receiving Royal Assent on 29th May 1830, as did Bills for The St. Helens & Runcorn Gap Railway and The Warrington & Newton Railway's Winwick branch.

The first meeting of the Wigan Directors occurred on 16th June 1830 at the *Eagle & Child* public house, Wigan. A second meeting at the *Horse & Jockey*, Newton, was followed up by a meeting at Liverpool on 21st July. Thereafter it was decided to meet once every month. Principal amongst their concerns were the invitations to tender for construction of the railway.

Charles Blacker Vignoles was appointed engineer on the Wigan Branch Railway at a salary of £500 per year in June 1830. He would already have had a familiarity with the area having guided the Liverpool & Manchester Railway Bill through parliament at its second attempt. Contractors for the Wigan branch were Pritchard & Hoof who were also awarded a two year contract for maintenance of the 6.9 mile route from Parkside East Junction, to Wigan, Chapel Lane.

Authorised capital was £70,000 in shares of £100 with a further £17,500 permitted in borrowing powers but all moneys had to be raised before construction could begin.

Provision was also made within the Act for a junction at Springs Branch which included north and south facing curves with the branch itself continuing to New Springs, North-East of Wigan, to serve a number of collieries in the area. In the event, none of these works were constructed as the Company found itself short of funds. The Springs Branch was eventually constructed, together with the south curve only, under the auspices of the North Union Railway and not opened until 31st October 1838, concomitantly with the opening of the North Union's Wigan to Preston line.

The Wigan Branch Railway Act also contained plans for a west facing curve at Parkside and, a connection with a proposed branch, some 1½ miles long, of the Warrington & Newton Railway from, or near to, the present Winwick Junction. The latter branch had been surveyed by Robert Stephenson who gave an estimate of £7,008 for its construction. The 1829 line plan for the Wigan Branch Railway seems to indicate that this proposed branch would intersect with the Liverpool & Manchester by a flat crossing between east and west junctions.

At this period the Warrington & Newton Railway was under construction and would meet the Liverpool & Manchester Railway at Earlestown by a west facing junction.

To this end, in October 1830, the Directors of the Wigan Branch Railway appointed representatives to confer with their Warrington & Newton counterparts regarding the arrangements for a junction between the two railways and negotiations were to continue on and off for some twelve months. However, there does not seem to have been a rush to acquire Wigan Branch shares for, in November of 1830, unappropriated shares to the value of £8,200 were offered to existing holders on a pro-rata basis and, strangely, the borrowing powers obtained within the Wigan Branch Act were never utilised.

In the event, therefore, both the Warrington & Newton, and Wigan Branch Railway Companies found themselves short of funds and the branch from Winwick, Parkside West curve, and the Springs Branch, were not proceeded with. The financial shortcomings of these two railway concerns were to have long lasting repercussions for railway travellers particularly on the north-south axis.

In January of 1831, the Directors of the Wigan Branch met only once and decided to oppose the construction of the Liverpool and Leeds Railway which would have bridged over the Wigan line in the vicinity of Westwood. This was often referred to as the 'North Line of Railway'

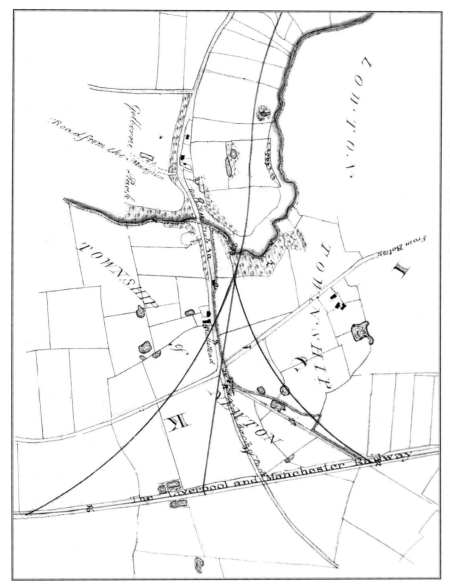

Fig 1. The line plan of the Wigan Branch Railway c1829 shows the arrangement of junctions as originally proposed. This differs considerably from the railway as built at this location. Not only were the west curve and flat crossing for the proposed connection with the Warrington & Newton Railway not built, it will be noted in comparison with the first series Ordnance Survey of 1845/7 *(see page 14)* that Lowton Junction was envisaged further north beyond Southworth Road and the alignment of railway beyond was built much closer to Golborne Dale Road.

and met opposition from many quarters, including the Liverpool & Manchester Railway, whose Directors objected on the grounds that their own railway, at this point only some four months in operation, had yet to establish itself and competition of another route from Liverpool was not needed at this stage. The fact remains, however, that income from the inter-city precursor for both passengers and goods exceeded all predictions and the Liverpool & Manchester Railway were doing very nicely thank you.

The 'North Line of Railway' would have taken a similar course to the later Lancashire & Yorkshire's Pendleton-Atherton-Crow Nest-Wigan route in an area which would see many railway proposals in the following 15-20 years most of which would come to nought.

Again in February 1831, the Wigan Branch Board met only once. Principal amongst their concerns was the fact that the engineer, Vignoles, had been approached by the Liverpool and Leeds Railway to render his services. The Wigan Board were aghast at this "indignant" proposal and reminded Vignoles of his duty to the Wigan Company. In the event, the proposed Liverpool and Leeds Railway was abandoned and Vignoles' predicament became academic.

In the light of experiences encountered on the Liverpool & Manchester Railway, the Board of the Wigan Branch Railway had discussed the distance between running lines and had decided, finally, in April 1831, that the distance between the two tracks should not be less than 6ft. *The Railway Gazette* of 16th September 1838, was undoubtedly right in suggesting that here was the origin of the '6ft Way'.

On the Liverpool & Manchester Railway the 'Way' between the rails varied from 4ft to 4ft-8in. Widening was, apparently, done gradually over a period of years and, for example, in an accident at Huyton in 1874, it was noted that the tracks were 4ft-4in apart.

In the early years of the railways, carriages were often wider than the locomotives, some projecting almost 2ft into the way. The Duke of Wellington's carriage which featured in the accident at Parkside on 15th September 1830, is one such example, the open door of his carriage actually being hit by the on-coming Rocket. Small wonder that Huskisson met with an untimely death and a miracle that others were not so fated.

Press reports of June 1831 indicating that the Wigan branch was nearing completion were somewhat wide of the mark. At this period the Directors were considering the best means of connecting, at Wigan, with the proposed Wigan & Preston Railway authorised in April 1831, and debating contracts for the supply of engines and coaches.

In August 1831, the shareholders of the Wigan Branch Railway met at the *Clarendon Rooms,* Liverpool, and the Secretary of the Company was ordered to inform the contractors that "if more energy was not displayed in carrying out the works they would be called upon to face the consequences". At this same meeting it was decided that it would be in their best interests if closer ties were formed with the Preston & Wigan Railway so that the railway might extend to Preston. It was therefore resolved to deposit a Bill in Parliament for consolidation of the two companies under the Title of 'The North Union Railway.' It was also decided that the Wigan branch should be only a single line of rails and 3,000 rails purchased for the second line should be sold off at cost.

At the Annual General Meeting of the Wigan Branch Railway on 19th April 1832 the line was said to be "still under construction."

The following month, consideration was being given to the conveyance of passengers between Wigan and the Liverpool & Manchester Railway. The proposal at this juncture was that the Wigan Branch Railway should find the engines and coaches to convey passengers from Wigan to Newton Junction and that the Liverpool & Manchester should carry them the rest of the journey. Also, that passengers were to be booked through and the total receipts divided between both companys in proportion to the distance carried.

This was, however, not quite how events transpired. Newton Junction was the connecting point where the Warrington & Newton Railway met with the Liverpool & Manchester line on a west facing junction (an east facing curve was not opened until 1837) and the reversal of Manchester bound trains in addition to those operating solely on the Manchester-Liverpool run would have caused operational problems. Therefore Parkside was to be the terminus for trains to/from Wigan for the foreseeable future.

As an aside to this, passengers on the Bolton & Leigh route were, from 18th June 1832, booked through to Manchester at 2/6d first class & 2/- second. The Liverpool & Manchester recieved two-thirds and the Bolton & Leigh one-third. The Liverpool & Manchester to convey passengers to/from Newton Junction and the Bolton & Leigh from Newton to Bolton and vice-versa.

However, just to add to the confusion at this early period of operations, the above arrangement was rescinded during the winter months, Bolton & Leigh Railway passengers having to change at Kenyon Junction.

Also in June 1832 the Wigan Branch Railway had requested the loan of six coaches from the Liverpool & Manchester which was agreed to. The former's junction at Parkside was now "being completed" but they were instructed by the Liverpool & Manchester to employ a "pointsman" at Parkside who would be held responsible for any accident connected with their workings. It had been proposed that in anticipation of the opening, special trains would be run from Wigan to Newton Races. How these trains would have traversed Parkside Junction is not made clear but in the event the plan was cancelled as it was thought "unwise" to proceed without completion of the "contract". This, presumably, refers to their contractors, Pritchard & Hoof.

By July it was said "The railway was now about to be opened for traffic". It had been anticipated that 1,000 passengers and 8,000 tons of goods per week would be carried. However, no mention was made of coal traffic, the reason given that it would cost £5/6,000 to make a connection with the collieries (a reference mainly, but not exclusively, to the Springs Branch) and the Directors did not see their way to find the money. It was envisaged that it would require only a "small engine" (of the *Rocket* type) and one or two coaches to run between Wigan and Parkside, passengers travelling onward in Liverpool & Manchester trains.

Finally, in August 1832, after further approaches from the Wigan Branch Railway, the Liverpool & Manchester Railway accepted a working agreement to provide locomotives and stock for passenger services to Wigan. As to goods, the Liverpool & Manchester Railway were to provide wagons and engines for services to Wigan from Liverpool and Manchester and to convey said goods at 5 shillings per ton. The Liverpool & Manchester Railway were to provide porters to *turn* the coaches at Parkside and the Wigan Branch Railway to provide the "establishment" at Wigan, a guard for each train, book all passengers and collect all moneys for passengers and goods. The receipts were apportioned two-thirds for the Liverpool & Manchester and one-third for the Wigan Company who seemed to be doing an awful lot for their one-third! A fare of 5/- was fixed for 1st class passengers travelling from Wigan to Manchester or Liverpool and 3/6d second class. The date for opening of the railway was fixed as 3rd September 1832.

Pressure was immediately applied by the coal proprietors to provide for the haulage of coal. The Wigan Branch Railway grudgingly conceded, indicating it might be conveyed from Wigan to Liverpool as "back loading" at 3/6d per ton.

However, this did not prevent colliery owners running their own trains on the Wigan branch as in the case of Richard Evans & Co. at Edge Green, more of which later, or Thomas Legh, who already had an agreement with the Liverpool & Manchester dating from August 1831 at 1d per ton mile for coal and 1½d for coke, to run his own coal trains from Haydock Collieries to Edge Hill, Liverpool, and to Liverpool Road, Manchester, providing he used his own locomotives and wagons.

Some two months later Thomas Legh approached the Liverpool & Manchester Board with a view to the purchase of *Rocket* but as they were themselves acutely short of engines this was declined.

On the Liverpool & Manchester Railway, Parkside and Eccles were the only places where locomotives could be fuelled and watered en-route, a practice in evidence from the very beginning of the line. The aforementioned Thomas Legh was not only a coal owner of collieries at Haydock and Edge Green but also M.P. for Newton-Le-Willows and, a Director of the railway. He had suggested that the watering place for locomotives should be at Newton Bridge station rather than Parkside, the former being "more convenient for passengers" and, perhaps, also for him. This idea was not taken up and Parkside continued to be the mid-point servicing station along the railway, and the interchange for Wigan services.

The Liverpool & Manchester Railway are said to have opened a one-road shed at Parkside in 1831 which, after closure was used as an outbuilding for the gas house.

The Wigan Branch Railway opened in its entirety on 3rd September 1832, and by so doing completed a remarkable phase in the establishment of railway connections between the major industrial centres of the North-West. At this early stage in the evolution of rail transport, all its major industrial towns - Liverpool, Manchester, Bolton, Warrington, St Helens and now Wigan, were the recipients of public mainline railways. The 'Railway Age' really had arrived.

Average journey time along the Wigan route with an engine of the "oldest" construction hauling four coaches was 15 minutes and, comments *The Manchester Guardian*, "The country through which the line passes has been well selected both by obviating abrupt curves and expensive cuttings and embankments. Inconvenience and danger have been avoided by bridges, by which the railway crosses over or under any thoroughfare. These bridges are built with great taste and some exhibit fine specimens of 'skew' on crossing in a very oblique line. Two iron bridges which cross the Leeds & Liverpool, and Manchester canals (at Wigan, and Bamfurlong) are fine specimens of perfection to which the art has been brought."

The line was constructed as single track with three passing loops per mile, but the trackbed made wide enough for double track. The rails were 'T' section at 45lbs per ft, in 15ft lengths, set on Parbold stone blocks 25in x 25in x 1ft thick, and chairs, which, said *The Manchester Guardian*, "to be heavier than those used on the Liverpool & Manchester Railway," and, "the line passes through country intersected by roads, rivers and canals and yet only in one instance does it cross any road on the level" (Golborne Gates). Cost of construction of the single track railway was put at £84,000.

In the following month, October, the Wigan Branch Railway announced it would now consider goods for transit and that a "glass coach" was arranged to run from Parkside to Newton Junction to meet the first class trains from Liverpool and Manchester in the morning. Arrangements were also made with a number of Preston stage-coach operators whereby passengers were collected at Preston and taken to Wigan for rail connections via Parkside to Liverpool and Manchester.

Construction of a goods warehouse was commenced at Wigan in October 1832. The coal owners along the route were asked to guarrantee either a minimum payment or a quota of traffic and in return the Wigan Directors were willing to make provision for transit.

By 1837 there were five tracks at Parkside - Up and Down Liverpool & Manchester lines, Up and Down Wigan lines (for by now the Wigan branch had been doubled in readiness for the opening of the Wigan - Preston line) plus an additional stub end siding between the Manchester and Wigan lines. The latter, that as was used for the engine shed but at what period it ceased to be used as such is not known.

On 31st October 1838, a new station was opened at Parkside, nearer East Junction, and east of the original station. This was constructed jointly by the Liverpool & Manchester, North Union, and Grand Junction Railways. Previously, on the 21st, as a precursor to the opening of North Union's route from Wigan to Preston, also on the 31st., a 'Directors Special' had run from Parkside to Preston, a distance of $22^{1/2}$ miles in 45 minutes hauled by 'Bury' type 2-2-0 locomotive No.2. Included in the party were Hardman Earl, after who the town of Earlestown was named, and T.W.Rathbone. The former station near Huskissons memorial became a 'Goods Station'.

The new station building at Parkside, nearer the junction for Wigan, was set at a distance of 9ft-10in from the inner rail with a paved 'platform' area 7ft wide leaving a distance of 2ft-10in to the rail. The two storey building was some 76 ft in length and 18ft wide. On the ground floor was a booking office, a general waiting room, a ladies room and an office room. The upper floor was occupied by the 'book-keeper.' This station was eventually to close in 1878, although the buildings continued to be occupied as cottages until the early years of the twentieth century.

Through Warrington-Earlestown-Wigan journeys required a reversal or change of locomotive at Parkside, often leading to delays, a cause of much complaint by the travelling public. (nothing really changes does it !)

There is some doubt as to what method of passenger transfer was employed in the early days of the single track Wigan Branch Railway and if at all, trains from the branch actually ran into the either the first or the second Parkside stations on the Liverpool & Manchester side. This would have been a complicated and time consuming manoeuvre and it maybe that passengers actually detrained here and simply walked across to the Liverpool & Manchester side or vice-versa. It was reported in October 1832 that passengers going from Wigan to Liverpool or Manchester had to change at Parkside and wait there for a considerable time, "absolutely without shelter". The

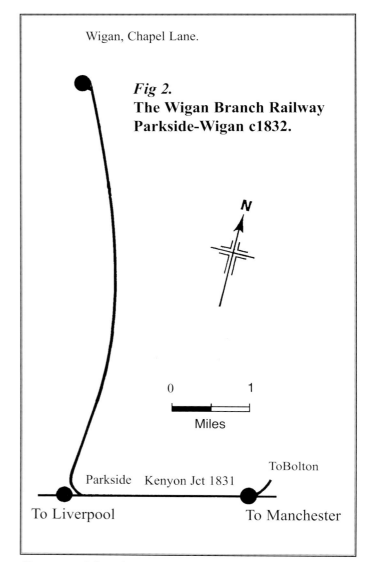

Fig 2.
The Wigan Branch Railway Parkside-Wigan c1832.

directors of the Liverpool & Manchester decided to build a "waiting shed", the Wigan Branch Railway contributing to the cost.

A comparison of the early views at this location as in **Plates 4 & 5,** would seem to give confirmation of this method of transfer. **Plate 4** is pre-1838 looking east and the engine stopped were Huskisson's Memorial now stands. In the later view westward by Tait from 1848, passengers are seen scurrying across the tracks with the new 1838 station on the left and the now double track Wigan branch on the right.

It seems likely that this usatisfactory arrangement continued for some years and it was not until 1847, when the London & North Western opened a west-facing curve onto the Liverpool & Manchester route, that some alleviation for passengers occured, albeit only for those travelling on a north-south axis.

An Act of 22nd April 1831, authorised the construction of the Preston & Wigan Railway of approx 15½ miles in length. On 8th August 1833, the Board of the Preston & Wigan Railway decided it would be to their advantage if they were to amalgamate with the Wigan Branch Railway. At a special General Meeting on 28th August 1833, the Directors of the Wigan Branch Railway agreed to the proposed merger with the Preston & Wigan Railway. The North Union Railway was therefore incorporated by Royal Assent on 22nd May 1834. This was the first merger between two Railway Companies to be sanctioned by a Parliamentary Act.

The first Chairman of the North Union Railway was Thomas Dalrymple Hesketh Bart, former Chairman of the Preston & Wigan Railway. Other prominent 'names' also elected to the North Union included T.W.Rathbone and Hardman Earle, who were also on both the Liverpool & Manchester, and Grand Junction Railway Boards.

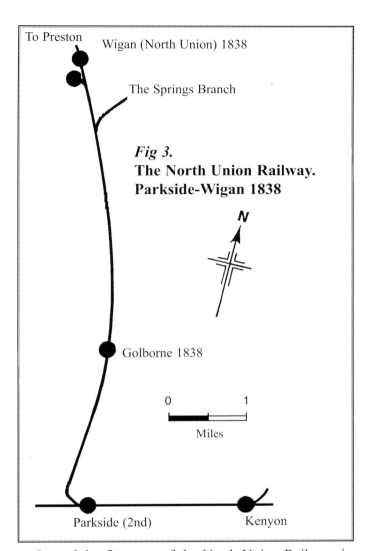

**Fig 3.
The North Union Railway.
Parkside-Wigan 1838**

Plate 2. Portrait, C.B.Vignoles. Vignoles had carried out the preliminary survey of the Wigan Branch Railway in 1829, and appointed as engineer for its construction in June 1830. The previous month he had undertaken the role as engineer for the projected St. Helens & Runcorn Gap Railway.

He is also credited with the invention of the flat bottom rail albeit in cast iron at the time which, in its steel form would ultimately become universal, although at this early period he was advocating longitudinal sleepers with tie bars between the rails to prevent spreading.

One of the first acts of the North Union Railway, in June 1834, was to appoint C.B.Vignoles as Engineer at a salary of £1,200, quite a hefty increase on his previous salary for the Wigan Branch Railway contract.

In September 1834 John Hargreaves, carrier, was offered the lease for freight services on the Wigan Branch Railway at £3,500 per year. Hargreaves and his son, also John, were established carriers from Bolton and already lessees for freight on the Bolton & Leigh Railway and the Bridgewater Canal amongst others. They had their fingers in many pies and were in prime position to take advantage of growing railway traffic. However, the approach was declined by Hargreaves who, in turn, offered to carry the goods on the line at revised terms as based on the previous years receipts, agreed to by the North Union. The contract for freight services was duly signed by John Hargreaves & John Hargreaves Jnr. However, as from July 1835, John Hargreaves Jnr.

became the sole lessee for freight services on the Wigan Branch Railway. The exception to this was the rights granted to various coal owners to run their own trains. Passenger traffic continued to be worked by the Liverpool & Manchester Railway as per the original agreement.

From 1835 there was a siding at Golborne - south of the later Golborne Junction - known as Bulls Head Coal Yard, first worked by Turner & Evans. It was still in operation prior to W.W.II, but seems to have closed in the late 1940s.

When the North Union's line to Preston had opened in 1838, some trains ran through to Manchester or Liverpool but these did not last long, maybe the problems of shunting across the lines at Parkside was far too cumbersome a procedure. In 1839, for example, the 7.30a.m. train from Manchester usually consisted of eight or ten coaches including two for Preston which "are left for the North Union at Parkside".

Also in 1838, the Grand Junction's London-Birmingham route had opened shortly before the Wigan-Preston line so it was now possible to travel the full 218 miles from London to Preston, but with the necessary reversal and delay at and Parkside, (as well as at Birmingham) it must often have been an endurance test. Although when compared to the journey by stage-coach from London to the North-West which took 2/3 days, the same journey would be accomplished in some 12 hours.

Through coaches between Preston and London were introduced on 19th August 1839, for 1st Class passengers only, at a fare of £2/14s/6d or £2/17s on the evening mail train. From Preston, departures were at 9.45a.m. and 6.27p.m., and from London at 8.45a.m. and 11.p.m. In total there were seven North Union southbound trains and six northbound on weekdays, all with connections at Parkside, and three each way on Sundays. The journey-time, Preston-Parkside was approximately one hour for 1st Class trains and 1¼ hours second class.

Whishaw quotes that in the first six months of operation some 68,587 passengers were carried over the North Union metals with reciepts of over £12,000. Some of these were carried by Liverpool & Manchester coaches but the North Union had been building up its coaching and locomotive stock and by the end of 1840 had twenty 1st class and fifteen second class coaches, plus horse boxes and other stock. Locomotives numbered thirteen, eleven being of 2-2-0 'Bury' type built by Haigh Foundry, Benjamin Hick of Bolton, and Jones, Turner & Evans. The other two engines were of 2-2-2 design and one of these, the *St. George* is also thought to have been built by the Haigh Foundry.

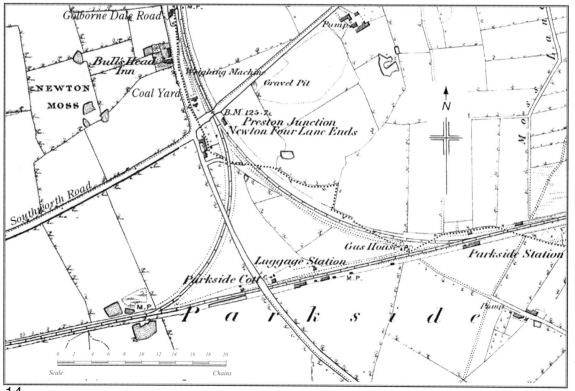

Fig 4. The first series Ordnance Survey compiled between 1845 and 1847 appeared in print in 1849. Parkside Junctions are therefore shown after the installation of Parkside West Junction built under the auspices of the London & North Western Railway. Preston Junction Station was to open here in 1849.

The original Parkside station has become a 'luggage station.' Note also the 'Gas House' chimney (this is sometimes referred to as a 'Pumphouse') clearly shown on the survey and also on Taits engraving, **Plate 5.**

A number of timed runs over the North Union are quoted in Whishaw's writings two of which are repeated here:-

Date, 1st August 1839, Parkside to Preston 22.25 miles. Engine No.5 plus three 1st class and two 2nd class carriages. Gross load = 54,012lbs. Seven stoppages:- Colborne (Golborne), Wigan, Standish, Cophall (Coppull), Euxton, Golden Hill (Leyland) and Farrington. Time, 66.5min, total stoppage time, 8.62min. Average speed = 23.05mph., Top speed on level plane 5 miles from Parkside (near the Springs Branch).

Date, 22nd November 1839, Preston to Parkside. Engine No.4 plus three 1st class carriages and one Post Office vehicle. Gross load = 46,380lbs. Time, 51.90 min., two stoppages 6.8min. Average speed = 29.26mph.

The Liverpool & Manchester, Bolton & Leigh, and Kenyon & Leigh Junction Railways had been absorbed by the Grand Junction Railway on 1st July 1845. On 1st January 1846, the North Union was leased jointly to the Grand Junction Railway and the Manchester & Leeds Railway, and on 16th July 1846, the London & North Western Railway was formed by the amalgamation of the Grand Junction, Manchester & Birmingham and London & Birmingham Railways. The Manchester & Leeds Railway became the Lancashire & Yorkshire Railway in July 1847 and from this date Parkside to Euxton Junction was worked by the London & North Western; Euxton Junction to Bolton by the Lancashire & Yorkshire and Euxton Junction to Preston jointly. However, it would not be until 7th August 1888 that the North Union Railway would cease to exist, being absorbed fully by the London & North Western and Lancashire & Yorkshire Railways on that date.

Eventually, a west facing curve was opened at Parkside in 1847, powers for which had been granted under an Act of 21st July 1845, obtained by the Grand Junction Railway.

This new curve, Parkside West Junction-Preston Junction, was a great boon to services allowing through

Plate 3. The Huskisson memorial was erected within a couple of years of his accident and is viewed here in 1965. The inscribed plaque was removed about the time of privatisation for restoration, completion of which occurred in 2001. The stonework of the memorial has been cleaned and restored to something like its former glory.   *J.A.Oldfield.*

Plate 4. One of a series of London & North Western postcards showing early railway scenes taken from the original artwork, depicts the scene at the first Parkside station in the early 1830s, with a Stephensonian type locomotive taking water. Note that there are water facilities for both directions. There is undoubtedly some degree of 'Artistic Licence' included in the view, as in the curve of the track, right background, which should be straight. Only beyond Parkside Lane bridge did it curve slightly, and not at all for some miles in the Manchester direction.
Author's Collection.

Plate 5. This contemporary view by Tait at Parkside c1848 is looking west with Parkside Lane overbridge in the background. Passengers gather under the canopy of the 1838 two-storey station building on the left to await their connection and there seems to be a general melee of bodies going from right to left, giving the impression of a recent train arrival from Wigan, Preston or beyond which has now gone forward (east) to Parkside Junction and on to Manchester or, has returned to Wigan. Is the building right of centre which clearly has a line running toward it the former engine shed ? Also of interest are the 'box' containers going westward, presumably carrying coal. The introduction of easily transferable loads from canal to rail/rail to ship was established very quickly on the Liverpool & Manchester Railway by means of "skeletal" wagons and movable "coal boxes".

In answering a query from Mr W. Hulton of Hulton Collieries regarding "what type of wagons would be suitable for the conveyance of coal on the Liverpool & Manchester Railway," the reply stated that "box wagons had to be used as those for the Manchester trade which have bottoms that would open to let out the coal to the stores underneath the railway". At Liverpool, he was informed "that boxes could be transferred to cart wheels according to the plan then in use at Bolton" (on the Bolton & Leigh Railway of which Wm. Hulton had been one of the principle promoters) but surely he would have known this!

It is of note that in November 1830 the familiar name of Messrs Pickford & Co. had offered £2.00 per trip for one wagon of "London goods," readily agreed to by the Liverpool & Manchester. The wagon had, apparently, a "movable body" which could be transferred to cart wheels at each end of the line.

north-south running, after which Parkside lost much of its importance as an 'interchange' station but it was not until 1864, on the opening of the Winwick cut-off, that true north-south journeys reached their full potential.

Where the East and West Parkside curves met, a new station was built, Preston Junction, opening on 26th September 1849, becoming Lowton & Preston on 1st February 1877. Later the same month, however, the London & North Western time-table gives it simply as Lowton Junction. The station was closed on 1st January 1917, only to re-open on 1st February 1919. Local Warrington-Earlestown-Wigan services used the route until final closure of Lowton Junction Station on 26th September 1949.

It would appear that neither the construction of the Wigan Branch Railway, or the maintenance of it by the contractors, Pritchard & Hoof, had been carried out to the satisfaction of the North Union Board. Therefore in May 1835, the firm of Smith & Eckersley were awarded the maintenance contract for one year at £400, later renewed for two years at £500 per year. That was not quite the end of the matter however. Ensuing legal action against the North Union Railway by Pritchard and Hoof resulted in the latter being awarded in excess of £6,000 in damages and costs.

The carriage of mail by the railways dates from November 1830 when 1½d per mile per bag was charged, later reduced to 1d, or approximately 2/6d per trip over the Liverpool & Manchester line. So from this very early date the Post Office were alive to the opportunity afforded by rail transport.

Early trials carried out in the dispatch of mails were successful and in May 1831 a contract had been signed between the Postmaster General and the Liverpool & Manchester Railway for the "conveyance of mails".

In the early years, mails for Wigan were dispatched to Parkside from Liverpool and Manchester. At Parkside the station attendant would hand over the mails to the guard of the Wigan train who now had the burden of responsibility for their safe arrival in Wigan.

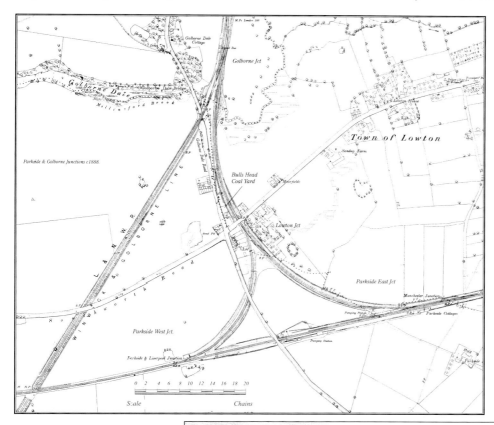

Fig 5. The second series Ordnance Survey of the area around Parkside was carried out in 1888, appearing in print in 1891. The Winwick cut-off route from Winwick Junction to Golborne Junction opened in 1864.

Of further interest is Bulls Head Coal Yard situated in a small triangle of land between Golborne Dale Road, Southworth Road and, what were by this period, the London & North Western's lines from Parkside Junctions. This coal yard had been in operation since 1835, first worked into by Turner & Evans locomotives from Edge Green and later by Richard Evans & Co. It was still in operation before W.W.II but seems to have closed sometime in the late 1940s.

Plate 6. This was the remarkable scene at Parkside on 11th August 1968 as Stanier Class '5' No.45110, working the 'Fifteen Guinea Special,' makes a photostop opposite the Huskisson Memorial. Everyone is anxious to get their picture of this 'famous' or 'infamous' special, dependant on your point of view. I don't think Network Rail would allow this sort of thing today! *Eddie Bellass.*

Plate 7. In December 1961, a six-car Trans-Pennine unit from Liverpool Lime Street passes the Parkside Memorial. These sets were built at Swindon principally for the Trans-Pennine services. Occasionally they would be seen working via the Kenyon Junction - Leigh - Tyldesley route at weekends. *Eddie Bellass.*

Plate 8. The Great Western Railway had running rights over the London & North Western route to Manchester Exchange from Walton Junction, Warrington, which had been in operation since 1860. It was not until 1943 that these were curtailed as a wartime necessity. At Parkside c1935, a return Manchester Exchange-Chester train is seen passing Huskissons Memorial hauled by a 'Hall' class locomotive.

I make some apology for the extremely blurred front end of the locomotive in this photo but it is a very rare shot of a Great Western engine at Parkside. *Author's Collection.*

At Wigan, a messenger met the train, retrieved the mail bags from the guard and took them to the main Post Office. The Post Office paid £5 yearly to both the station attendant and the messenger at Wigan, plus £20 per annum to the North Union Railway. After the North Union line to Preston was opened mail coaches ran through, being added or detached as was necessary at Parkside.

Apart from Huskisson's Memorial there is little remaining at Parkside to give the observer any inkling of the former importance that this location played in the formative years of Britain's railways. Sidings that were still extant in the 1970s have gone and the whole area returned to nature. Occasionally the steam locomotive will pass by with a special, and the main lines can be busy at times. The Parkside curves see occasional use as diversionary routes but little scheduled traffic is to be seen on them.

Plate 9. Stanier Class '5' No.45285 passes the Parkside memorial, westbound in April 1965. Parkside East signal cabin is just visible beyond the train. The sidings here are long gone and nature has reclaimed all but the main lines. *Eddie Bellass.*

Plate 10. Hughes 'Crab' No.42863 is seen eastbound at Parkside with a horse box train in August 1960. On the extreme left is Huskisson's memorial and the bridge on Parkside Lane under which the train is passing, one of Stephenson's original Liverpool & Manchester Railway constructions. This is the site of the first Parkside station where, in those pioneering days, locomotives were serviced and watered. Passengers, as in Tate's engraving, *Plate 5,* wandered freely about, unhindered by todays often paranoid restrictions. *Brian Magilton.*

Plate 11. A pair of Stanier Class '5s' Nos.44734 & 44927 work the Royal Train off Parkside East curve toward East Junction in May 1961 conveying H.M. Queen Elizabeth II to a Manchester engagement. *Eddie Bellass.*

Plate 12. 'Patriot' Class No.45527 *Southport* appears to be in sparkling condition when passing Parkside East Junction in October 1960 with a Trans-Pennine express for Lime St. *Brian Magilton.*

Plate 14. (Opposite). A northbound WCML diversion sees Stanier 'Pacific' No.46231 *Duchess of Montrose* take Parkside West curve on a dismal January day in 1961. In the background are the sidings to Parkside Colliery, still under construction at this time, the last deep mine to be sunk in Lancashire. Connections have already been made with the Manchester-Liverpool route east of Newton-le-Willows station. Note also that this is pre-motorway days, the view now obscured by a bridge and embankments of the M6 which were built on an alignment between the signal box and the colliery sidings. *Eddie Bellass.*

Plate 13. One of the unrebuilt 'Patriot' Class 4-6-0s No.45520 *Llandudno*, comes off Parkside West curve to join the Liverpool-Manchester route working a diverted WCML Blackpool North to London Euston train in January 1961. The train will diverge at Earlestown East Junction to rejoin the main lines at Winwick Junction. *Eddie Bellass.*

Plate 15. In December 1960, one of the B.R. Standard Class '4' 2-6-0s No.76075 traverses Parkside West curve from Lowton Junction. The working is an Earlestown Carriage & Works test train returning to Earlestown. This was nececessary to test the road worthiness of repaired vehicles before they were released back into traffic. Every weekday a test train ran from the works to either Ribble Sidings or Horwich. Lowton Junction signal box is on the extreme left *Eddie Bellass.*

Plate 16. At Parkside East Junction on 19th June 1983, a W.C.M.L diversion from Preston hauled by Class '47' No.47 547, has A.C Electric No.86 255 *Penrith Beacon* in tow. The train will work via Ordsall Lane to Manchester Piccadilly where it will revert to electric traction. *Author.*

Plate 17. An Edwardian view at Lowton Junction Station where the east and west Parkside curves met. The view is looking north toward Golborne Junction, the exceptionally tall signal box giving a view of the station over the A572 bridge on Southworth Road, Lowton. The bridge dates from the single track Wigan Branch Railway of 1832, wide enough for a double - track railway although at first only a single track was laid. In the event, the bridge succumbed to explosives on 7th May 1972 when additional clearances were required for the W.C.M.L. electrification project which entailed electrifying the route from Golborne Junction, through Lowton Junction and west curve and, a section of former Liverpool & Manchester Railway from Parkside West Junction through Newton-Le-Willows and Earlestown East curve to Winwick Junction. Note the London & North Western lower quadrant signals and how steep the signal box steps are. The present day scene is again one of uncontrolled greenery taking over and long gone are the station buildings and signal box. On the far side of the junction however, the platforms remain in situ despite there being no passenger service since 1949.

In 1847 the London & North Western introduced services using both east and west Parkside curves, to make connections at Preston Junction, with trains from Preston which contained through coaches for Liverpool and Manchester*. It may be that this only applied to certain 1st class trains for by this period there were seventeen trains daily in each direction between Liverpool and Manchester and the obvious complications involved by shunting movements at Preston Junction for all of these (and the added delays therein) would not have gone down well with the fare paying passenger. *P.Collier.*

* 1st class through coaches had been run from Preston to London from 1839, off the 9.45a.m. and 6.27p.m. trains from Preston, interchanged at Parkside. From London, through coaches to Preston left at 9.30a.m. and 8.30p.m.

Plate 18. A pair of Lancashire United Transport double-decker buses add to the scene at Lowton Junction as Class '5' No.44838 passes by light engine routed for Parkside West Junction in April 1965. It has, in fact, worked empty carriage stock into Lowton Siding for stabling and has run-round in the Parkside triangle

The signal cabin at this location remained until September of 1972 when, along with a number of other signal cabins in the area, it became redundant when Warrington Power Box was commissioned.
Eddie Bellass.

Plate 19 (below). Some 50 years after closure, Lowton Junction station, still with the remnants of its platforms, plays host to the Preston - Manchester Victoria - Crewe leg of "The Dalesman" railtour special on 11th June 1999 with 'Deltic' 55 019 at the head and sister locomotive 50 009 at the rear.

Bulls Head Coal Yard was sited on the left c1835-1940s.
Author.

Plate 21.(opposite). An unidentified ex- 'WD' 2-8-0 approaches Golborne Junction from Lowton Junction in February 1965 with a coal train from Parkside Colliery. The rear of the train is out of sight on the curve back toward Lowton. *Eddie Bellass.*

Plate 20. In June 1966 the diesel prototype DP2 emerged from Vulcan Locomotive Works and underwent a series of trial runs over the WCML. Under the watchful eye of signalman Jack Wardle, one of these trial runs is seen departing from Lowton Carriage Siding heading for Golborne Junction with DP2 in 'Deltic' colours. This siding was quite a long one and could hold eighteen coaches, almost extending to Parkside East Junction, but not accessible from it. Even at this period, Lowton Junction signal box was still lit by paraffin lamps.
Eddie Bellass.

Plate 22. A Type '4' diesel, later Class '47,' at Golborne Junction in September 1965 working the 1S61, 08.55 Motorail service to Stirling from Newton-Le-Willows. The introduction of this service in 1965, Wednesdays, Thursdays and Saturdays only, was, initially, a success although operational difficulties were encountered at departure and, more severely, on arrival with the 'Up' service at Newton-le-Willows. For departure, empty stock would arrive from Edge Hill with the car-flats at the rear which were shunted up against the loading ramp, train and stock then uncoupled and shunted into the 'Up' siding allowing passengers to board the last coach and walk through to their respective seats. The return working from Stirling at 16.30 as 1M36 presented quite a problem on arrival at its destination. Passengers de-trained onto the 'Down' platform, engine and stock then away to Edge Hill. The car-flats were left on the main line awaiting the arrival of a light engine to couple-up, shunt across to the 'Up' side and into the siding. All this took time and very often, Trans-Pennine expresses would be standing for 15-20 minutes waiting for the road. By 1972, departure was at 21.35 but now going to Inverness, Tuesdays and Fridays only with return workings on Wednesday and Thursdays. *Eddie Bellass.*

GOLBORNE JUNCTION

Golborne Junction came into being when the Winwick cut-off route, Winwick Junction-Golborne Junction, opened in 1864. The line had been inspected by Colonel Yolland on 17th July 1864, on the same day that the Eccles-Tyldesley-Wigan and the Tyldesley-Leigh-Pennington Junction routes were inspected and likewise, opening officially on the same date, 1st September 1864.

The Winwick cut-off provided a means for express passenger and freight trains to avoid Lowton, Parkside and Earlestown Junctions. In the 1880s, local trains, all stations Warrington Bank Quay-Wigan took 40 minutes for the journey, calling en route at Earlestown, Newton Bridge, Lowton Junction, Golborne and Bamfurlong. At the same period, express trains using the new route took only 16 minutes. Newton, on the Liverpool-Manchester route had been renamed Newton Bridge in June 1868 and finally, on 14th June 1888, becoming Newton-Le-Willows.

The London & North Western had built a 'Telegraph Cabin' at Golborne Junction in 1866. By 1879, this had been replaced by an early type signal cabin, possibly a Saxby & Farmer design as many of these were at the time. In February 1888, this in turn was replaced by a London & North Western Type '4' signal box with a 48 lever tumbler frame, surviving intact until decommissioned on 17th September 1972, due to the impending electrification of the West Coast Main Line.

Designated as a Class '3' cabin, northbound trains were were wired from Stafford, Crewe and Warrington. Southbound trains were wired from Carlisle, Lancaster and Preston. In the steam era, northbound passenger trains not stopping at Wigan were required to whistle when passing Golborne Junction box. Likewise, southbound freights requiring water at Warrington, or those routed to North Wales be they passenger or freight, also whistled on passing Golborne Junction cabin, a different whistle for each destination. A wrong whistle could cause disruption to following services for the information received at Golborne Junction was immediately passed on to Winwick Junction cabin where the signalman would route the train onto the appropriate line. All northbound freight trains were wired from Winwick Junction to Golborne Junction and then to Bamfurlong Junction, vice versa for southbound freights. Even on night turn during the 1940-50 period 80 to 100 trains would pass through section. Willesden-Carlisle freights for example, usually worked Down Fast line from Golborne Junction, whereas trains needing relief crews went Down Slow line to Bamfurlong.

All northbound express passenger trains passing Golborne Junction were belled on as 4 beats and, whether stopping at Wigan or not, trains would give the necessary whistle when passing the box.

Now if, for example, the train was a non-stop express passenger through Wigan, Golborne Junction box, instead of giving ordinary section 2 beats, gave a 3/2 beat to Golborne No.1 cabin, who in turn sent a 1/3/2 'Through Wigan' approach signal to Bamfurlong Junction. Bamfurlong Junction then altered this signal to 4/4/4, and sent it on to Springs Branch Nos. 1&2 and Wigan Nos.1&2. This told the signal boxes concerned that the train approaching was a non-stop, through Wigan express. In the meantime, the signalman in Wigan No.1 cabin rang the bell at North Western station giving warning of the oncoming express.

This was also the signal for the army of schoolboy spotters to gather at the south end of Wigan station, Ian Allan notebooks at the ready. In similar fashion, Wigan No2 cabin operated the bell for southbound expresses. Those really were the days! A couple of sandwiches, a bottle of pop and a return ticket from Tyldesley to Wigan at 9d (3p). It really was a thrill to see those great locomotives arriving at Wigan. It couldn't last of course, the sheer numbers of schoolboy spotters crowding the platforms

Plate 23. (Opposite). 'Royal Scot' No.46115 *Scots Guardsman* rounds the curve at Golborne Junction on Saturday 13th February 1965 with a Railway Correspondence & Travel Society (RCTS) special, the 'Rebuilt Scot Commemorative Railtour' which began at Crewe for a run over the Settle & Carlisle via Boars Head Junction, Blackburn and Hellifield then back south from Carlisle on the WCML to Crewe. The locomotive originally scheduled for this tour was to have been sister engine No.46160 *Queens Westminster Rifleman* which, unfortunately, had failed and was on Holbeck shed. Despite numerous 'slacks' on the tour route, the engine performed well when allowed to run freely for which due credit must be given to the enthusiastic footplatemen. In January 1966 No.46115 was withdrawn, the last of its class to remain in service. That was not quite the end, however, as 46115 was rescued for preservation and performed a number of mainline steam runs in the 1980s. On Saturday 16th August 2008, *Scots Guardsman,* having undergone restoration at Carnforth, hauled its first excursion over the main lines, between Hellifield and Carlisle, returning by the same route later in the day
Eddie Bellass.

eventually resulted in a ban from spotting on Wigan North Western so it was back to the bike, but those memories are something to treasure.

I now find it rather poignant that one of the signalmen who rang the bell at Wigan would, some forty years later, become a very good friend - namely Bill Paxford, whose recollections of signalling operations on the railway have provided so much information for this book.

Mileposts for the route to Preston began at Parkside East Junction and are positioned on the west (Down) side of the line, so ordained by the Grand Junction Railway, London being zero, since the formation of the Trent Valley route. This was not always so, however, for the Ordnance Surveys of the 1840s clearly show the mileposts at some locations alongside the 'Up' line. The Grand Junction Railway was incorporated on 6th May 1833 with the Birmingham - Warrington route of 78 miles. Milepost 188 from Euston is located a few yards north of Golborne Junction S.B.

* A brief word of explanation for those not familiar with signalling operations on the former British Railways.

All train movements on the main lines were identified by a bell code, passed forward from signal box to signal box as the train progressed. Each type of train, i.e. local passenger, express passenger, fast freight etc. all having a different bell code. Generally the signalman at any particular location knew from practice, allied to his knowledge of the working timetable, which train was which, and the time it should pass; the train 'whistle,' as at Golborne Junction, being a reminder to him and useful at busy locations, particularly at night.

Plate 24. Golborne Junction signal box surrounded by a tranquil environment is still in situ in late summer 1972, but as can be seen electrification is not far away. Although the signal box has long since gone the overall scene has changed little with the passing years. The nearby A580, East Lancashire Road overbridge, built in the 1930s, provided a convenient vantage point for engine spotters to congregate. To observe one of Sir William Stanier's 'Pacifics' majestically round the curve at Golborne Junction, sweep past the box and thunder northward was the highlight of the spotters day.

Alan Hart.

Plate 25. An inside view of Golborne Junction signalbox c1970. There are four bell-code boxes on the shelf, one for each main line here. The signal levers most identifiable in this monotone photo are the distant signals with the arrows, Up and Down Fast line distants. Red levers are home signals, black are points and blue are locking bars. There are two white 'spares' next to the Down line distant.
Peter Hampson.

Plate 26. 'Jubilee' class No.45629 *Straits Settlements* heads north at Golborne Junction in June 1964 with an express freight routed onto the Down Fast line.
Eddie Bellass.

Plate 27. An earlier view of Golborne Junction signal box as Stanier Class '5' No.45136 is seen southbound at Golborne Junction in December 1959 taking the route to Lowton Junction. *Eddie Bellass.*

Plate 28. A view from Golborne Junction signal cabin as 'Mickey Mouse' No.46447, one of the Ivatt designed 2-6-0s, approaches from Parkside with a through freight in June 1964. *Eddie Bellass.*

Plate 29. HST fashion, a pair of Stanier Class '5s' are seen signal checked near Golborne Junction in December 1959. The East Lancashire Road, A580 bridge is in the left background. *Eddie Bellass.*

Plate 30. BR Type '2' diesel No.7639 is seen just north of Golborne Junction with a train of cement tankers for the WCML construction project in the Summer of 1970. One of the concrete bases for the electrification masts can be seen extreme right. As in this case, these workings were done at weekends. The signal box can be seen in the right background as can the towers of Parkside Colliery. *Alan Hart.*

Plate 31. One of the few locations to remain relatively unchanged with the passing years, apart from the overhead equipment, is the view south towards Golborne Junction. On 14th September 2002 L.M.S Stanier. 'Pacific' No.6233 *Duchess of Sutherland* is seen on the Down Fast with a Leicester-Blackpool special. *Author.*

Plate 32. This is how it used to be. Stanier 'Pacific' No.46223 *Princess Alice* is seen, unusually, on the Down Slow just north of Golborne Junction about 1954. *Princess Alice* was amongst the first batch of blue streamliners to be built, entering traffic in July 1937. De-streamlining of this example occurred in August 1946, hence the cut-away smokebox. Loco spotters often called these examples 'Semis,' meaning semi-streamlined, a term which sent the purists into fits of rage. *Princess Alice* received the green livery in which it is seen here in October 1952. *G.Mellor.*

Plate 33. With the withdrawal of the last Stanier 'Pacifics' in September 1964 the Anglo-Scottish services were often in the hands of less than reliable diesel locomotives and it was not until the arrival of the Class '50s' on the scene in 1968, that some measure of performance returned to the WCML. In August 1971, No.401 approaches Golborne Junction working 1A75, the Saturdays only 16.53 Blackpool North - Euston. The East Lancashire Road-bridge, built in the 1930s, is seen in the background devoid of passing traffic; you would be hard pressed to get a similar photograph today!

The Class '50', was a development of 'DP2' which had performed consistently well over both the West Coast and East Coast Main Lines. In appearance, however, the 50s' differed considerably from their progenitor having flat ends, roof mounted indicator panels and additional BR specifications of automatic tractive effort, slow speed control and dynamic braking. The engine was basically that as used in the English Electric Type '4' (Class '40') diesel, uprated from 2,000h.p. to 2,700.h.p. by intercooling which had proved so successful in DP2. Built at the Newton-Le-Willows Vulcan works between 1967/8, all were originally allocated to the WCML as mixed traffic locomotives. However, in traffic, the performance of the '50s' did not always live up to expectations. *Alan Hart.*

Plate 34. In October 1964, ex-LNER 4-6-2 'Pacific' No.4498 *Sir Nigel Gresley,* makes a rare appearance over the West Coast Main Line with a northbound special.

Tony Oldfield.

Plate 35. A more recent view at Golborne Dale taken from a higher vantage point adjacent to the A580 than *Plate 32,* is this shot of A.C. Electric No.85 030, with a returning Rugby League Wembley special to Wigan North Western on 29th April 1989, composed of B.R.MkI stock in Network Southeast livery. Like their steam predecessors, these locomotives have also been subjected to the cutters torch. Note also Parkside Colliery in the background the sinking of which began in 1957, No.1 shaft completed on 13th February 1959 and No.2 shaft completed on 3rd March 1959, production beginning in April 1964. Closure occurred in 1993 amidst great controversy, Parkside being one of the pits condemned in the coal review of 1992. Clearance of the site began in May 1994. Plans for a new Freightliner Depot on the site were put forward in 2007. *Author.*

Plate 36. 'Coronation Pacific' No.46242 *City of Glasgow* heads southbound on the approach to Golborne Junction on 25th March 1961 with an Up express. *Jim Peden Collection.*

Plate 37. Class '50' No.429 heads north with 1P 70, the 15.05 Euston - Blackpool express in July 1972, and is seen passing over Mill Lane bridge, Golborne. The bridge in the background is a farm overbridge and beyond that, the A580 bridge. *Alan Hart.*

Plate 38. Mill Lane bridge, left, as constructed by the Wigan Branch Railway, survives today. It originally carried only one track but built wide enough for two, instituted during the period before the completion of the North Union route to Preston c1838. This is as viewed from the western side. The monotone reproduction here does not do the bridge stonework justice. *Alan Hart.*

Plate 39. Mill Lane bridge, right, as viewed from the eastern side, constructed by the London & North Western under the 1883 Acts for the Golborne Junction - Springs Branch widening, showing a noticable difference in construction methods; no arch and no stone parapet walls. *Author.*

Plate 40. Golborne No1, or station box, was situated alongside the Up Fast line at the south end of the station at a distance of 1,640 yards from Golborne Junction and controlled access to Golborne Goods Yard.

This particular cabin had opened in 1888 on completion of quadrupling of the lines from Golborne Junction to Springs Branch. *Alan Hart.*

Plate 41. Golborne station box can be seen in the right background as Class '50' No.417 approaches Mill Lane working 1A63, the 12.47 Blackpool North - Euston in July 1971. *Alan Hart.*

GOLBORNE STATION

Whishaw gives the opening of Golborne Station as 31st October 1838, to co-incide with the opening of the North Union's Wigan to Preston railway. The Wigan Branch Railway crossed the Warrington-Golborne-Wigan Turnpike Road on the level, the crossing known locally as Golborne Gates. A bridge over the railway (the present one) immediately north of Golborne Station, was not constructed until the lines northbound from Golborne to Springs Branch Junction were quadrupled under the Act of 1883.

Golborne station's first cabin was again one of the early Telegraph type dating from 1866, this being replaced by a new cabin by 1879, designated as Golborne No.1 and, in 1888, by a second Golborne No.1, a London & North Western Type '4' cabin measuring 18ft - 9 in x 12ft - 0in with a 26 lever tumbler frame. The box was situated at the south end of Golborne station and worked the Up and Down Fast and Up and Down Slow lines. Off the slow lines, access was gained into Golborne Goods Yard from the south and three sidings ran towards the goods warehouse in a northward direction near Golborne station and, until the 1950s, was a busy yard, used by the local firm of Naylors amongst others. At the south end of the yard was a well used coal baggers siding where wagons would be shunted in to be unloaded by the various coal merchants. The yard was closed to traffic on 22nd May 1967.

Golborne No.2 cabin opened in November 1877, and with the track quadrupling of the 1880s, found itself situated between the Fast and Slow lines at the north end of Golborne station. No.2 box controlled the Up and Down Slow lines and Golborne Colliery Sidings which were accessible only from the slow lines.

There had been private sidings at Golborne, south of Tanner's Lane from 1856. Initially Brewis' Siding, it served the cotton mill adjacent to the main lines. A number ber of firms owned these premises over the followingyears and in 1920, it passed into the hands of Messrs Harbers Ltd, recieving acid and wood pulp. The last owners of the mill from 1963 were Wm. Tatton & Co.Ltd.

Golborne Colliery had been sunk in 1876/7 by one Edward Johnson and a connection provided by the London & North Western on 24th September 1877, off the Down line, north of Golborne Station. The colliery was to become the property of Richard Evans & Sons in August 1880 and the new owners sank a second shaft at Golborne in 1886.

Plate 42. Golborne South station as viewed from the centre of the Up Slow line looking north toward Wigan in the Edwardian period. Golborne No.2 cabin, at 470 yards from Golborne No.1, can be seen on the far side of the bridge. Before the tracks were quadrupled a level crossing sufficed here. The main station buildings and footbridge are identical to those at Bamfurlong and undoubtedly date from quadrupling days. There are coal wagons in Golborne Colliery Sidings in the distance and, note the signal controlling access to the sidings, prominent just beyond the platform. *Authors Collection.*

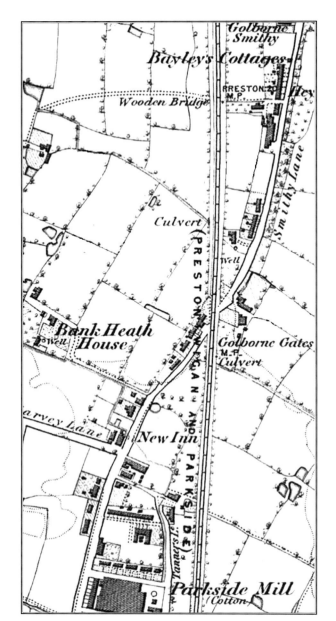

Fig 6. The original level crossing at 'Golborne Gates' is still in evidence as per the 1849 ordnance survey. Strangely, the location of Golborne Station, immediatley south of the crossing, is not shown.

Richard Evans, a successful printer of Paternoster Row, London, arrived in South Lancashire in 1830 and began to acquire an interest in collieries at Edge Green from Thomas Legh M.P. of the firm Legh & Turner, it thus becoming Turner & Evans in 1833.

The history of Richard Evans, his mining and engineering interests, together with his sons and their collective partnerships including salt mining at Winsford, are often complicated and wide ranging affairs outside the scope of this work. Suffice to say that with the acquisition of further collieries at Haydock and Golborne, Richard Evans had secured the mining rights to some 6,000 acres of South Lancashire and by 1850 the firm Richard Evans & Co. were established as the principal mining concern in the Haydock and Golborne areas.

In the 1880s, trips were worked by Evans from Golborne colliery to Haydock, and to Dover Basin on the Leeds-Liverpool Canal by 0-4-2 tender engine *Haydock*, built in 1842 by the Vulcan Foundry at Newton -Le-Willows. Well tank locomotives *Makerfield* and *Bellorophon* were also worked main line to Edge Green and return.

In L.M.S. days, Golborne No.2 cabin was a Porter/Signalman's post, one of the duties of which included the number taking of traffic from Golborne Colliery. No.2 box closed in 1959.

The Golborne Colliery trips were worked from Springs Branch, No.1 trip in LMS & BR days at about 9.30 a.m. If the colliery had any loads for Liverpool these would be picked up, then to Golborne Yard to shunt and re-marshall the train. Next it was off to Earlestown and shunt if required, then to St Helens Junction, shunt again and pick up any 'norths' for Wigan or Bamfurlong, calling again at Golborne on the return journey and pick up any for Wigan Canal Sidings. The whole process would be repeated on the afternoon trip.

Plate 43. The view south from Golborne Station in 1951 as a freight train approaches on the Down Fast line. *Stations U.K.*

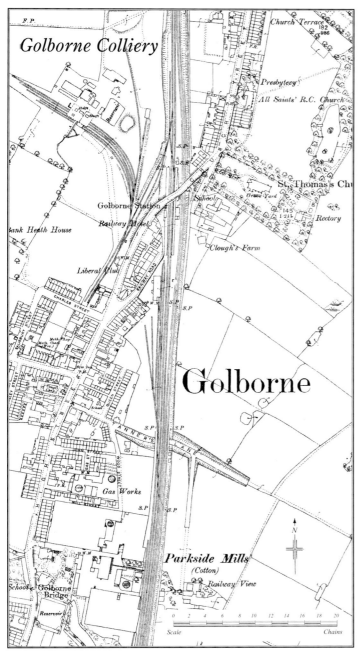

Fig 7. The late 1880s Ordnance Survey of Golborne with Golborne Colliery on the west side of the main lines and its connection with the London & North Western north of Golborne Station. By this period the flat crossing at Golborne Gates has been removed in conjunction with the Golborne Junction-Springs Branch widening and a new bridge carries the A573 over the railway. The goods yard south of Golborne Station has two roads, later increased to three.

Plate 44. One of the North British 0-4-0 dieselshunters is seen at Golborne Colliery on 13th June 1959 with Yard Foreman Bob Dinsdale and Shunter Stan Berry alongside.
Peter Eckersley.

The Golborne pits would later be served by connections with the Manchester, Sheffield & Lincolnshire Railway's Lowton-St.-Mary's to St. Helens branch which opened for goods in 1895. Much traffic was to go out by this route, a spur being laid from Golborne Colliery to connect with the new line at Edge Green. From 4th August 1905 this route was absorbed by the Great Central Railway.

On 1st January 1947, nationalisation of Britain's mines occurred and all Richard Evans' collieries came under the auspices of the National Coal Board who reserved the right to work their own trains over the London Midland & Scottish lines from Golborne and Haydock to Dallam and return. In fact, upon nationalisation of the railways in 1948, the new owners, British Railways, did not dispute that right, only asking that 'token' trips no longer need be undertaken as they were unnecessary. The trips that did run were only lightly loaded workings, all the heavy coal trains were hauled by mainline locomotives. However, some traffic which normally went via the ex-LNER route between Haydock and Golborne was routed via Parkside West Junction in 1952 due to a fire at Old Boston pit, Haydock.

Golborne Colliery was a particularly long-lived mine and continued to wind coal until 1977. From 1975 it had been linked to Bickershaw Colliery by underground tunnelling, as was Parsonage Colliery at Leigh, all coal to be wound at Bickershaw from the three collieries. After a life of 112 years, production ceased at Golborne as from 31st March 1989. The shafts were filled in later that year and the site quickly cleared to make way for industrial units and housing.

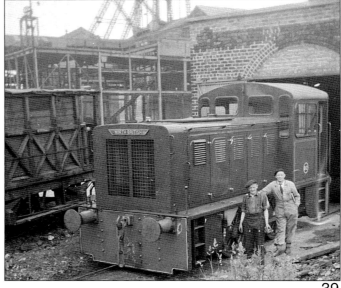

Plate 45. Pre - W.W.II, one of the Hughes designed, Horwich built 'Crab' 2-6-0s No.2880, passes Golborne No.2 cabin on the Up Fast line. Beyond the train is the footbridge from May Street which gave pedestrian passage across the railway. In the far background is Ashton Road bridge. *J.Muir.*

Plate 46. Seen heading north past the dismantled platforms of Golborne Station which had closed on 6th February 1961, is Class '50' No.455, working 1P70, the 15.05 Euston - Blackpool North in August 1971. Golborne Station cabin can be seen beyond the train and the sidings into the redundant goods yard over on the extreme right. *Alan Hart.*

Plate 47. Golborne Goods Shed, seen here in 1972, had been closed for some years and over that period has suffered from the usual mindless vandalism which seems to affect any property which has been vacated by its owners and left empty. *Alan Hart.*

Plate 48. Type '4' No.223 passes the site of Golborne Station with 8G 80, the 05.05 Carlisle - Bescot van train in August 1972. In Wigan Branch Railway days the level crossing at Golborne Gates would have been here. The 1880s built bridge on High Street carrying the new road alignment can be seen in the background. Golborne Colliery headgear is on the left. *Alan Hart.*

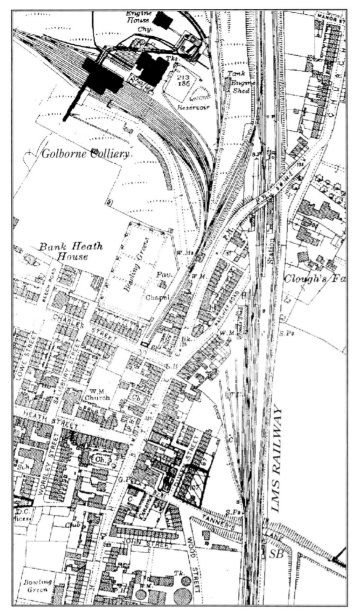

Fig 8. The 1920s Ordnance Survey shows how Golborne Colliery had expanded in the intervening years. The colliery was particularly long-lived and continued in operation until 1989. Golborne Station closed in 1961. However, at the time of writing a call for its re-opening has received some support from the local authorities. The problem is though that no local service operates along the route and it is hard to see how, in the privatised era, any company taking on the mantle of service could get it off the ground in isolation without a complete survey of other much needed railway investment in the surrounding area. Further, Network Rail have stated that the idea is a non-starter!

North of Golborne Station lies the area known as Edge Green, adjacent to the present Haydock Branch Junction. A number small collieries had been sunk here in the first quarter of the nineteenth century, on the western side of what was later to become the West Coast Main Line. An Edge Green Colliery is shown here on the 1829 line plan for the Wigan Branch Railway and is believed to be amongst those that came into the hands of Richard Evans in 1830. There are no colliery tramways or plateways shown on this plan.

In 1833, Evans also acquired an interest in a new colliery at Edge Green on land owned by Thomas Legh on whose behalf Evans worked the coal. This mine is shown on the Golborne Tithe Map of 1838, connected to the North Union by a branch railway. It is likely that this branch to Edge Green was put in during construction of the Wigan Branch Railway as Evans was running his trains over the main line in 1832, for it appears that a locomotive from Evans' collieries at Edge Green was in a head-on collision at Parkside with a Wigan Branch Railway passenger train worked by the Liverpool & Manchester locomotive *Rocket,* working to Wigan in November 1832. It seems that Evans' train was working over the line outside its 'allotted hours'. *Rocket* was reported as badly damaged.

On the subject of accidents, Thomas Legh's engines were also involved in a number of collisions on the Liverpool & Manchester lines. In January 1832 his locomotive *Black Diamond* was involved in an incident working from Edge Hill to Haydock when, at Whiston, a number of wagons broke loose, running into a following train. The second of Legh's locomotives, *Shrigley,* was in collision at Liverpool Road, Manchester, with *Venus,* one of George Stephenson's locomotives, and in May 1833 one of Legh's engines was involved in a fatal accident at Golborne Gates whilst propelling a train of wagons.

By the time the first 6in Ordnance Survey was carried out in 1845 another colliery had been sunk at Edge Green and is shown as 'New Coal Pits'. This also had a branch railway which crossed the North Union Railway, and Windy Bank Lane (later A573) on the level. The tramway ran parallel with the lane to terminate at Smithy Bridge, at the junction with Ashton Road (B5207), and here a landsale yard for coal sales was established. In later years, part of this railway trackbed on the east side of the main lines would be used for line maintenance access and is still in use for that purpose today. *(See* **Fig 9** *page 46)*

Plate 49. One of the Brush Type '4s' in the early two-tone green livery No.D1631, is seen on the Down Fast after passing through Golborne working cartic 4S 34, the 15.16 Kings Norton - Bathgate in July 1971. The siding into Golborne Colliery is on the extreme right on this side of the overbridge.
Alan Hart.

Plate 50. Stanier Class '8F' No.48620 passing Golborne Colliery Sidings on the Up Slow with a block freight on 7th June 1967. The photographer is being carefully watched by the fireman taking it easy for a while on the falling gradient. The North West of England was the last outpost of steam traction and many of these '8Fs' continued in service until the very end of steam workings in August 1968.
W.D.Cooper.

Plate 51. Stanier Class '5' No.45425 is seen on the Down Slow with a freight for Bamfurlong Sidings about 1962. On the right is the lead into Golborne Colliery and just beyond the A573 bridge in the background was Golborne South Station. This shot is taken from a point near the footbridge visible in *Plate 52 (opposite)* replaced some years ago by a more modern structure.

Jim Carter.

As previously mentioned, coal proprietors along the route with running rights were required to find their own engines and wagons. In July 1833, Richard Evans asked the Liverpool & Manchester to "lend" him ten wagons to which request the company declined, saying that they did not have enough themselves. An employee of the Liverpool & Manchester was therefore sent to Edge Green by train to take a census of wagons where 301 were counted. Certainly not a large number considering Evans' collieries had moved 100,000 tons of coal over the Wigan line in the last six months, even allowing for a few on the road or in sidings elsewhere!

Further mines were sunk at Edge Green by Richard Evans in the 1840s. In the 1850s, a new connection was made with the main line on the eastern side, opposite the original 'tramway' junction, and a line of colliery railway was constructed from this junction to serve a new wharf on the Leeds-Liverpool Canal at Dover Basin. Richard Evans & Co. were thus able to work their own traffic, by reverse shunting movements over the main lines to Dover Basin from Edge Green, and also from his other collieries at Haydock. Working via Parkside, coal was also transported to Crewe and Winsford from Edge Green.

These 'shunts' were, apparently, an irritant to the London & North Western Railway and during the quadrupling of tracks under the 1883 Acts, a bridge was constructed, at the expense of the Company, to take the Edge Green colliery railway under the main running lines, thereby eliminating the need for connections with the new Fast lines. Once the quadrupling of lines here was completed in 1889, the colliery railway only had connections with the slow lines.

Plate 52. As can be determined from the previous two photographs, beyond Golborne Station the railway passed through a shallow cutting extenuated on the west side by Golborne Colliery spoil heap. In August 1972, a pair of Class '50s' Nos.D447&418, speed northwards on the Down Fast with a Euston - Glasgow express. Using pairs of these locomotives on the Crewe-Glasgow route from the Summer of 1970 led to an acceleration in timings - a foretaste of what was to come when the route was eventually electrified in 1972. Through Euston - Glasgow services using electric traction began in 1974. *Alan Hart.*

Plate 53. A Sunday working, 1P 55, the 11.00 Euston - Blackpool North is seen at the same location as above in May 1971 hauled by Type '4' No.D1848. This had been diverted from its normal Crewe - Warrington route, working via Chester because of engineering work north of Weaver Junction. *Alan Hart.*

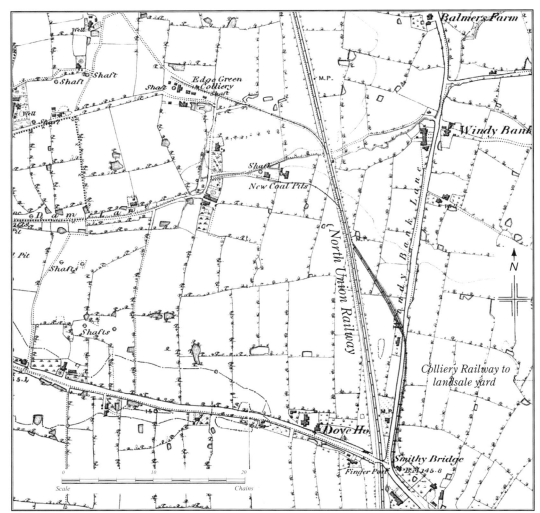

Fig 9. This section of the 1840s 6in Ordnance Survey shows the Edge Green pits worked by Richard Evans from 1833 and connected by a standard gauge branch line from the North Union Railway. To the south of these are 'New Coal Pits' sunk between 1838 and 1845, also connected by a branch railway. As this railway was worked by Evans it is presumed to have been standard gauge. The railway crossed the North Union and nearby Windy Bank Lane ((A573) on the level. It then ran parallel with the lane to terminate at Smithy Bridge, often referred to as Golborne Smithies, at the junction with Ashton Road (B5207). The portion of trackbed between road and railway which formed the original connection can still be seen today and is used by line maintenance road traffic.

In later years, Evans' colliery railway would be extended and re-routed as in *Fig 10* to form a new junction with what would become the London & North Western Railway.

Plate 54. One of the Haydock built 0-6-0 well tanks, *Bellorophon*, is seen on the Haydock Colliery's railway system on 26th May 1958. The locomotive ended its working life at Lea Green Colliery in August, 1964. It would eventually be preserved on the Keighley & Worth Valley Railway, arriving there in 1966. It seems remarkable that these engines had running powers on B.R. lines from Earlestown and Haydock in the 1960s. *Peter Eckersley.*

Plate 55. Ex-Lancashire & Yorkshire Railway 0-6-0 No.52225 on the Up Slow descending from Golborne Summit in July 1959. The fireman views the surroundings from the footplate of this ancient class of engine which was designed by Aspinall and first introduced in 1889. The train is passing beneath Ashton Road bridge which makes a junction with the A573, at which point the Lancashire United bus is seen, complete with period advertising for 'Magee's Ale'. Magee's Brewery had a rail connection on the original alignment of the Bolton & Leigh Railway, at Daubhill, water for the brewery arriving by rail from Burton-on-Trent, Staffs. After being worked into Springs Branch and tripped worked via Howe Bridge and Bag Lane to Crook Street Yard, the water tankers were shunted up the steep incline to Magee's Siding, for which the locomotive's crew were rewarded with a free 'sample' a practice that would make today's Health & Safety Executive go bananas. Sorry if I digress, but what a pint! *Eddie Bellass.*

Colliery owners had reached agreements with the Liverpool & Manchester, and later, the Wigan Branch Railway to work their own trains from early days and these agreements were consolidated on the formation of the North Union in 1834 under Section 95 of the Act.

The various coal owners managed to have inserted in the North Union Act a section which gave all owners of land adjoining the line, and their tenants, the right to make connections with the railway and run their own trains over it. Richard Evans & Co. used the Wigan Branch Railway to gain access to the Liverpool & Manchester Railway from their Edge Green mines.

The provisions of the 1834 Act, relating to all the local coal companies, was rescinded by section 75 of the London & North Western's Act of 1888, except, that is, for those of the Wigan Coal & Iron Company which were preserved by section 76 of the same Act. It appears, however, that this did not effect workings on the Springs Branch.

Apparently, the London & North Western had gone to great lengths to determine the rights and provisions of the 1834 North Union Act for there were a number of colliery railways in the area before the Wigan Branch Railway was constructed. In all probability it was this 'first on the scene status' of the collieries that induced the London & North Western to put in the necessary infrastructure to divert Richard Evans' colliery railway. The trackbed of this colliery railway to Dover Basin, east of the West Coast Main Line, is still discernable and you might, if you're quick, be able to spot the bridge amongst the vegetation from the comfort of a passing train.

Also of note is that between 1869 and 1887 Richard Evans & Co. built a number of their own locomotives. These were 0-6-0 well tanks with 4ft wheels and 16in x

Plate 56. This elevated view at Golborne on 28th July 1972 is of Type '4' No.400 (no D prefix) hauling an southbound express descending from Golborne Summit. In the foreground is the B5207 near its junction with the A573, where, in the early 19th century Edge Green Collieries had their coal staithes, the line of which ran parallel to the A573 before crossing toward the main lines and intersecting at the extreme top left hand. The second and third last coaches are passing the site of the Great Central's Lowton-St.-Mary's to St. Helens route overbridge which had been demolished in 1971. Some of the rubble from this bridge, and the A573 overbridge can be seen nearby. *Tom Heavyside.*

22in cylinders, and in all, six were constructed. Designed by Josiah Evans, one of Richard's sons, they were specifically intended to work over the main lines. *Hercules* was the first to be built in 1869, followed by *Amazon* 1871, *Bellorophon* 1874, *Makerfield* 1876, *Parr* 1886 and finally *Golborne* in 1888. In the 1880s, *Bellorophon* and *Makerfield* worked Evans' trips to Edge Green and Dover Basin. Five of these well tanks - *Amazon* being the exception, would survive to be taken over by the National Coal Board in 1947. One - *Bellorophon* escaped the scrap merchants and survives in preservation at Keighley.

Although Evans' rights to run his trains over the main lines had, supposedly, been rescinded, this appears to have applied only to the new fast lines. On the former Wigan Branch Railway lines, which now became the slow lines, he continued to work two trains per day from Haydock to Edge Green and return, plus return trips between Golborne Colliery and Dover Basin, which would require shunting into Edge Green Colliery Sidings off the Down Slow in order to work to Dover Basin, and one return trip between Golborne and Earlestown. These arrangements seem to be confirmed by the insistence of the newly formed National Coal Board in 1947 on continuing their rights to run traffic over certain sections of the London Midland & Scottish Railway.

Around the turn of the twentieth century, Evans' workings over the London & North Western lines had diminished owing to the arrival of the Manchester, Sheffield & Lincolnshire's branch railway from Lowton - St- Mary's to St. Helens which opened for goods on 1st July 1895.

Plate 57. One of the much acclaimed B.R. designed Standard '9Fs' No.92008, is seen on the Down Fast line passing beneath Ashton Road (B5207) bridge on the approach to Golborne Summit on 5th August 1966, with a train composed mostly of I.C.I. tankers. In the opinion of many, these locomotives were the finest of the B.R. designed Standard Classes. *W.D.Cooper.*

Plate 58. A Freightliner train, 4G70, the 16.57 Heysham - Birmingham Lawley Street is hauled by Type '4' No. D1813, seen passing the remains of the Great Central overbridge north of Golborne in June 1971. *Alan Hart.*

Plate 59. 'Britannia' Class 4-6-2 No. 70031 *Byron* gallops along the Down Fast and is seen passing beneath the former Great Central lines at Golborne on 27th July 1966. The bridge in the background carries the B5207. *W.D.Cooper.*

Richard Evans negotiated agreements for a number of connections with the Manchester, Sheffield & Lincolnshire. As a result of that, the London & North Western time-table for 1906 shows only one Golborne-Edge Green train and an occasional train to Earlestown. It may be that he wished to preserve whatever rights he still had with the London & North Western by continuing to work these trains.

Evans' branch to Smithy Bridge landsale yard closed sometime in the 1860s, his Edge Green Collieries closing in 1928. The line to Dover Basin on the Leeds-Liverpool Canal continued in use by Richard Evans & Co. to work trains from their Haydock and Golborne Collieries to Dover Basin until early 1933 when the branch was dismantled and connections to what was now the London Midland & Scottish Railway main line lifted.

Traffic at Edge Green from the Evans' collieries had been controlled by the similarly named Edge Green Colliery Sidings signal box, the first of which was open by 1879. This was replaced in 1887 by a second box of the same name with 16 working levers. This cabin was to close on 6th February 1933.

A foundry was constructed on the Edge Green site in the mid 1930s by T. Crompton & Sons Ltd. and the agreement in respect of mainline connections came into effect on 11th September 1935. The foundry became known as Edge Green Rolling Mills and in 1961 the company was acquired by the Guest, Keen & Nettlefolds group. However, connections with the London Midland & Scottish Railway were not reinstated. Any traffic using the works went by the Great Central route to Edge Green.

Approximately 800 yards North of Golborne station the Manchester, Sheffield & Lincolnshire's Lowton-St-Mary's to St Helens line of railway, opened on 1st July 1895, crossed the London & North Western lines by an over-bridge, the Manchester, Sheffield & Lincolnshire itself being eventually absorbed by the Great Central Railway.

The Great Central's Golborne station was situated on the eastern side of the Parkside-Wigan route and not until 1st February 1949 were both Golborne stations renamed, the Great Central station becoming Golborne North and the former North Union station becoming Golborne South. Golborne North closed on 3rd March 1952, Golborne South closing on 6th February 1961.

Plate 60. In the first year of Nationalisation, ex-LMS 'Pacific' No.46230 *Duchess of Buccleuch,* heads south on the Up Fast at Golborne Summit on 22nd September 1948. The locomotive, one of the first batch of non-streamliners, is seen in the BR blue livery as applied in May 1948 with the legend "BRITISH RAILWAYS" in full on the tender. This livery was carried until May 1952 when the engine was outshopped in the BR green livery. It is often said that the only true colour for these Stanier 'Pacifics' was maroon but I thought that the blue livery sat well on these locomotives.   *W.D.Cooper.*

Plate 61. 'Coronation Pacific' No.46225 *Duchess of Gloucester* is seen on the Down Fast at Golborne Summit on 12th April 1958 with a 16 coach train. In the background is the Great Central overbridge. The present Haydock Branch Junction chord is sited on the right, in front of the P.W. hut.   *Dr.J.G.Blears.*

Plate 62. On a fine summers day in August 1946, one of Sir William Staniers 'Coronation Pacifics' No. 6228 *Duchess of Rutland*, is seen in its original streamlined form at Golborne Summit heading north with 15 vehicles on. These locomotives were first introduced in 1937 as an enlargement of the 'Princess Royal' class and, for a short time, one of them No.6229, held the world speed record for a steam locomotive of 114 mph, until eclipsed by Gresley's 'A4' *Mallard* on the much easier alignment of the East Coast Main Line. In the event, the streamlining of 6228 and her class was of little aerodynamic use at speeds under 90mph and was a hindrance to maintenance, thus being removed from 1946 onward. By 1949 all the streamliners had been converted to normal. The feature which identified all the former streamliners was the cut-away smokebox as in *Plate 32*.

This elevated shot from the nearby footbridge gives a clearer view of the point of former connections to Richard Evans' Edge Green Collieries, on the right. The second coach is passing over the late1880s built colliery railway underbridge by which Richard Evans & Co transferred their coals to Dover Basin on the Leeds-Liverpool Canal. *(see Plate 64 opposite)* Note also the track, not a blade of grass to be seen anywhere, in stark contrast with the railway today.   *W.D.Cooper.*

Plate 63. Taken from a lower viewpoint at the same location is one of the ancient Barton-Wright 0-6-0 tender engines of 1887 No.12063, heading north on the Down Slow with a short freight on 10th September 1945.

W.D.Cooper.

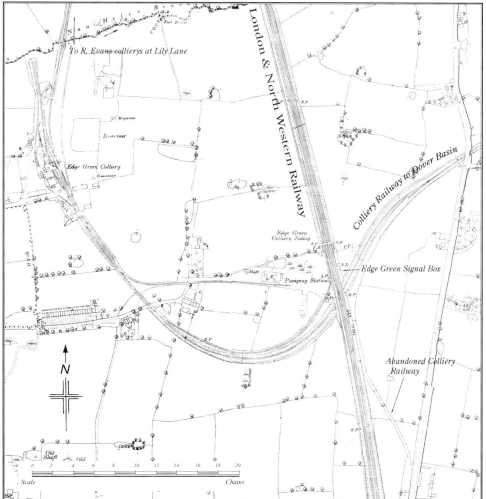

Plate 64. This is a 1930s view of Richard Evans' colliery railway to Dover Basin on the Leeds-Liverpool Canal, Leigh branch. It is taken from the western side of the WCML showing the bridge as constructed by the London & North Western Railway under the new arrangements of the 1888 Act.
Author's Collection.

Fig 10. The new Edge Green colliery connections which came into operation after the track quadrupling of the 1880s gave access only to the slow lines eliminating the previous 'shunts' carried out by the Colliery Co. over the main lines. Richard Evans' railway to Dover Basin on the Leeds-Liverpool Canal now passes beneath the London & North Western lines near the old connection to 'New Coal Pits' now shown as a 'Pumping Station'. The former railway to Golborne Smithies has been abandoned, as has the original branch to Edge Green Colliery, but R.Evans & Co. have extended their colliery railway beyond Edge Green to other mines at Lily lane. By the time of the second survey from which this section is taken, the replacement signal box of 1887 would have been in operation at Edge Green.

Plate 65. A view from the occupation bridge at Golborne Summit to illustrate the new pointwork which had been installed for the Haydock Branch Junction Chord in 1968. Type '4' No.D382 heads north in the evening sunshine in June 1970 with 4S14, the 19.30 Crewe South -Glasgow parcels which has a new MKII coach in the middle. On Saturdays this train terminated at Carlisle, running as 4P27. *Alan Hart.*

Plate 66. Ex L&NW 'G2' No.9304 is seen in late LMS days at Golborne Summit on the Down Fast with an oil train from Stanlow. The occupation footbridge seen here was built to give access over the railway to Edge Green and was the vantage point from which *Plates 62, 65 & 67* were taken. Note on the far left distance, the water tower on the Lowton St Marys - St. Helens G.C. route near their Golborne station. (Golborne North from 1.2.1949). *W.D.Cooper.*

Plate 67. This view northward from the footbridge at Golborne Summit toward Bamfurlong is taken about 1965 as B.R. Standard, 'Britannia' Class No.70047, heads south on the Up Fast with a Carlisle-Crewe parcels train. This engine was the only member of the 55 strong class never to receive a name. Many of the footplate staff were critical of the rough riding characteristics of these locomotives, particularly when the trailing bogie became worn, the noise likened to sledge hammer blows on the cab!

The first of the 'Britannia' Class engines emerged from Crewe works in January 1951 and the last in September 1954. One of the class, No. 70004, *William Shakespeare*, received an exhibition finish with brass fittings and chrome plate for display at the Festival of Britain in 1951. Another of the class, No.70013 *Oliver Cromwell* would have the distinction of working the Leeds to Carlisle portion of the 'last' steam excursion over B.R. metals on 11th August 1968.
Jim Carter.

Plate 68. A another L.M.S period view at Golborne Summit as one of F.W.Webb's delightful 0-6-2 Coal Tanks No.2766, approaches the camera working a Warrington-Wigan North Western local train in 1946. Again in the background the Great Central overbridge is in view. *W.D.Cooper.*

Plate 69 (below). A complete contrast in motive power sees Class '37' No.37 706 *Conidae* at the head of 'The Institute of Mining Engineers' railtour on 21st September 1991 returning from the Kelbit Works with Class '47' No.47 479 *Track 29* bringing up the rear. The tour also traversed the Bickershaw branch on the same day. *Author.*

On 22nd April 1968, the former Great Central line between Lowton-St-Marys and Edge Green, Golborne, closed. On the same day a new chord was opened from a junction with the W. C. M. L. slow lines at Golborne Summit (Haydock Branch Junction). In fact, the section of route between Ashton-in-Makerfield to St Helens had closed on 4th January 1965. However, with the opening of this new curve and the easier working arrangements it presented, the section from Ashton-in-Makerfield to the Shell/B.P.* oil terminal at Haydock re-opened in July 1968. Also served by this chord was the Lowton Metals scrap works at Haydock. The release frame for this new junction was controlled by Golborne No.1 cabin.

Workings to Lowton Metals ceased in March 1987 whilst trains to the oil depot had ceased in February 1983. However, in the period April-June 1987, track was relaid on the former Great Central's connection to the Edge Green Rolling Mill site which had been taken over by Kelbit Ltd for deliveries of bitumen arriving from Humberside, the first train running over this relaid section to the works on 17th July 1987. In 2005, this traffic was transferred to a new terminal at Preston, accessed from the former Preston Docks branch line.

Race specials to Ashton-in-Makerfield for Haydock races also used this new chord running on 22.5.1975, 7.6.1975, 7.75, 9.8.1975 & 4.10.1975, the last time race trains ran. **Haydock Br. Jct. - Ashton-in-Makerfield @ 1m 373 yds Haydock Br. Jct. - Haydock Oil Terminal Sdgs. @ 1m 230yds.*

Plate 70. The construction of the new chord from Haydock Branch Junction is underway in April 1968, the new earthworks curving left to the WCML. On the extreme left the trackwork to Edge Green which met the Great Central's lines. It was later lifted, only to be re-laid in 1987.
Eddie Bellass.

Plate 71. Type '3' diesel No.D369 is seen propelling a ballast train along the new chord.
Eddie Bellass.

Plate 72. The men who carry out the P.W. Works are not often photographed. Here two platelayers attend to the job with tracklaying well underway.
Eddie Bellass.

North of Richard Evans Edge Green connections a further two main line outlets served collieries which again were to the west of the North Union Railway and joined the latter by north facing curves.

Brynn Hall Collieries were initially owned by John Smith & Sons between 1856 and 1866, at which latter date the firm was declared bankrupt. However, a succession of owners followed and a number of new mines sunk in the same area. Although much of Smith's colliery railway alignment is conjectural, their connection to the North Union line, made in 1856, was south of the Mains Colliery connections and a 'Telegraph' box was in operation by 1866, listed as Bryn Hall Colliery Sidings.

A second connection with the North Union in 1859, close to Smiths, was made by Mercer & Evans from new mine workings at Lily Lane and Park Lane collieries, all of which were again on the western side of the main lines and both of these colliery railways ran parallel on approaching the North Union, separated only by a few yards.

By 1869, both of these connections with the North Union had been dismantled and new connections made with the recently opened Lancashire Union Railway authorised in 1865. The Lancashire Union's line ran from St. Helens on a north-easterly course making connections with the North Union at Springs Branch, passing over the latters lines on a rising gradient from Ince Moss Junction. The original Lancashire Union proposal of 1864, although authorised, would have cut across the Edge Green coalfield and made a connection with the North Union south of Bamfurlong bridge. In the event, it was not proceeded with and the amended Bill, as passed in 1865, took a more northerley route as described.

Mercer & Evans, however, put in a branch railway from their new workings at Lily Lane to Richard Evans' Edge Green railway thereby continuing to work over the North Union's lines, and to the Dover Basin canal branch.

Mercer & Evans sold their Park Lane colliery to The Garswood Coal & Iron Co. in 1873. However, in the early 1890s, the latter sank a new colliery, Long Lane, south-west of the former's Lily Lane colliery. A new line of colliery railway was built from Long Lane towards Mercer & Evans Lily Lane colliery and by re-instating the old branch as formerly used by Mercer & Evans between 1859 and 1869, re-connected with the North Union by a south facing curve on 26th November 1893. Workings into this connection and sidings had been controlled by Long Lane signal box which was commissioned on 26th January 1893. Sited alongside the Up Fast line the box had 14 working levers and controlled access to the sidings, the Up and Down Slow lines, a cross-over road between the Slow lines and signals for the Fast lines. The cross-over here was often used to work a goods train from the Down Slow, by reversal, onto the Up Slow, thus allowing a following, more urgent goods train to pass, and/or gain access to Bamfurlong Sidings.

By the outbreak of W.W.II. the Garswood Hall mines in the area had ceased production and Long Lane signal box was eventually closed on 8th October 1945 and the block section extended to Cross Tetleys.

Cross Tetley's Mains Collieries were situated close to the main running lines. The collieries here, dating from the 1840s were, initially, small concerns under various ownerships that transported their coals to a wharf on the Leeds-Liverpool Canal near Bamfurlong bridge.

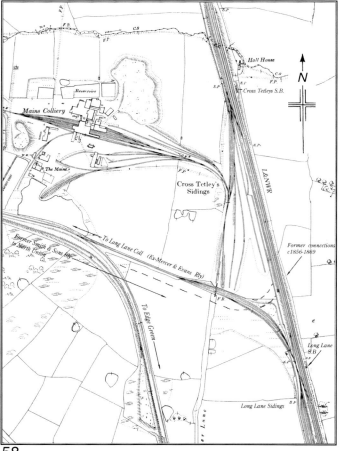

Fig 11. The expanded Mains Colliery, sidings and connections with the London & North Western, and those of the Garswood Coal & Iron Co. to Long Lane, are illustrated by the revised Ordnance Survey of 1906. Cross Tetley's signal cabin was sited 1 mile 1,235 yards from Golborne No.2 and 1,387 yards from Bamfurlong Junction (1888) cabin. Garswood Coal & Iron Co. eventually became Garswood Hall Collieries in 1929.

Plate 73. Stanier Class '5', No.44892 is seen at Cross Tetleys on the Down Fast line in the mid 1950s and by this date it is apparent that the signal box had seen better days. The pointwork giving access to Cross Tetley's Sidings can be seen to the right of the train. Also in view toward the rear is the footbridge at Golborne Summit and the signals as seen in *Plate 64* photographed from Richard Evans' colliery branch. *G.Mellor.*

The firm of Cross Tetley & Co. was formed in 1864 and they quickly set in motion a period of renewal and expansion having taken over a number of old workings, most of which were closed and new shafts sunk.

Line plans of the North Union c1864 show a series of sidings and a main line connection which had served the early collieries. In the 1860s & 70s these sidings were extended and around the same period Cross Tetleys took control of other mines in the vicinity.

As recession took hold in the 1920s and 30s a number of amalgamations within the mining industry occurred and Cross Tetley's mines were taken over by the Wigan Coal Corporation in 1934, with Mains collieries continuing in production under N.C.B. ownership until 1960. A siding had been retained at this location as a relief road, allowing trains scheduled to work into the overcrowded Bamfurlong Sidings to reverse into, off the Down Slow line, and await further instructions.

Cross Tetley's signal box was situated 1m 1,235 yards north of Golborne No.2 box, controlling the outlet from Cross Tetley's Mains Collieries, access to which was gained from the Down Slow. A cross-over between the Down Slow line and the Up Slow was also controlled by Cross Tetley's box and in addition there were signals here for the Fast lines. The first signal cabin at this location was in operation by 1875 having 18 levers. This was replaced by a second cabin in December 1887, during the quadrupling era, a London & North Western Type '4' having a 25 lever tumbler frame. This cabin lasted until 6th May 1961, by which time the mines in the vicinity had closed and connections with the main lines removed.

Plate 74. When taken over by the NCB, 0-6-0 *Bobs*, RS/2991/00, was aquired by Wigan Coal Corporation in 1934, given the No.1 and the name removed. It seen in that guise at Mains Colliery on 8th September 1959. *Peter Eckersley*

Plate 75. Type '4' No. D231 climbs the gradient from Bamfurlong towards Haydock Branch Junction on the Up Slow line with a tanker train for the Shell terminal at Haydock on 2nd September 1972. These English Electric locomotives were introduced in 1958 and weighed in at 133 tons. Although generally reliable, they needed to be worked at full power to maintain schedules, yet in many instances the maximum power available at the drawbar was much less than the steam engines they were meant to replace, the one advantage being that the power was more readily available. *Alan Hart.*

Plate 76. This view at Bamfurlong Station dates from 1951 and is looking north. The station was opened by the London & North Western Railway on 1st April 1878. With the onset of electrification in the early 1970s, the bridge in the background carrying Lily Lane over the railway would, like many others along the route, be rebuilt to give the extra clearance required. Over on the extreme left is Cross Tetley's single track from Mains Sidings to their Bamfurlong mines. *Stations U.K.*

BAMFURLONG

Cross Tetley's also had mines at Bamfurlong on the western side of the North Union Railway near the Leeds-Liverpool Canal, dating from the 1860s on sites which had seen earlier mining and industrial activity. The sidings connection at Bamfurlong dates from 1875. However, the sidings schedule also record that alterations had to be made to these siding under a seperate agreement of 6th September 1877. These were required because of the construction work for the new Bamfurlong station, sited south of Lily Lane bridge, in the period 1877/8.

Prior to quadrupling of the lines, Cross Tetleys worked their own trains between Mains Sidings and Bamfurlong Collieries, on a third line of rail opened between those two points in 1881, and retained after quadrupling. This line was first used by Cross Tetley locomotives on 14th May 1881 and by London & North Western locomotives a week later.

A signal box at Bamfurlong was in operation in 1878 and is shown on the Golborne - Springs Branch widening plans. It was sited at the junction of Cross Tetley's Bamfurlong Colliery Sidings south of the canal bridge at Bamfurlong. More levers were added to the box between 1881 and 1883 as new sidings and loop connections were laid, the total number of levers being 24.

In November 1888 a new cabin at Bamfurlong Junction opened in conjunction with the Platt Bridge Junction Railway, making the previous cabin redundant. This new box originally had 49 levers, extended to 66 in 1889 and to 74 in 1892. .

Although the Bamfurlong pits closed in 1936 the sidings connection at Bamfurlong was retained to serve a landsale yard and, during W.W.II., the sidings were taken over by the Ministry of Supply. Additional sidings were laid by the M.o.S. to cope with war traffic. The sidings agreement at this location was terminated in 1962, but they had been out of use for some time.

Bamfurlong Station was opened by the London & North Western on 1st April 1878, but not before the inspecting officer required that certain levers be brought together and not on separate platforms.

North of the station the railway crossed over the Leeds-Liverpool Canal (Leigh Branch) and the canal was spanned by a "skew bridge" of which contemporary reporting says was "a fine example." It is a great pity that subsequent developments and expansion of railway infrastructure at Bamfurlong swept it away.

North of the skew bridge, on the eastern side of the main lines, an arm of the canal had been served by a colliery tramway from mines at Strangeways Hall which were situated on the eastern side of the Wigan-Hindley (A577) road. By the early 1850s this had been converted to a standard gauge railway, extended, and a connection made with the North Union in 1853. The firm of Crompton & Shawcross were to take over Strangeways Hall Colliery in 1875.

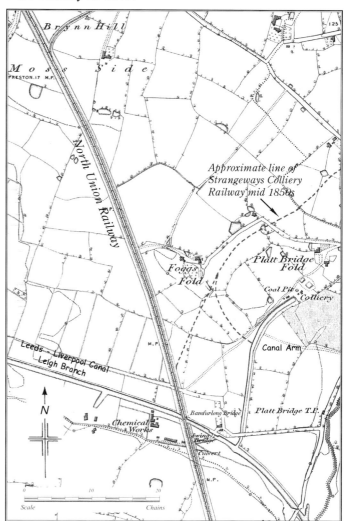

Fig 12. The connection to Strangeways Hall collieries from Bamfurlong met the North Union just north of the canal bridge and the approximate line is shown here superimposed on the 1840s survey. By the edition of the second series in the late 1880s it had been lifted. It is not shown on the Golborne-Springs Branch widening plans but the trackbed is clearly visible.

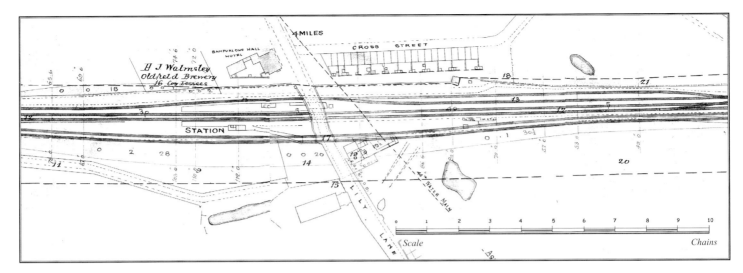

Fig 13. Bamfurlong Station opened on 1st April 1878, a portion of the platforms extending under Lily Lane bridge. The above is extracted from the Golborne-Springs Branch widening plans of 1886 showing the Cross Tetley line from their Mains Colliery to Bamfurlong which ran along the western side of the platform, the platforms themselves served by the slow lines only, these the original tracks of the Wigan Branch Railway. The new running lines which will become the Up and Down Fast are at the bottom.

Plate 77. The present day Bamfurlong Bridge still shows a 'skew' of sorts, but a far cry from that as built by Vignoles for the Wigan Branch Railway, successive alterations have destroyed that. The doyen of its class No.70000 *Britannia*, crosses the Leigh Branch of the Leeds-Liverpool Canal about 1965 with a van train and a good head of steam working north. *Tom Sutch.*

In 1881 the Strangeways Hall Colliery connection with the North Union line at Bamfurlong was removed, perhaps as a preparatory measure preceding the 1883 Acts which allowed the quadrupling of lines from Golborne Junction to Springs Branch Junction, and other works which extended sidings facilities at Bamfurlong. However, by this period, Crompton & Shawcross had other outlets, at Crompton's Sidings with the Tyldesley route, at Amberswood West Junction with the Lancashire Union line and at Strangeways West Junction on the Wigan Junction route, so the removal of the North Union link was of little consequence.

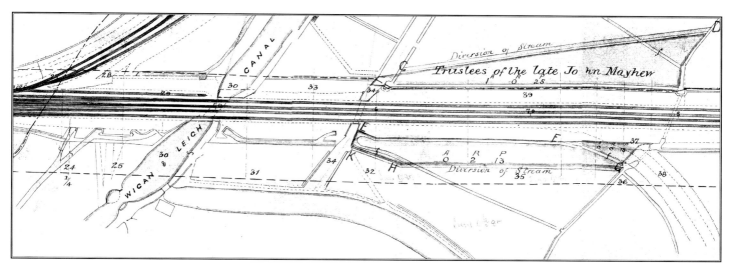

Fig 14. The line continuation of the 1886 document shows the railway passing over the Leeds-Liverpool Canal (Leigh Branch) just north of Bamfurlong station. Cross Tetley's lines into their Bamfurlong Colliery are at top left. At bottom right is the now abandoned trackbed of Strangeway's Hall Colliery's branch line where it had connected with the North Union. This had been severed in 1881 in advance of the widening works and quite obviously the London & North Western did not want colliery workings blocking up the fast lines with slow moving coal trains. The Strangeways Hall Colliery owners, Crompton & Shawcross already had another outlet with the Lancashire Union line at Amberswood West Junction from 1882, and with the Wigan Junction Railway at Strangeways.

Plate 78. Brush Type '4' No.1511 passes under Lily Lane bridge at Bamfurlong in 1972 working a northbound cartic train laden with Vauxhall products, 4S32 the 15.10 Gosford Green - Johnstone. The two vehicles on the upper deck being Vauxhal Viva HA vans. Lily Lane bridge had been completely rebuilt in the 1970/1 period to give the clearances required for electrification of the WCML northward from Weaver Junction. *Alan Hart.*

On 6th May 1961, a new box was commissioned at Bamfurlong Junction, a B.R/L.M.R. Type 15, flat top, all timber, (some of this type had a brick base) measuring 45ft -3in x 13ft -10in x 10ft, having 75 levers.

Bamfurlong Junction was an extremely busy cabin, controlling the Up and Down Fast lines, the junction to Bamfurlong Sorting Sidings, Down Whelley line, crossover roads between Fast and Slow lines, outlets from Nos.1,2&3 sidings onto the Up Slow, Up and Down Goods Loops to Bamfurlong Sorting Sidings, Up Through Siding, a road off the Down Slow to 'Bank' and the sorting sidings themselves.

Every train breaking up at Bamfurlong went onto this 'Bank' road which was permissive, worked by a block bell. The Up Through Road from Bamfurlong Sorting Sidings, and Up and Down Goods Loops were also permissive. A cross-over between the Up and Down Slow was situated on the Bamfurlong side of the cabin. The Bamfurlong Colliery Siding ran parallel to the Down Slow, in the direction of Cross Tetley's cabin.

Bamfurlong Junction cabin was in continuous operation, working shifts identical to those at Platt Bridge Junction. A Box Lad was employed to take telephone messages and train bookings. Goods trains, both north and southbound were relieved at Bamfurlong. Sometimes it was just a case of crews exchanging trains but as many as twenty sets of engine crews could often be waiting for their charges here in the 1940s, the relief cabin overflowing with bodies.

Bank engine No.62 was stabled at Bamfurlong Junction to give assistance to trains working over the Whelley route, either through freights off the main lines, or those out of Bamfurlong Sorting Sidings. Bank engines Nos.60, 61 & 63, 64 were stabled at Ince Moss for the same purpose. Trains for Manchester via Golborne, Lowton and Parkside East Junctions had a special "train entering section" code of 2/2/2/2.

During W.W.II troop trains were lettered "S" for British and "L" for American. The American trains were always routed onto the Down Slow line if possible, and obviously so when needing to relieve crews, enabling a bit of light hearted banter to take place between the U.S. troops and the Box Lad as the train slowly drew to a halt at the cabin, which went something like this:-

Plate 79. Stanier Class '5' No.45268 crosses over the Leeds-Liverpool Canal at Bamfurlong on 10th May 1966 with a Down excursion special. The lines from Bamfurlong Sorting Sidings can be seen on the extreme right. *W.D.Cooper.*

Fig 15. The complexity that was Bamfurlong and the surrounding area is illustrated by the Ordnance Survey edition of 1905, the arrangement of sidings, junctions and flyovers making this an extremely busy location until the late 1960s. Come the 1970s and electrification of the WCML, many of the sidings and connecting lines had been lifted. Some sidings remained at North End until the late 1980s and were used for the storage of withdrawn vehicles but these too have been lifted. The Platt Bridge Junction route has gone in its entirety, the last part of it being a short headshunt and single line spur to the CWS glass works.

Connections remain between Bamfurlong Junction slow lines and Ince Moss Junction/ Springs Branch goods lines.

Note also Fir Tree House Sidings, top right, and the colliery line from Amberswood passing under the former Lancashire Union Lines.

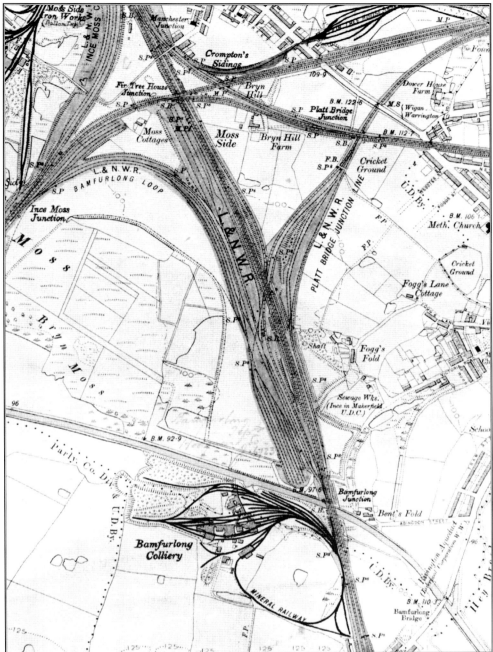

"Where are we bud," " you're on the approach to Wigan" came the reply. "Is this the place with the pier?" "aye but we've taken it in aatu't rain. Hey Yank, throw us a parcel," "why sure." These parcels contained food and other 'essential' items for the servicemen. "How many d'ya want," "oh just a couple," the box lad would answer and a shower of parcels rained down around the cabin to be quickly gathered up and shared out amongst the signalmen.

Fast southbound freight trains which had left the WCML at Standish Junction to work over the Up Whelley thus avoiding the congested central area of Wigan, were routed via Amberswood West Junction onto the Platt Bridge Junction Railway and via 'Flying Junction' onto the Up Fast at Bamfurlong. These trains would have to keep good time as they were interspaced with the express passenger trains.

Illustrative of the usefulness of this Wigan avoiding route, and of the serious traffic congestion through Wigan North Western up until the late 1960s, was the 2.30a.m., Spring Branch, North Sidings, to Blackburn freight. The train did not have enough pathing time to work through Wigan and up to Boars Head Junction for the Blackburn route via Red Rock and Cherry Tree.

The train would draw forward out of North Sidings onto the Down Slow where a banking engine would be attached to draw the train round to Ince Moss Junction. From Ince Moss the train was banked towards Amberswood West Junction and, if required, all the way over Whelley and the 1:60 Brinscall Bank.

Plate 80. The scene at Bamfurlong Junction on 29th March 1966 as Stanier Class '5' No.44911 heads south on the Up Fast with a Post Office parcels train. *W.D.Cooper.*

Powers had been granted, in 1883, for the quadrupling of tracks between Golborne Junction and Springs Branch Junction, a distance of 4 miles 48 chains, brought into use on 29th October 1888*. The Down Bamfurlong connection from Bamfurlong Junction to the Platt Bridge Junction Railway had opened in full by October 1889, having been authorised on 18th July 1887.

By an Act of 4th August 1890, the London & North Western Railway were authorised to widen the main lines from Springs Branch for a distance of 1 mile 22 chains towards Wigan. The same Act empowered the Company to purchase the land bordering the main running lines, the Leeds-Liverpool Canal and the Lancashire Union's Ince Moss-St. Helens route. It was in this area that Bamfurlong Sorting Sidings, Pemberton Corner, and Loop lines were set out.

Ince Moss North Sidings were completed in 1892. On 17th February that year the contract for the widening of the main lines into Wigan was awarded to J.Wilson & Sons for £13,184.10s, completed in the autumn of 1894. The Bamfurlong Loop and Sidings were completed in 1895. Goods trains usually arrived at Bamfurlong Screens after working over the Whelley route from Standish Junction via Amberswood West and Platt Bridge. The slower through freights working via Platt Bridge and Bamfurlong to southern destinations were routed over the Through Road and onto the Up Slow line at Bamfurlong Junction. The common term used by the signalmen for this manoeuvre was to "Bend it," indicative of the track alignment at this location as the train slowly wound its way beneath the main running lines, passing Bamfurlong Sorting Sidings cabin en-route before climbing the steep gradient from this lower level to access the Up Slow at Bamfurlong Junction.

Bamfurlong Sorting Sidings cabin had opened in April 1892 having 51 levers and controlled the access and egress to the complex of sidings including the Up and Down Loops to Whelley, Bamfurlong Junction and Springs Branch. * *see also Chapter III, PBJR*

Plate 81. This may well be a Sunday working as a Type '2' diesel trundles along the Up Fast south of Bamfurlong Junctions. The ensamble consists only of two wagons, a 16 ton steel variety and an older wooden bodied type, plus a small removable container and guards van. As the wires are up and the semaphore signalling still intact it is probably engaged on WCML electrification works in the Spring of 1972. *Alan Hart.*

Southbound trains departed from North End via the Up Through Road which was a block road, then onto the Up Slow at Bamfurlong Junction. Conversely, northbound trains departed from South End, working via the West Loop to access the Down Slow at a point where the route from Ince Moss to Fir Tree House Junction ascended over the West Coast lines or, if diagrammed to work over Whelley, onto the Down Whelley line via Platt Bridge. The Up and Down Whelley lines were absolute block, necessary to protect passenger trains (excursions & diversions) working over the route.

A ground frame gave access, c1950s, to the C.W.S. Glass Works from the Up Whelley route, and, one train per day worked in and out of Bamfurlong Sidings from the Great Central Railway via Hindley & Platt Bridge and Amberswood West Junction. All block roads at Bamfurlong Sidings were permissively worked. Bamfurlong Sorting Sidings cabin closed on 1st October 1972, on completion of electrification works for the W.C.M.L. modernisation.

In the late 1930s, Bamfurlong Sorting Sidings was one of a number of cabins for which the National Union of Railwaymen sought to have upgraded and a report detail-ing the complexity of working this busy cabin was put before the Railway Staff National Tribunal in 1938.

At that period, Sorting Sidings cabin was a Class '2' box, so designated since the classification of signal boxes was introduced in 1922. It then consisted of 54 working levers, four permissive block instruments, one single needle absolute block instrument, two circuit telephones and one control circuit telephone. The box was opened at 5a.m Monday until 6a.m. Sunday and was staffed by three signalmen working eight hour shifts. It had a reputation for being heavy and complex to work which had been eased only slightly by the downturn in the South Lancashire Coal Trade as a direct result of economic depression. That effect would be far outweighed by the onset of W.W.II and the additional freight movements generally on the railways.

Resulting economies put in place by the L.M.S. - better timing of freight trains and the elimination of unnecessary passage through the sidings of trains, were said to have eliminated some congestion and delay. However, about 80 freights worked into the sidings in any 24 hour period, the majority of which were terminating or starting trains from the sidings; and in any event, many light engine movements from Spring Branch shed were involved in these arrivals and dispatches which added considerably to the workload of Bamfurlong S.S. signalmen. In addition, there were through freights working 'Whelley' in order to avoid Wigan. The report continued "A few trains detach or attach in passing, leaving rear portions on the running lines when so doing and the signal box also deals with those engines which pass through entirely on the loops, the box for this purpose being a block post."

Mention was made of the strain that the signalmen were under, having to resort to a "primitive method of keeping check on the state of the necks" (conjunction of points in sidings). "To help keep a check they have a number of empty 20 cigarette packets." Written on these would be "neck 1 blocked," "neck 1 engine and van," "crossing engines," and so on. Evidently, the size of the cigarette packet fitted nicely over the lever handles. "It is only by continually and consistently mentally auditing his every movement by taking into consideration almost every lever in the his box that the signalman can carry on safely at all." In the event, the box was not upgraded, probably because there were no regular passenger trains booked over the route, and those specials that occasionaly did went on the Through Road.

Plate 82. On the approach to Bamfurlong bridge is Class '50' No.D402 working 4S57 the 18.35 Trafford Park Freightliner train to Glasgow in 1972. This working would change to electric traction at Wigan. *Alan Hart.*

Plate 83. One of the M.o.S. 'W.D' 2-8-0 locomotives labours its way along the Up Slow on the approach to Bamfurlong bridge in 1965, an ECS movement with twenty on. Generally unkempt and unloved these engines long outlived their intended lifetime. In the foreground is 'Flying Junction' where the Platt Bridge Junction Railway made connections at Bamfurlong. *Tom Sutch.*

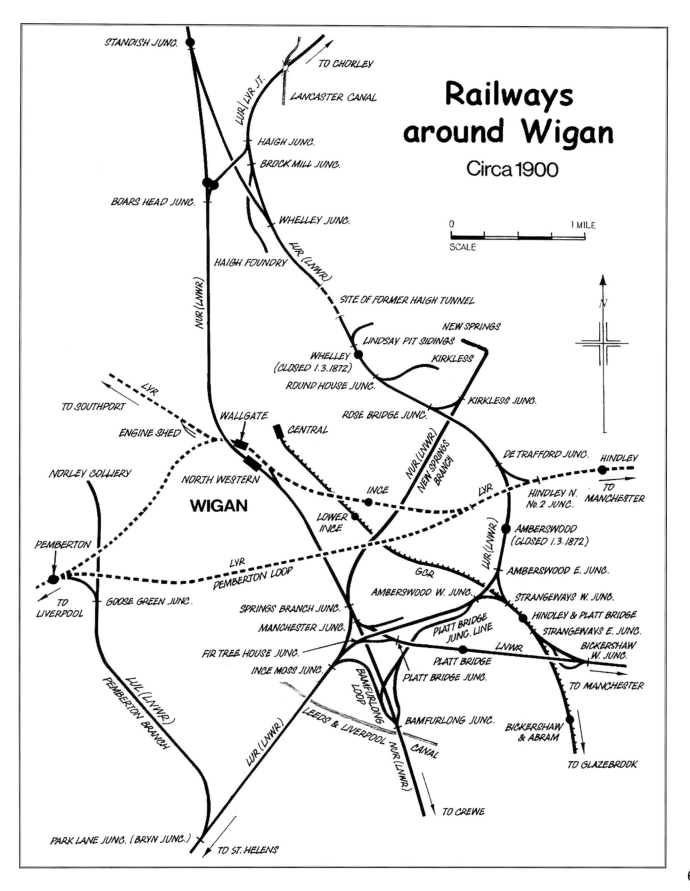

One Richard Blundell sank the Amberswood Collieries in 1842 on a site east of the North Union lines and his colliery railway connected with the North Union some 600 yards south of Springs Branch Junction by a south facing curve. Blundell worked his own trains to Preston in the 1840s, which again would mean shunting over the main running lines. One of his locomotives, *Ace of Trumps,* was involved in at least two accidents; one at Coppull in 1844 when returning from Preston with empty wagons, and a second at Preston in 1849. Blundell had also been authorised to work his own trains to Liverpool and Winsford via Parkside.

On the death of Richard Blundell in 1853, the firm was taken over by his son, Henry. However, by 1857, Henry was only using North Union metals as far as Wigan.

In the early 1860s construction of the Eccles-Tyldesley-Springs Branch line began which would cut across Blundells colliery railway west of Warrington Road and therefore a new connection was provided at Cromptons Sidings on the Tyldesley route.

Henry Blundell's pits were eventually to be taken over by Crompton & Shawcross who, as previously stated, were already mining in the same area at Strangeways. Later, as from 6th October 1908, the London & North Western Railway would work some 800 yards of the Crompton & Shawcross' mineral line from Crompton's Sidings Junction at Springs Branch, over Warrington Road level crossing (A573) into new exchange sidings at Fir Tree House.

In the late 1870s a wagon works was established - Fir Tree House Wagon & Iron Co., who later constructed premises alongside the branch on the eastern side of Warrington Road. Wagon Repair Co. are recorded as owners of the site in the 1920s. Shortly after W.W.II the wagon repair activity here ceased. However, the firm of Messrs Hodgson of Liverpool had built a coke cleaning and grading plant alongside the former Crompton & Shawcross' sidings in 1928. In the 1940s this was the only traffic being worked on the branch, tripped every day into Springs Branch Shed Yard Sidings for marshalling. The branch was still in use, intermittently, up to the early 1960s when, in 1962, after termination of sidings agreements, the level crossing over Warrington Road was removed and the branch closed.

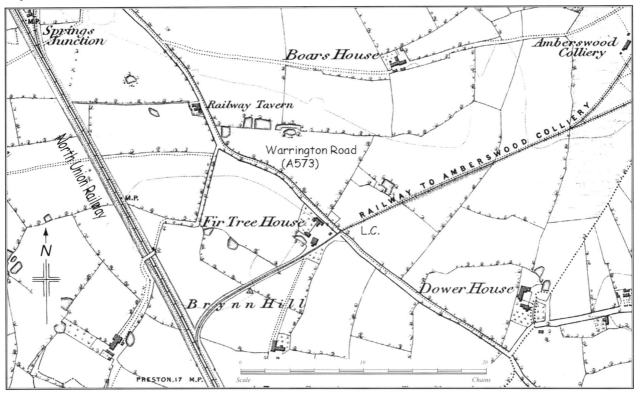

Fig16. Blundell's Colliery Railway to Amberswood c1845 showing the original connection with the North Union Railway some 600 yards south of Springs Branch. In the 1860s this whole area would be transformed with the construction of the Eccles-Tyldesley-Springs Branch route, the Lancashire Union's route from Ince Moss to Haigh Junction and the Platt Bridge Junction Railway. By way of colliery railways from Amberswood, Blundell's would have an outlet relocated to Crompton's Sidings on the Tyldesley line.

Plate 84. The Bamfurlong Junction cabin as seen here, is that as instituted on 6th May 1961, a BR/LMR Type '15', constructed in timber. Just beyond the box access was gained to Bamfurlong Sorting Sidings, the Down Whelley or Platt Bridge lines and the Goods lines to Springs Branch. In August 1970, Brush Type '4' No.D280, passes southbound on the Up Fast working 1M29, the 14.55 Glasgow Central - Liverpool Lime St. which was routed via Lowton and Parkside Junctions. Note, over on the far left Westwood Power Station. *Alan Hart.*

Plate 85. Bamfurlong Junction Cabin is seen from the opposite direction as Stanier Class '5' No.45371 heads north on the Up Fast in 1965. On the extreme right is the relief cabin. *Tom Sutch.*

Plate 86. 'Britannia' Class No.70027 *Rising Star* is seen on the Up Fast at Bamfurlong with a van train on 27th September 1962, about to pass over the burrowing lines from Bamfurlong Junction to Platt Bridge and Springs Branch. Over on the left, out of shot, are Bamfurlong North End Sidings. The bridge in the far background carried the Lancashire Union lines from Ince Moss via Fir Tree House Junction toward Amberswood Junctions and Whelley. *W.D.Cooper.*

Plate 88. An unidentified Class '8F' slowly manoeuvres its train from Bamfurlong South End, passing North End Sidings, through West Loop and onto the Down Slow about 1960. Above, is the Lancashire Union route with Fir Tree House cabin in view. The engine carries a Class '3' lamp and may only be going to Springs Branch North Sidings to shunt. The vans are thought to be return fish vans for Wire Dock. *Alex Mann.*

Plate 87 (left). The 1.30p.m. Crewe-Carlisle fast freight with Stanier Class '5' No.44680 in charge, is seen passing the Down Through Road connection at Bamfurlong, or West Loop as it was often referred to. The bolt lock and signal for access to the West Coast Down Slow at this location were operated by Springs Branch No.1 cabin, but the points were operated from Fir Tree House Junction cabin.

Through workings from Bamfurlong Sorting Sidings to Springs Branch or beyond meant that the signalman at Bamfurlong S.S. would have to contact Springs Branch No.1 and inform the signalman there of the type of train and its destination before being allowed to proceed. Once the train had cleared Springs Branch No.1 box, a return call would be made informing Bamfurlong that West Loop was now clear.

At this point the fireman of 44680 would be stoking up for the climb to Boars Head. The photographer, railwayman Jim Carter, is standing with his back to the Fir Tree House Junction flyover. On the far left at Bamfurlong Screens, an assortment of vehicles can be seen in the sidings. Signals in the 'off' position are Springs Branch No.1 home and Springs Branch No.2 distant. *Jim Carter.*

Plate 89. An unidentified Type '4' diesel passes the Fir Tree House overbridge which is seen in the throes of demolition about 1971. There will be no more Long Meg workings over this route! *Gerry Bent.*

Plate 90. Now stripped of its identity, 'Britannia' Class 4-6-2 No.70014 *Iron Duke* approaches Springs Branch in 1967 on the Down Fast with a Carlisle bound freight. *Mike Taylor.*

Plate 91. It is not only the steam locomotive that has, apart from special excursions, disappeared from the WCML, most of the A.C. Electrics have gone the same way. Whilst there is still the opportunity to see Class '86s' working freight, the '87s' are, apart, from special workings, almost extinct, some having been sold to Bulgaria and others scrapped. On 1st May 1991, Class '87' No.87 011, *The Black Prince*, heads north with an express for Glasgow and is passing the site of the Lancashire Union overbridge. *Author.*

SPRINGS BRANCH JUNCTIONS

The Springs Branch, synonymous with the New Springs area of Wigan from which it undoubtedly derives its name, a name which, perhaps, had we not been relating it to railways, altogether conjures in the imagination a leafy glade where clear waters flow, a place where contentment and inner peace may flourish.

Not so however; here, from the earliest days of the railway era, geography dictated that this was to be a hub of activity, in railways, in mining, in industrial engineering. A continuous expansion of the railways is in evidence until the early years of the 20th century when, as it has often been said, they had reached a state of 'complacent maturity.'

The branch line to New Springs and Kirkless was opened by the North Union Railway in 1838, this the true Springs Branch Junction. The route to Manchester Exchange via Tyldesley, Manchester Lines Junction, was opened by the London & North Western Railway in 1864, providing a much needed passenger service to the local populace, in addition to opening up the coalfields in the Tyldesley area. The Lancashire Union's St. Helens-Haigh route was built at the behest of Wigan coal proprietors anxious to gain other markets for their produce. This passed over the Parkside-Wigan lines at Bamfurlong North End by a steeply inclined gradient which began at Ince Moss Junction, also making a junction with the main

Plate 92. Class '8F', No.48211, complete with ballast plough, takes the London & North Western's Springs Branch-Tyldesley-Eccles Junction route at Manchester Lines Junction, Springs Branch, with coal empties from Lostock Hall for Howe Bridge West Sidings about 1962. Springs Branch No.1 cabin is in view far left. *Alex Mann.*

Plate 93. In the 1930s an unidentified 'Claughton' takes the Manchester route via Tyldesley and is photographed from Taylor's Lane bridge, which still affords a good view of the running lines at Springs Branch. Note the L&NW lower quadrant signalling in the background and the period lamp in the foreground.
Author's Collection.

lines, St. Helens Lines Junction, in 1869. Quadrupling of the tracks, expansions of sidings capacity, rebuilding of engine shed capacity and construction of goods loops all added to the crowded railway scene at Springs Branch. It is easy to see why the central area through Wigan became so congested.

All this railway infrastructure required signalling to control increasing traffic movements and from the 1870s to the turn of the century the proliferation of running lines and sidings at, and near Springs Branch, necessitated that provision was made for the safe running of the railway.

There had been one of the early Telegraph cabins at Springs Branch by 1866. By 1875, this had been replaced by Springs Branch No.1 and this in turn was replaced by a second No.1 on 17th September 1883, having 99 working levers and 13 spare. A third No.1 followed after only twelve years, in September 1895, initially having 65 levers, later increased to 80.

The first Springs Branch No.2 was opened in January 1877, receiving a new 48 lever frame in November 1889. In July 1895 this was replaced by a new cabin having 75 levers. On 1st March 1936, a Midland pattern cabin replaced the former London & North Western type at this location.

The expansion of the railways, not only in the Wigan area, but the country as a whole, gave to the world an oft forgotten benefit; that of measured time.

In the 1840s, Parliament was petitioned for the adoption of "Universal Time" by the railway companies who were supported by many sections of industry and commerce.

Speed and Time, science instructs, are relevant to the observer. However, time, in the formative years of Britain's railways, had become a source of exasperation to many travellers. Time in southern Scotland for example, was 20 minutes behind that in London, with greater variation between east and west. Many connections were missed due entirely to time variations in different parts of the land, and travellers stranded in out of the way locations, often for hours.

Yet it was to be nearly 40 years before the necessary Act to achieve this uniformity of time was passed. In 1880, under the Statutes (Definition of Time) Act, time was to be determined from the Greenwich Observatory in London and this became the standard, legal time for the railways, and for Great Britain as a whole.

This was of immense value to the railways when one considers the advent of telephonic communications which were rapidly being installed on the railways at that period, and the advances in signalling techniques, resulting in speeding up of many services, in particular, long distance travel.

In 1912, at an International conference in Paris, Greenwich Mean Time, (G.M.T) it was decided, was to become the basis for world time. Thus, this very concept, which we in the modern world take so very much for granted, stems from the early railway companies and the need of " Running to Time."

In L.M.S./B.R days, Springs Branch No.1 cabin was situated in the triangle at the junction of the branch to St Helens and Liverpool, alongside the Up Slow Main Line, and opposite the junction for the Tyldesley route. It controlled the Up and Down Slow, Up and Down Fast, Up and Down Goods lines, traffic worked via West Loop from Bamfurlong Sidings, an outlet from Springs Branch Yard onto the Down Goods and access into the yard from the Up Goods line. During W.W.II., this cabin was double manned continuously, later reverting to single manning on the Sunday 8a.m.-7p.m. turn, followed by a

7p.m.-8a.m. Monday shift, although at 10p.m. a second man came on shift who worked through to 6a.m. on Monday morning.

Similar hours were worked by Springs Branch No.2 cabin which was situated between the Down Goods line and the Up Fast Main line, at 417 yards north of No.1.

Again, Branch No.2 controlled the Up and Down Fast, Up and Down Slow and Up and Down Goods lines. From the Down Slow, access could be gained, by reversal, into Springs Branch North Sidings. A loop line running round from Ince Moss, permissive and wrong line worked, also connected with the Down Slow.

From Springs Branch North Sidings trains went 'Right Away' to Carnforth or Blackburn and all points North.

Crossings were provided between Down Goods to Down Slow, Down Slow to Down Fast and Up Fast to Up Slow. Fast and slow lines were absolute block and the goods lines permissive, an arrangement which also applied to No.1 cabin. No.2 was, from mid L.M.S., days a Midland pattern cabin which had replaced the earlier 'Wessy' design of 1895, as was nearby Cromptons Sidings cabin.

Off the goods lines trains could be run to Engine Shed Crossing on the branch to New Springs and shunted into Brewery Sidings. This branch, sometimes referred to as the 'Kirkless Branch' by enginemen was, as stated earlier, a part of the original Wigan Branch Railway Act of 1830, so authorised to connect collieries in the area with the main lines but not opened until 1838.

Plate 94. Class '5' 45243 is seen on the Up Goods Loop passing Manchester Lines Junction in the early 1960s with a through freight. Over on the left is the Yardmaster's Office. Every week an engine came off shed and crossed over to Ince Moss where a guard and van, and sometimes, a brake van cleaner would be collected; the van loaded with stores from the Yardmasters Office and delivered to each of the signal boxes over the Whelley line. The items were, soap, metal polish, paraffin, buckets, dusters, mops and weekly notices, but most importantly water as none of the signalboxes had mains connections.   *Alex Mann.*

Plate 95. An early 1960s shot at Springs Branch as Class '5' No.45092 passes No.2 cabin with the 1.30p.m. Crewe-Carlisle freight on the Down Fast line. Taylor's Lane overbridge is in the far background and on the far right a 'W.D.' creeps toward the Down Slow junction. In Springs Branch No.2 box the signalman can be seen silhouetted against the light. *Jim Carter.*

Plate 96. One of the BR built, Derby designed, 2-6-2 tank engines No.84000, passes Springs Branch sheds on the Up Slow about 1960 with a local train, possibly for the St. Helens route. This engine, along with Nos.84001-4, were allocated to Plodder Lane Shed when new in 1953, replacing the LMS built 2-6-2Ts which were transferred to other depots.
Brian Nichols.

Plate 97. A very well-cared for 'Jubilee' Class No.45666 *Cornwallis*, passes Springs Branch No.2 cabin on 19th November 1962 on the Up Fast line as a DMU approaches on the Up Slow bound for Liverpool Lime Street via St. Helens Shaw Street.

W.D.Cooper.

Plate 98. 'Britannia' Class 4-6-0 No.70034, minus its *Thomas Hardy* nameplates, is seen in the dilapidated condition so typical of the last years of steam passing Springs Branch No.1 box on the Up Goods Loop with a parcels train on 3rd September 1965.

Eddie Bellass.

Plate 99. Springs Branch No.2 as photographed in July 1872. This Midland pattern box replaced the one opened in 1895 and the re-positioning of signal boxes here has contributed to the line discrepancies on the Springs Branch route. *Alan Hart.*

Plate 100. Type '4' No.244 passes Springs Branch No.2 signal box on 16th August 1971 with a mixed freight on the Down Slow line. As yet, there is no sign here of the on-going electrification of the route which was steadily proceeding northward. Also, note in the foreground the line to Crow Orchard Coal Yard still in situ alongside the Goods Lines and, the intersection it makes with the Springs Branch lines just beyond No.2 box. *Tom Heavyside.*

Plate 101. A late afternoon scene at Springs Branch on 6th April 1962, as 'Royal Scot' Class 4-6-0 No.46162 *Queens Westminster Rifleman,* makes its way from the Up Fast to the Up Slow line thence via St Helens Line Junction to Ince Moss North Sidings with the empty stock for the workers trains between Wigan North Western and the Royal Ordnance factory at Chorley. These trains worked via Boar's Head, Haigh and Adlington Junctions to Chorley, where a platform had been specially constructed at the ROF Sidings to accommodate them. The signals. far left, are for Springs Branch North Sidings. *Jm Carter.*

Plate 102. A four car class '108' DMU, off the St. Helens route, passes Springs Branch No.2 box en-route to Wigan North Western in July 1971 with the 18.00 from Liverpool Lime St. Springs Branch North Sidings are still in situ on the right, as is the similarly named signal box which was worked by a shunter. Note the National Coal Board sign which says "Ince Moss Sidings" Tel.66419. Compare this to the photo above and note also that the Springs Branch Sidings signal arms have been removed from the post alongside the Down Slow. *Alan Hart.*

Plate 103. One of the Barton-Wright Class '25' 0-6-0 locomotives of 1877, No.52053 in early British Railways livery, is seen shunting a train of wooden bodied wagons at Springs Branch North Sidings in June 1950. By 1959 only one of this class remained in service (52044) and the wooden wagons had not long to go before being replaced in their thousands by the ubiquitous 16 ton all steel variety. *W.D.Cooper.*

Plate 104. An ex-LMS 2-6-4T No.42343 is seen shunting at Springs Branch North Sidings about 1960. This is one of the Fowler versions introduced in 1927, later versions had a cab window. The Stanier design with taper boiler and three cylinders appeared in 1933; these were built for the London, Tilbury & Southend Railway. In 1935 the Stanier two cylinder type came on the scene, and lastly, the Fairburn development in 1945. Also of interest is the line of wagons in Springs Branch Sidings which may be for scrapping at Central Wagon as all but one, an all steel 'Lancashire Steel - Irlam', are the old planked variety.

Alex Mann.

Plate 105. The Crow Orchard siding is still in situ c1964 as a BR Standard Class '3' stands alongside during some P.W. works. The bridge in the background carries the Pemberton Loop over the WCML, beyond that is Westwood Lane bridge. *N.Dyckhoff.*

Plate 106. Type '4' No.290 is seen on the Up Goods line approaching Springs Branch on 16th August 1971. The former Lancashire & Yorkshire's Wigan avoiding line (Pemberton Loop) had previously crossed over the WCML here as can be seen from the partly demolished bridge. In the background Westwood Power Station looms large against the skyline. *Tom Heavyside.*

H & E. Hilton had taken over 'Ince Hall Colliery' situated on the eastern side of the North Union in 1838. This particular Ince Hall Colliery, of which there were a number with identical names in the same area, had been sunk about 1820. By 1840 a connection with the North Union had been made north of Springs Branch. H & E. Hilton were declared bankrupt in 1842, and their mines taken over by Pearson & Knowles. These mines became better known as Crow Orchard Collieries. By 1864, the colliery railway had been extended to run parallel with the main lines southward where a connection was made at Springs Branch Junction

In 1840 Pearson & Knowles had sunk Springs Colliery, alongside the Springs Branch and were known to be working their own trains to Preston in the 1840s having purchased 'Planet' type 2-2-0 locomotive No.19 *Vulcan* from the Liverpool & Manchester Railway in 1841. Like most other colliery companies operating their own trains over the main lines, accidents seemed to be inevitable. Their locomotive *ASA* was in collision with a stage coach on a level crossing at Euxton in September 1841, whilst working empty wagons from Preston to Springs Colliery and, in February 1844, a Pearson & Knowles coal train suffered a rear end collision by one of Henry Blundell's coal trains worked by *Ace of Trumps* in which a brakesman from Golborne was killed.

In 1863, Pearson & Knowles sank the first of their shafts at Ince Moss, on the western side of the North Union and connections made with the latter opposite the Springs Branch in 1865. Eventually there would be six shafts on this site and was probably their most successful mining venture.

Pearson & Knowles amalgamated with Dallam Forge, Warrington, and the Warrington Iron Co., becoming the Pearson & Knowles Iron & Coal Co. in 1874. Dallam Forge had built their Ince Moss Ironworks alongside the Ince Moss Collieries in 1872 and a separate connection made with the North Union slightly north of the Ince Moss Collieries connection.

Since the opening of the Springs Branch the area has seen much mainline building activity firstly by the Lancashire & Yorkshire in 1848 with their line to Wigan Wallgate, and later by their Pemberton Loop, seen running across the top of the map in *Fig 17*. The Wigan Junction's line to Darlington Street opened in 1879 and is seen top right passing under both the Springs Branch and the Lancashire & Yorkshire lines.

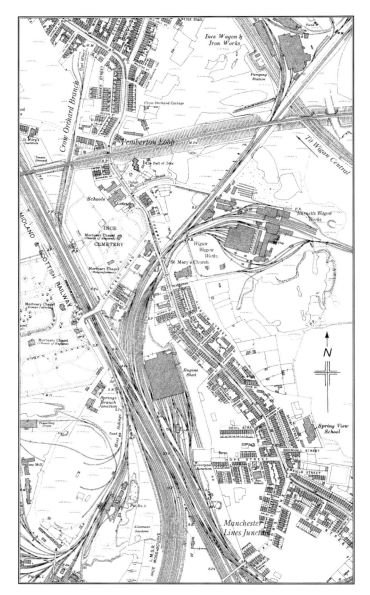

Fig 17. Crow Orchard Colliery and its line alongside the former North Union to Springs Branch is shown here at top left about 1925 continuing in use as a landsales yard until 1956.

The Ince Moss Colleiry connections were north of those of the Lancashire Union, the latter opening in 1869. The former Lancashire & Yorkshire's Pemberton Loop from Hindley to Pemberton Junction crosses both the WCML and the Crow Orchard Colliery branch line.

Also, middle right, is the site on which Springs Colliery was established in the 1840s, eventually to become Burnetts Works. It, and the adjacent Wigan Wagon Works of 1873/4, are shown with the 1896 connection south of the original Pearson & Knowles link to their Springs Colliery.

House building commenced on these sites, and the site of St. Mary's Church in 2006.

In the reorganisation of the 1930s carried out to counteract the increasing depression, Pearson & Knowles Iron Co., its subsidiary companies, the Wigan Coal & Iron Co. and Partington Steel & Iron Co., were amalgamated. The collieries became the property of the Wigan Coal Corporation Ltd., whilst the iron and steel works at Kirkless, Partington and Warrington, became the Lancashire Steel Corporation Ltd. These new companies came into being on 1st August 1930.

Pearson & Knowles Springs Colliery closed in 1870, Crow Orchard Colliery in the 1890s. However, the branch line alongside the main running lines continued in use to serve a landsales yard at Crow Orchard, worked into from their other collieries. The yard would eventually be taken into National Coal Board ownership in 1947, traffic worked into it by mainline locomotives until 1956, possibly later, as the branch line into the yard was still in situ in the mid 1960s.

Westwood Power Station, on the Down side of the approach to Wigan, had six roads, access to which was gained off the Down Slow. A ground frame here was controlled by Springs Branch No.2. Coal traffic had been worked directly into these sidings from Bickershaw Collieries for a number of years. However, a reversal of fortunes (to the railways) occurred in the 1960s when this traffic was lost to the canals and coal transported direct from Plank Lane to Westwood by barge until 1971.

There were also deliveries to Westwood via connections with the ex-Lancashire & Yorkshire's Pemberton Loop line and a number of reception sidings for traffic.

The power station itself was demolished in 1988, the cooling towers making a dramatic exit from the topography of Wigan when they were demolished by explosives

Plate 107. On 17th August 1971, Type '4' No.404 passes under Westwood Lane bridge with a southbound express. These engines were built at Vulcan Foundry, Newton-Le-Willows in the late 1960s and became designated class '50s' under the 'tops' renumbering scheme. Is it really over forty years since the first of these emerged from Vulcan works! *Tom Heavyside.*

Plate 108. Having recently emerged from Crewe works sporting a double chimney, 'Jubilee' Class 2-6-0 No.45596 *Bahamas*, is seen on the Down Fast passing Westwood Sidings with a fitted freight for Carlisle. *Jim Carter.*

Plate 109. The Stanier Class '5s' numbered 842 in total and were first introduced by the L.M.S. in 1934. Most had the conventional Walshaert's valve gear and single chimney, as in *Plate 112* for example. Here, seen at rest opposite Westwood Power Station, is one of the class, No.44686, as fitted with Capprotti valve gear, Skefko roller bearings and double chimney. The first Capprotti types Nos.44740-44757 appeared in 1948 after nationalisation, some with Timken bearings and/or double chimney. Nos. 44686 & 44687 were introduced in 1951, the only examples fitted as described above. Nos. 44668-44685 also had the Skefko type of bearings, some on the coupled axles only, but with conventional Walshaert's valve gear. *Alex Mann..*

Plate 110. Towards the end of their life the Stanier 'Pacifics' were relegated to much more mundane duties other than the Top Link express turns which had been their preserve until the new diesels gradually began to make inroads into these.

No.46237 *City of Bristol* heads north on the Down Slow with a Carlisle bound freight in the summer of 1963 and is seen passing Westwood Sidings. The locomotive was withdrawn for scrap in September 1964. *Jim Carter.*

Plate 111. The going away shot gives a good view of the amount of railway once to be seen on the approach to Wigan North Western Station. Also of interest is the load on the second vehicle of 46237's train - a boat no less. Now when was the last time you saw a boat going by rail? *Jim Carter.*

Wigan, Canal Bridge, (Sidings) first cabin had opened in June 1876 and appears to have been short lived, either being replaced by a second cabin of the same name in October 1879 or, the existing cabin receiving a new frame which in turn was superseded by a third cabin at this location in 1894, a Saxby & Farmer type cabin with a 54 lever frame which was to close about 1916.

On 31st May 1880, a new London & North Western-Lancashire & Yorkshire connecting line from Wigan, Canal Bridge, had been commissioned and on the Lancashire & Yorkshire side their Wigan No.1 cabin having a 48 lever frame, 40 working, 8 spare, seems to have come into use on the same date.

A first, North Union side, Wigan No.1 cabin is in evidence by the 1870s but in July 1880, a second No.1, an overhead cabin having 30 levers was opened. Yet a third No.1, a London & North Western Type '4' having 70 levers was commissioned in October 1894. This was built near to the Leeds-Liverpool Canal bridge, on the east side of the Goods Loops and it seems likely that the Canal Bridge Sidings cabin operations were eventually incorporated into this.

Just to summarise for a moment. In 1866 there were Telegraph boxes at the following locations between Parkside and Wigan at:- Golborne Junction, Golborne Station, (No.1) Bryn Hall Sidings, Springs Branch and Wigan (North Union) Station.

The 1866 Telegraph box at Wigan seems to have been extant until the substantial rebuilding of the North Union Station in the 1890s, more of which later. Wigan No.3 cabin opened in February 1894, an overhead Type '4' cabin having 19 levers, straddling the roads adjacent to platform No.8., south end. It was to close on 27th July 1941. Wigan No.4 had opened in July 1894 and was sited at the north end of the station and had a 66 lever frame. This was also a London & North Western Type '4' box.

Plate 112. With Wigan Gasworks in the background, a Carlisle-Crewe fast freight hauled by Stanier Class '5' No.45034, heads south on the Up Fast line about 1962 opposite Canal Bridge Sidings, left. Wigan No.1 ARP cabin is visible to the rear of the train in front of the gas holders. To the right of the engine are the Up and Down Goods Loops which ran from Bamfurlong northward to Wigan. Note also the wagon tippler in the gasworks yard, level with the top of the locomotive's smokebox. *Jim Carter.*

Plate 113. 'Royal Scot' Class No.46118, *Royal Welch Fusilier* leaves the environs of Wigan North Western with a Carlisle-Crewe parcels train on the Up Fast line about 1962, passing Wigan No.1ARP signal cabin. The 1894 built Wigan No.2 box had been situated between the Fast & Slow lines near Chapel Lane bridge. *Jim Carter.*

Plate 115. (overleaf) 'Patriot' Class No.45524 *Blackpool*, is seen approaching Wigan North Western in the early 1960s with a heavy Crewe-Carlisle fast freight the tail-end of which is still out of sight round the bend. Both locomotive and fireman are working hard at this point for the steady incline northwards through Wigan toward Boar's Head. Sometimes referred to as 'Baby Scots' by enginemen, this particular locomotive is as built with parallel boiler, never receiving the taper boiler as many of its class did. Note also the gas works sidings on the left. *Jim Carter.*

Plate 114. The present day structure that carries the W.C.M.L over the Leeds-Liverpool Canal on the south side of Wigan North Western station has seen at least two reconstructions carried out for widening of the route. There still remains, however, a portion of the original Wigan Branch Railway stonework as designed by the engineer Vignoles, which in its elegance stands head and shoulders above consequent rebuilds. It is unfortunate that a monotone reproduction does not convey the range of delicate colour still to be seen in this sandstone some seven generations after its construction. The angled masonry with its five panels a testament to the builders of Wigan's first railway. Hundreds of people walk the canal footpath passing this work each day, but I wonder how many actually notice it! Go and have a look.........
Author.

WIGAN, CHAPEL LANE

Wigan's first station had been at Chapel Lane, opened by the Wigan Branch Railway on 3rd September 1832, on a site now occupied by Do-it-All. It would undoubtedly have been spartan in its appearance with only basic facilities and not at all as we today imagine a station of today to be. Initially, it is likely that, as at most other early railway stations, these facilities consisted of something resembling a shed, for want of a better word. It may be that an engine shed, Wigan's first, was also constructed here by the Liverpool & Manchester Railway in 1832 but the hard evidence for its exact location remains elusive.

Plate 116. Wigan, Chapel Lane, as viewed from the approaches off the main lines on 14th August 1957. The site of the original Wigan Branch Railway terminus which had opened on 3rd September 1832, then a single track railway from Parkside was to the right of the later goods shed, close to the present day running lines. The opening of the North Union's Wigan Station on 21st October 1838, relegated the Wigan Branch terminus to a goods yard, a role it was to fulfil until the end of its days. Over the years, particularly in London & North Western days, it would be considerably enlarged to cope with the increase in traffic. Where the large goods shed stands is now the home for Do-It-All warehouse and car park. The former railway approaches to it in the foreground are derelict. Over on the right hand, between stanchion and gas holder, one of the large boilered ex Lancashire & Yorkshire designed freight engines is seen approaching from Wigan Wallgate, whilst a small saddle tank shunts the gas works sidings.

Plate 117. This early 1950s B.R. view of the traditional 'Goods Yard' could be replicated nationwide. This was to change, however, all too soon. The rail strike of 1955 lost much traffic to the roads which never returned and with the coming of the motorways yards like these would shut in droves.

Nevertheless, a view such as this at Wigan Chapel Lane portrays all the paraphernalia of yesterdays railway. The ubiquitous three wheeled Scammells, box vans, yard lamps, and cobbled yard all reflect an era long gone. *B.R.*

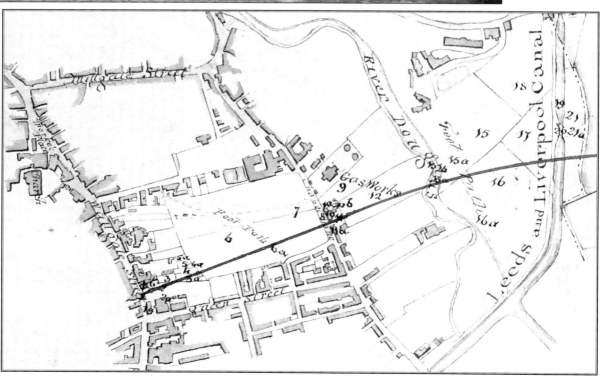

Fig 18. The 1829 plan of the Wigan Branch Railway differs, at Wigan, in one important feature from that as eventually built. It is shown terminating at Wallgate, not Chapel Lane, although the line of railway as built to Preston in 1838 by the North Union follows a similar course alongside Queen Street.

WIGAN NORTH WESTERN

The Romans are reputed to have established an out-station here, Coccium, on the banks of the River Douglas. Unfortunately, much of the evidence of this has been disturbed by later building and mining activity. Its fairs date from the time of Henry III, and a charter obtained in 1246 gave to Wigan the status of a Free Borough.

Coal is known to have been mined here from the fourteenth century and, in the sixteenth, Wigan was regarded as a 'Spa Town', the sick and maimed visiting its hot and cold springs. Eventually the waters were drained away by mine workings.

Part of the River Douglas had been made navigable in the eighteenth century to connect it with the River Ribble. In the later years of the the same century the construction of the Leeds-Liverpool Canal allowed mining activity to expand and by 1820 some 200,00 tons of coal were being transported along its waters, greatly helped by the number of wagonways or tramways which served the canal.

Robert Daglish constructed his first locomotive at Haigh Foundry, Wigan, in 1812, for use on Clarke's wagonway to Crooke on the Leeds-Liverpool Canal. Daglish would later set out the Bolton & Leigh Railway, the first Public Railway in Lancashire, part of which from Chequerbent to Bolton opened in 1828, to the instructions of George Stephenson. Another of Wigan's early wagonways ran from Stone House Colliery at Pemberton, to the north of Wigan, to a pier-head on the canal, this the Wigan Pier of much Music Hall hilarity.

When the Wigan Branch Railway opened its terminus at Chapel Lane in 1832, the population of Wigan was 21,000. By 1900, this had become 60,000 and has continued to expand ever since, and now (2008) being about 90,000.

On the outbreak of W.W.I. some 12,000 were employed in Wigan's mining industry but the recession of the 1920s and 30s reduced this to around 7,500.

It can be seen, therefore, that Wigan was ideally placed to become a hub of railway activity, for as Crewe was to Cheshire as a railway intersection, Wigan was to Lancashire as a mining conglomerate, and the need to move this self-generated fuel for industry ensured that the railway companies would not be too slow in providing the necessary infrastructure and, as the population of Wigan expanded, the dire need for a much larger station was met in the 1890s.

Plate 118. In 1873 a serious accident occured at the North Union built station at Wigan involving the 8.00pm from Euston - 'The Tourist'. The train was composed of two locomotives and 25 vehicles. As the train passed through the station at speed, the sixteenth vehicle suddenly broke loose and turned towards the Down platform causing considerable damage in which thirteen people were killed. Although the cause was never fully established the Board of Trade ordered facing point locks to be fitted on all passenger lines. The engraving shown may again contain some degree of 'Artistic Licence' but is the only known view of the event.

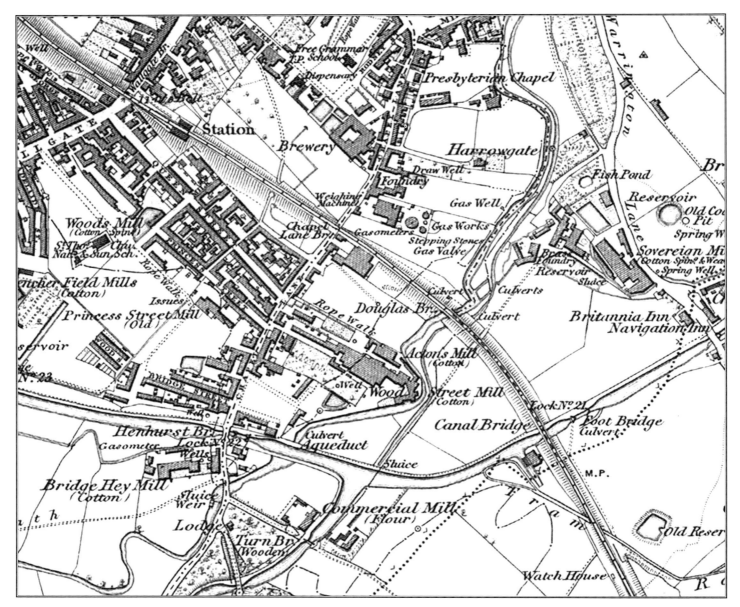

Fig 19. Although the orientation of this 1840s Ordnance Survey is quite different from that as drawn up for the Wigan Branch Railway on *Fig 18*, **Page 92**, the line of railway is virtually identical. A goods warehouse has been built alongside the railway bordering on Chapel Lane, (by the Liverpool & Manchester Railway) but strangely, no sidings into it are shown. It is also possible that this same building may have been used as an overnight stabling point for engines before the line to Preston was completed in 1838. There is no evidence to support an engine shed at Springs Branch at that period and, once the services to Preston began an engine or two would have been stabled there.

As previously mentioned, the North Union Railway had been incorporated by Royal Assent on 22nd May 1834, by the amalgamation of the Preston & Wigan Railway, whose plans for construction of the Wigan-Preston route had already been assented to, and The Wigan Branch Railway. This was the first amalgamation to be sanctioned by Parliamentary Act.

Authorised capital for the construction of the line to Preston was £320,000 with additional borrowing powers of £160,000. This was later amended to £460,000 share capital and £20,000 in loans. A further Act of 23rd March 1840, authorised a further £250,000 to be raised.

The North Union's line from Wigan to Preston opened on 31st October 1838, but it was not a cheap railway to build. There were substantial embankments to be constructed at Wigan, over Wallgate, to connect the North Union with the Wigan Branch Railway, forming an almost fortress like barrier on the western side of the town. Deep cuttings were necessary to the north, at Worthington, Boar's Head and Farington, and of course, substantial bridge construction over the River Ribble immediately south of Preston.

By the North Union Act of 1834, provisions were made for the interests of the colliery proprietors and landowners, allowing them to construct new sidings and connections with powers to run their own locomotives and trains over the North Union Railway. At least seven different colliery owners exercised these rights to work coal traffic to Preston, some still in evidence in the 1870s. These powers were finally revoked by Section 75 of the London & North Western Railway's Act of 1888. However, Section 76 of this Act preserved the rights of the Wigan Coal & Iron Co. to work their traffic along the New Springs Branch and over the North Union line between Rylands Sidings and Broomfield Colliery.

Stations on the route to Preston were:- Standish, Coppull, (sometimes given as Cophall) Euxton, Golden Hill, Farrington and Preston. Golden Hill became Leyland in 1839 and Farrington became Farington in late 1857. Standish became Standish Lane sometime before 1844, closing on 23rd May 1949. Coppull's original station was replaced by a new station on 2nd September 1895, this in turn closed on 6th October 1969. Euxton was replaced by Balshaw Lane and Euxton, 3/4 mile south of the original in 1895, also closing on 6th October 1969. A new Euxton & Balshaw Lane opened on 15th December 1997, served only by the slow lines. Leyland station remains open for local services only. Farington station closed on 7th March 1960.

At Wigan, the bridge over Wallgate was 45ft in length and 26ft wide with iron beams supported intermediately by two rows of cast-iron, fluted, Doric columns, six on each side, which separated the footways from the carriageways.

Whishaw in his narrative of 1840 writes "The station at Wigan is approached by a sloping road from Wallgate 24ft wide. On each side of the railway is a paved platform 8ft-6in wide covered by a colonnade in front of each building, the whole length is about 70ft. On the Wigan side is a booking office, a first class waiting room, a second class waiting room and a ladies private room. On the other (Preston bound) side the chief part is a 'carriage house' 24ft wide having two lines of (rail) way which run into the main line. The remainder of the ground floor is occupied by a general waiting room and booking office. In the basement are cellars for wood and coals etc." As to locomotives he states that " all are on Bury's plan of construction with four wheels, except the *St. George* which has six wheels".

The Bolton & Preston Railway Act of 1838, authorised the construction of a branch end on from the Manchester, Bolton & Bury Canal Company's railway at Bolton, which had opened for traffic on 29th May 1838, to join with the North Union at Euxton thereby providing for the Company to reach Preston over North Union metals. The previous Bolton & Preston Act of 1837 had intended to use the trackbed of the Walton & Summit Tramway in order to reach Preston. In the event the completed railway from Bolton to Chorley opened by 22nd December 1841, and the alteration to the route, so authorised under the 1838 Act between Chorley and Euxton Junction, opened on 22nd June 1843.

The Bolton & Preston Railway Company was purchased by the North Union in 1844. From 1st January 1846, the North Union had been leased jointly by the Grand Junction Railway and the Manchester & Leeds Railway, and from July 1846, vested jointly in them. The Manchester & Leeds Railway became the Lancashire & Yorkshire Railway on 23rd July 1847.

On 16th July 1846, The London & North Western Railway was formed with the amalgamation of the Grand Junction, London & Birmingham and Manchester & Birmingham Railways.

The North Union Railway was dissolved in 1888, becoming London & North Western and Lancashire & Yorkshire joint property on 7th August of that year. On 26th July 1889, the assets of the former North Union Railway were transferred to the two lessees. Euxton

Plate 119. The Wigan North Western Station as rebuilt in the 1890s is seen here during a quiet period in the mid-1930s looking north. Alongside bay 4 platform a set of local passenger stock awaits further use whilst in the centre road there appears to be a couple of wooden planked wagons, possibly for some local trip working or P.W. works. Apart from the main platforms, all that you see here was swept away for the electrification of the WCML, the first services through Wigan beginning on 11th May 1974.

Authors Collection.

Junction-Bolton, previously worked by the Lancashire & Yorkshire Railway was transferred to them. Parkside-Euxton, previously worked by the North Union became the property of the London & North Western Railway, as did the New Springs Branch line. Euxton-Preston, which had been worked and maintained jointly by the Lancashire & Yorkshire and North Union Railways was vested equally in the London & North Western and Lancashire & Yorkshire Railways.

In the mid to late 19th century many of the North-South 'Scotch' expresses would connect at Wigan with Liverpool and Manchester services and, as the volume of passenger and freight trains increased, Wigan was to become something of a bottleneck. The opening of the final link in the Wigan avoiding, or 'Whelley' route, in 1886 - the London & North Western's Platt Bridge Junction Railway - did allow some alleviation, particularly for freight and excursion traffic, but still the central area through Wigan was increasingly congested and although the mantle of providing interchange connections was increasingly being shared with Preston, something had to be done.

The North Union station of 1838 had, by the 1880s, long outlived its usefulness and the London & North Western set about a complete rebuild of the station. On 18th December 1889, a contract for the enlargement of the station was issued to the firm of Holme & King at a price of £21,983/15s.

When completed in 1894, the new station had five through platforms and five bay platforms. A second approach to the station had been constructed on the western side, namely Queen Street, but only opened for access to the station 8a.m. - 10p.m. On this side, arches carrying the station above were formed in blue engineering brick and used as bonded warehouses, stables, general storage and one utilised to house the hydraulic lifts installed at the rebuilt station.

The main entrance continued to be on Wallgate, diagonally opposite to that of the Lancashire & Yorkshire station. Subways gave passenger access to the platforms, and fish vaults under the station had separate lifts to the platforms. Milk and other market produce was also dealt with in similar fashion.

A passenger footbridge crossing the adjacent Lancashire & Yorkshire lines and Goods Yard linked platform 1 with King Street, a main business quarter of the town. Platforms 2 & 3 served the Up and Down main lines respectively, No.1 platform generally used for Up workings also. Bays 2 & 3, south facing, used for local passenger services to Liverpool, Manchester and Warrington. No.4 platform provided relief for Down workings and was bi-directional. Two more south facing bay platforms, Nos. 3 & 4, mostly used for local passenger arrivals, with a centre road between these allowing extra shunting capacity for run-round movements. No.5 bay, north facing, was used for Blackburn and East Lancashire trains.

No.5 platform was used for mostly for excursion traffic and relief trains, mostly in the Down direction, but also for goods and mineral traffic to work through the station when other lines were busy. At the south end of this, access could be gained to the turntable and a bank engine siding. At the north end of the station, parallel to the Up Main and platform No.1 roads, a horse dock and carriage sidings were situated.

Lengths of platforms were as follows:-

No.1 Platform	194	yards
No.2 "	251	do
No.3 "	294	do
No.4 "	310	do
No.5 "	265	do
No.1 Bay	92	do
No.2 "	109	do
No.3 "	149	do
No.4 "	149	do
No.5 "	99	do

Plate 120. The WCML passes over the Lancashire & Yorkshire lines north of W.N.W. Station as seen here in this view from Wigan Wallgate in the 1930s. One of the Lancashire & Yorkshire large boilered 'Baltic' 4-6-4 tank engines runs alongside some period advertising. *Authors Collection.*

Plate 121. Former London & North Western ' Prince of Wales' class 4-6-0 No.5770 calls at Wigan North Western with a northbound express during the Easter holiday period of 1926.   *W.D.Cooper.*

No.3 signal box was situated on platform 5 with a gantry spanning over platform 4 & 5 roads. No.4 box controlled access to lines at the north end, whilst No.2 box, the largest signal box here, controlled lines at the south end.

In the early twentieth century, by far the busiest period was during the night with heavy parcels, luggage, mail and newspaper trains converging on Wigan from all directions, all needing to be loaded or unloaded, as the case may be, often re-marshalled, and sent on their way.

Although most of the day express trains met connecting services at Preston, a number of the 'Scotch' expresses still connected at Wigan, particularly during the Summer season at night, beginning soon after 10p.m. with the arrival of the 9.15p.m. from Manchester and the 9.30p.m. from Liverpool. Both of these are stopping trains but with them come considerable quantities of luggage and parcels all of which required sorting at Wigan.

The yearly escapade of the landed gentry for the 'Glorious' 12th of August sees the arrival of special 'grouse' expresses which depart from Liverpool at 10.p.m. and from Manchester at 10.15p.m. These departed Wigan at 11.30p.m. as a combined train for Perth.

Shortly before the Perth train departed, further trains from Liverpool and Manchester have arrived followed by the 8.p.m. from Euston. Enormous volumes of parcels and packages for the north have to be loaded onto the latter in the respective vans for Aberdeen, Dundee, Oban, Stranraer and Glasgow in just a few minutes, this train departing at 12.10a.m.

At 1.29a.m., the 8.50pm Scotch Express from Euston arrives followed at 1.51a.m. by the 9.p.m. from Euston which has worked via Birmingham. Connecting with these are the 1.22a.m. from Liverpool and the 1.23a.m. from Manchester, each with through coaches for Glasgow.

A less hectic period followed until about 3am when another rush began with mountains of newspapers, parcels, fish, meat and market produce as expresses from London and Carlisle arrived. The 3.05a.m. from Wigan conveyed London vans for Preston and Whitehaven, some of these vans arriving on earlier trains from Liverpool and Manchester. Fish vans for Lancaster, Blackpool and the Furness line were attached along with two passenger coaches. There would be anything from twelve to twenty vehicles on this train. After the departure of a parcels train for East Lancashire around 3.30a.m. the workload eased off again and several of the Scotch Expresses were non-stop through Wigan.

At 5.a.m. a special colliers train departed for Abram Colliery for which old North London Railway coaches were used. It is worthy of note that the (wooden) seats of these had been padded to suit the ideas to which it was said "Lancashire colliers are accustomed"!

At 5.30a.m., a stopper for Preston departed conveying mill girls for Coppull, which in the summer months was also composed of ex-North London stock, but in the winter used steam-heated coaches. This was followed by the midnight train from Euston, arriving at 5.38a.m. At 6.23a.m. a slow train from Preston arrived, departing at 6.28a.m. for Crewe, Chester and other parts of the London & North Western system.

The first local from Warrington via Earlestown arrived minutes later followed by the 6.49a.m. departure of the Belfast Boat train from Fleetwood bound for London, with connections for Liverpool and Manchester. The 7.45a.m. and 8.a.m. from Liverpool and Manchester respectively, arrived and combine to form a 'Commercial Express' for Lancaster, Carlisle, Barrow and Kendal.

An interesting working, Mondays and Saturdays only, consisting of North Staffordshire Railway stock, passed through, working from Stoke to Blackpool. Mondays, Wednesdays and Saturdays express for Morcambe departed at 9.10a.m. with connections from Liverpool and Manchester, followed at 9.53 by a Liverpool - Blackpool train.

At 10.14a.m. the 5.a.m. from Euston arrived for Glasgow with connections from Liverpool Exchange (via Preston) and Manchester Victoria. This train included a luncheon car. A Crewe - Blackpool called at 10.40a.m., followed by the 'Lake District Express' from Liverpool at 10.10a.m., and Manchester 10.15a.m. Another notable train calling at Wigan was the 9.42a.m. from Cambridge which arrived at 2.38p.m. during the summer months only.

The above are only a sample of the traffic which was interspaced with the more mundane local trains, express and semi-fast workings; summers specials from all parts of Lancashire, Yorkshire, the Midlands and points north of Wigan. There were the regular football and other 'specials' to places of interest including the not to be forgotten 'Pigeon Race' specials. Consisting of 12 to 20 vans, these trains would often require re-marshalling at Wigan for various destinations within the U.K. and also to the continent via boat trains. In any twenty-four hour period there would be some 230 arrivals and departures, excluding through passenger, freight and local trip workings.

It would not be until the late 1950s and early 1960s that that the numbers were seriously reduced. Long gone now the parcels, mail, newspaper, fish and market trains, not only from Wigan, but the rail system as a whole and whilst some resurgence of passenger traffic has occurred in recent years, they really are a very pale shadow of what once was.

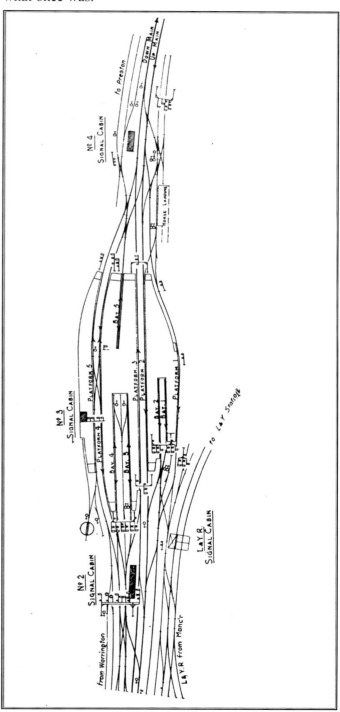

Fig 20. Station arrangements and track layout at Wigan North Western c1912.

Plate 122. This pre-W.W.II view from the south end of Wigan North Western clearly shows the juxtapositions of the 19th century-built signal boxes with, on the ex-Lancashire & Yorkshire side, left, their No.1 cabin, and the ex-London & North Western No.2 cabin of 1894, centre. As can be seen when compared to *Plate 1,* the cabin is much closer to the station than the later Wigan No.1 ARP box.
Authors Collection.

In the 1930s, plans were approved for the modernisation and resignalling of parts of the WCML at, amongst other locations, Preston and Wigan.

At the south end of Wigan North Western station the London & North Western No.2 and Lancashire & Yorkshire No.1 were located within a few yards of each other and shared control of the connections between the two routes. The proposed scheme was to install colour light signalling and to replace the existing cabins by three new ones. The new Wigan Nos.1 & 2 would be sited at the South and North ends of Wigan North Western respectively. The third new cabin would be sited at the North end of Wigan Wallgate station, where the Liverpool and Southport lines diverged.

At Preston, the proposals involved the installation of colour light signalling throughout and a total of eight cabins in the ex-London & North Western and ex-Lancashire & Yorkshire station areas were to be replaced by two new power boxes at the south and north ends of Preston station. In the event, the Preston scheme was cancelled at the outbreak of W.W.II. before much site work had been done. The signalling equipment which had been delivered was recovered and eventually used at Euston and Cannon Street in 1951 and 1959 respectively.

By the time war did break out in 1939, much of the preliminary work for the Wigan scheme had been done and the decision was taken to complete the resignalling work in full.

The three Wigan signalboxes were designed to the London Midland & Scottish Region ARP (Air Raid Precaution) specification with solid 14inch brickwork and a flat concrete roof built to withstand the bombing during W.W.II. Unusually for a war-time installation, concrete name panels using large embossed lettering were set beneath the signal box windows but these were speedily boarded up and remained so for the duration of the war. In the event of invasion, this was supposed to confuse the enemy!

Wigan Wallgate was the first of these new cabins to be commissioned on 27th July 1941, followed by Wigan No.2 in August 1941 and lastly, Wigan No.1 on 24th May 1942. At this period no less than twelve older signal cabins, including some on the former Lancashire & Yorkshire lines, having a total of 472 levers, were replaced by the three L.M.S types having 200 working levers.

All roads through Wigan North Western were worked as 'Station Yard Working,' thus allowing more than one train on each line.

Off the Down Slow, access was gained into Wigan, Chapel Lane Goods Yard which, by the 1930s, had nine sidings, No.1 being nearest to the slow lines. Access could also be gained off the Down Slow into Wigan Canal Sidings which had two roads running parallel to the Down Slow called 'Front Road and Back Road.' It was also possible to work to/from the Up Slow line at this location.

At the north end of Canal Sidings was a Down Slow to Down Fast connection and south of Wigan No.1 were Down Goods to Down Fast and Up Fast to Up Goods connections. The Up & Down former Lancashire & Yorkshire lines were also under the control of Wigan No.1 ARP box as was the entrance into Wigan Gas Works, off the Up line. C1940s the gas works had three sidings putting out about twenty wagons of coke per day.

All the signals controlled by these new boxes were electrically operated but the points were mechanical although some had motorised apparatus.

The 1942 built Wigan No.1 had in fact replaced the former 130 lever London & North Western Type 4 cabin, Wigan No.2 of December 1894, which had been sited near Chapel Lane bridge, *(Plate 122)* the third Wigan No.1 of 1894, and the Lancashire & Yorkshire's Wigan No.1 cabin. The 'Wessey,' Wigan No.2 had itself replaced the first, earlier, No.2, known to be in operation by 1875.

Wigan No.1 ARP cabin had dimensions of 55ft x 24ft-4in x12ft and controlled the Up & Down Goods Loops, Up & Down Fast lines, Up & Down Slow lines, all platforms and bays at the south end of Wigan North Western and the entrance to Top Yard. Up & Down Goods were permissively worked whilst the Up & Down Slow and Fast lines were absolute block. In addition, Wigan No.1 ARP controlled traffic on both the former London & North Western and Lancashire & Yorkshire routes.

On the London & North Western or 'Wessy' side of the cabin there were 70 working levers with 15 spare plus 74 switches, whilst the Lancashire & Yorkshire or 'Lanky' side had 30 working and 10 spare with 39 switches. It was continuously manned having three signalmen on duty each turn, two 'Wessey' and one 'Lanky'. Two men were on duty Sundays working 8a.m.-7p.m., replaced by two men at change of shift with the third man coming on at 10p.m. until 6a.m. Monday morning.

The Wigan No.2 L.M.S. ARP Type was smaller than the Wigan No.1 ARP box previously mentioned, having dimensions of 41ft x 13ft -7in x12ft. It was built adjacent to the old Wigan No.4, alongside the Down line and had a 65 REC tappet frame, 45 working levers and 20 spare with 15 switches. New and old boxes at this location opened and closed simultaneously on 3rd August 1941.

Wigan No.2 ARP cabin could turn a train from the Up Fast into No.1 platform, had a cross-over road situated north of the cabin, controlled the Up & Down Fast lines and the junction off Nos. 8 & 10 roads to the Down Fast. From Nos. 8 & 10 roads it was also possible to work into the sidings which ran behind Wigan No.2 ARP box. There were also two sidings on the Up side, opposite No.2 cabin which could be shunted into off No.1 platform or the Up Main. No.2 was a one man job, continuously operated in three shifts and again, as at Wigan No.1 ARP box, the signals were electrically operated with mechanical points operation. A box lad was also employed here and during W.W.II. was required to work Sundays.

From the opening of Wigan No.2 ARP cabin in 1941, until its closure with the onset of the 1970s modernisation, it was not unknown for the signalman on the day turn or afternoon turn to be constantly engaged with

E.R.O. 47916/2
No. 1100. G.

LONDON MIDLAND AND SCOTTISH RAILWAY COMPANY
(WESTERN AND CENTRAL DIVISIONS)

SPECIAL NOTICE

THIS NOTICE MUST BE KEPT STRICTLY PRIVATE, AND MUST NOT BE GIVEN TO THE PUBLIC

NOTICE TO DRIVERS, GUARDS, SIGNALMEN AND OTHERS RESPECTING THE INTRODUCTION OF COLOUR LIGHT SIGNALS WIGAN (NW) AND WIGAN (WALLGATE) STATIONS.
STAGE I.

The diagram attached to this notice should be retained for reference until the whole of the signalling shown thereon has been brought into use. Notices of the carrying out of the various stages of the work will be issued as these are brought into use, but no further issue of the diagram will be made.

IMPORTANT:—This notice to be acknowledged IMMEDIATELY on receipt to "TRAINS F. B. CREWE" using the code:—
"DERWENT 1100. G."

shunting movements for parcels traffic. These parcels trains were nearly always worked into Nos.8 or 10 roads and the necessary shunting arrivals and departures kept the Platform Inspectors, his assistant, and the Parcels Foreman well occupied. Also, two Coach Shunters and a Tail Lamp Man were employed on each shift.

The late p.m. Fleetwood-Crewe fish train is a good example of the shunting carried out at Wigan North Western at the time. The train would be split into three loads, the first portion for Crewe, the middle portion for Chester and the rear part of the train for Bolton and Manchester. This latter part would be shunted into No.1 platform and worked out via the cross-over at the south end of the station onto the ex-Lancashire & Yorkshire lines.

As viewed from a northbound approach to the station the platforms were arranged, from the 1940s resignalling as follows, working east to west:-
No.1 Platform.
No.2 Bay, South facing.
No.3 Bay, South facing.
No.4 Platform, Up Main.
No.5 Platform, Down Main.
No.6 Bay, South Facing.
Middle Road.
No.7 Bay, South facing.
No.8 Platform, Through Road, Up & Down working.
No.9 Bay, North facing.
No.10 Platform, Through Road, Down only. *

Midway between Nos.8 & 10 there was a scissors cross-over with motorised apparatus, worked from Wigan No.1 ARP cabin. Here, previous to the 1940s signalling modernisation had been Wigan No.3 cabin, elevated and spanning Nos. 8 & 10 roads. No.8 road was called Up & Down, covered by 'Station Yard Working.' There was a locomotive turntable at the south end of No.10 road.

Access to the west side, south facing roads could be gained from either Down Fast or Down Slow lines.

Plate 123. At the north end of Wigan North Western 'Royal Scot' Class No.6132 *Phoenix* waits to depart from No.3 Down Main platform northbound about 1934/5. The locomotive has the parallel boiler as built but has received angled-top smoke deflectors as against the first applications of the straight sided type in 1932/3. In 1936 the locomotive was renamed *The Kings Regiment Liverpool*.

Note also Wigan No.4 cabin of 1894 in the background. This would be replaced by the LMSR ARP type, Wigan No.2 in 1941. *Authors Collection.*

Middle Road, situate between Nos. 6 & 7 Bays was often utilised to stable parcels traffic shunted in during remarshalling operations.

Warrington-Wigan and Manchester-Tyldesley-Wigan locals arriving here were worked into the appropriate platform, dependent on the next booked destination. On the Up, or east side, traffic being remarshalled was shunted into platform Nos.1,2 & 3 as necessary.

Dependant upon the next rostered working, the Wigan-Tyldesley-Manchester locals, for example, arrived or departed from platform Nos.1,5, 6 or 7, but in later years, until withdrawl of the Wigan-Tyldesley-Manchester services in 1964, No.1 platform seemed to be used mostly for these departures.

* *Also see Pages 106-109, Wigan Signalling Alterations c1941.*

Plate 124. The view northward from No.5, Down Main platform at Wigan North Western. This appears to date from about 1940 as again Wigan No.4 cabin can be seen but behind it the new ARP box is well under construction. Over on the extreme left one of the 'Patriot' class engines makes ready to depart from the old No.4 platform. These engines were rebuilds of the 'Claughton' class first introduced in 1912, two of which, Nos.5500 & 5501, retained their original wheels and although it cannot be determined which of the two engines this is, the driving wheels have the larger axle bosses. Interestingly, the engine is still paired with a 'Claughton' tender. *Authors Collection.*

Plate 125. At the south end of Wigan North Western about 1960, Stanier Class '5' No.44986 arrives with an excursion special as the spotters gather.
Alex Mann.

Plate 126. The platforms at the south end of Wigan North Western gave a good view of trains in and out of Wigan Wallgate. In this mid 1930s photograph one of the Hughes 4-6-0s passes, Manchester bound. These locomotives were built by the Lancashire & Yorkshire Railway at their Horwich works from 1908 onward, having only just been rebuilt in 1921, before the Company became part of the L.M.S.
Author's Collection.

Plate 127. The only BR Standard Class '8' No.71000 *Duke of Gloucester* takes water at Wigan N.W. about 1960 whilst working a southbound parcels train, an ex-GW siphon van next the engine. This locomotive was built a Crewe in 1954 as a replacement for ex-LMS 'Pacific' No.46202 *Princess Anne* damaged beyond repair in the disastrous Harrow accident of 1952. The design was based on that of the 'Britannia' class, but with 3 cylinders, Capprotti valve gear, enlarged grate and double chimney. As the diesel era grew nearer in the form of the 1955 modernisation plan, No.71000 was expected to be the climax of British passenger locomotive design. Unfortunately it did not live up to expectations. It was placed in the 'Pacific' link at Crewe North and gained a reputation as a heavy coal burner and poor steamer. Only since, in preservation, has it performed to its full potential. The locomotive was withdrawn from BR service in 1962, rescued from Barry scrapyard in 1973 and restored at Loughborough.
Authors Collection,

Plate 128. Now here's a photograph which turned up at almost the last minute. Taken in the Edwardian period at North Western the station staff have, it appears, been specially assembled to pose for the cameraman. There are three Inspectors in the group, first and third left, standing, and far right. I presume the Station Master is wearing the bowler hat (maybe he ought to have had a larger size!). Poignantly, I find the five boys, who are probably train reporting or telegraph boys, illustrate the era all too well. The one next to the station master looks a little older and much more 'streetwise' than the other four who themselves can't be more than twelve years old. Sill, I suppose it was better than being sent down a mine. *Alan Grundy.*

Plate 129. Slowly but surely diesel locomotives began to make inroads into workings once the preserve of the steam engine. At first very intermittently and my first sight of a diesel was at North Western in 1958 when one of the new 'Peak' class of locomotives, No.D7, passed through southbound, probably on test. In May 1960 D5058, (later class '24') arrives at Wigan with an 'Up' passenger train.
Jim Peden Collection.
(Ron Stephens).

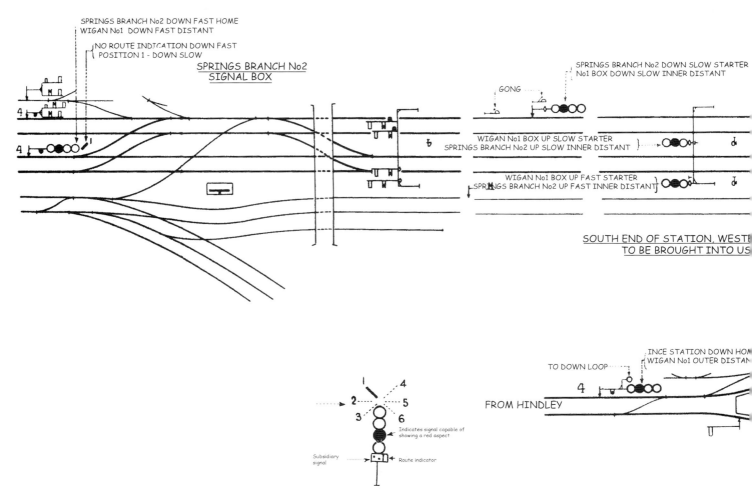

Notes:-
A junction indicator exhibits a line of white lights when a proceeed aspect is given for a diverging route. (Rule 35e)
Thus:-
A junction indicator is never illuminated with a subsidiary signal. Small route indicators are generally associated with subsidiary signals except for bay departure signals where they may be associated with both the main and subsidiary aspects.
Large route indicators are in all cases associated with main and subsidiary signals.

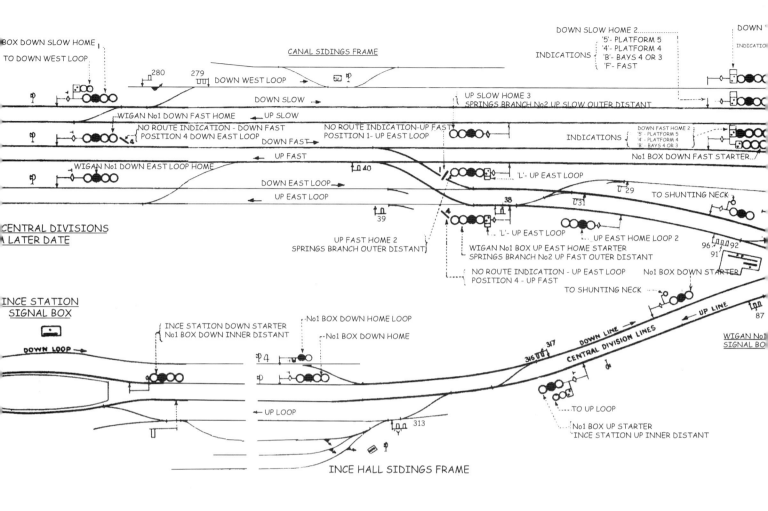

Wigan No.1 had the additional feature of controlling traffic on both the London & North Western and Lancashire & Yorkshire lines at Wigan.

On the London & North Western or 'Wessy' side of the cabin there were 70 working levers with 15 spare plus 74 switches, whilst the Lancashire & Yorkshire or 'Lanky' side had 30 working and 10 spare with 39 switches. It was continuously manned having three signalmen on duty each turn, two 'Wessey' and one 'Lanky'. Two men were on duty Sundays working 8a.m.-7p.m., and replaced by two men at change of shift with the third man coming on at 10p.m. until 6a.m. Monday morning.

Wigan No.1 ARP cabin had dimensions of 55ft x 24ft -4in x 12ft and controlled the Up & Down Goods Loops, Up & Down Fast lines, Up & Down Slow lines, all platforms and bays at the south end of Wigan North Western and the entrance to Top Yard. Up & Down Goods were permissively worked whilst Up & Down Slow and Fast lines were absolute block.

All roads through Wigan North Western were worked as 'Station Yard Working,' thus allowing more than one train on each line.

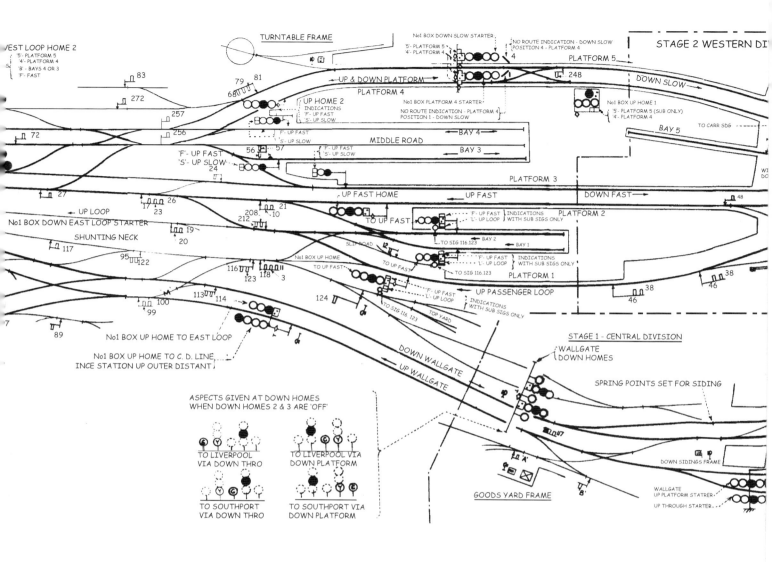

Plate 133. A DMU waits in the south facing bay platform No.6 on 25th April 1968. In the middle road a type '2' No.5152 idles away.
John Sloane.

Plate 134. Stanier 'Jubilee' Class No.45653 *Barham* calls at Wigan North Western about 1960 with a southbound special and looks to be in extremely good condition.
Brian Nichols.

Plate 135. A typically wet Summers day at Wigan as one of the Huges designed 2-6-0 Horwich built 'Crab' engines calls at North Western on 14th July 1957 working a southbound special.
Jim Peden collection..

Plate 136. The High Speed Trains which were used on the Cross-Country services have also disappeared from the WCML scene being replaced by the 'Voyager' sets. Power car No.43 087 stands at platform 4 at Wigan North Western on 4th May 1996, awaiting the right-away on the 06.50 Edinburgh - Bournemouth.
Author.

Plate 137. The demolition of the western side of Wigan North Western station is underway in this view of the bay platforms on 25th April 1971. Type '2', later class '25' No.D5256 is on duty with an engineers train in preparation for electrification of the route.
Ian Isherwood.

Plate 138. Named Stanier Class '5'No.45154 *Lanarkshire Yeomanry* arrives at Wigan North Western with the Railway Correspondence & Travel Society 'South Lancashire Railtour' on 24th September 1966. Over on the extreme right are Top Yard and the lines to Wigan Wallgate.
Jim Peden Collection (B.Barlow).

WIGAN NORTH WESTERN TRAIN MOVEMENTS SUMMER MID 50s (WEEK DAYS) Arranged as freight/passenger & other.
DOWN LINE

AM/PM	Route From	Line	Time Arr.	Time Dept.	Except.	Type	From	Route To	To
AM		SL		12.26	MX	H	WIGAN SPRINGS BRANCH	MAIN	PRESTON FARINGTON Jct
AM	MAIN	FL		12.31	MX	E	BIRKENHEAD SOUTH RESERVE SIDINGS	MAIN	CARLISLE VIADUCT YARD
AM		GL		1.16	MX	H	WIGAN BAMFURLONG Jct & SIDINGS	WG	LIVERPOOL AINTREE
AM		SL		2.20	MO	J	WIGAN SPRINGS BRANCH	MAIN	CARNFORTH
AM		SL		2.25	MX	H	2.25am FROM SPRINGS BRANCH		BLACKBURN VIA INCE MOSS Jct
AM		GL		2.30	MX	G LE G	WIGAN BAMFURLONG Jct & SIDINGS	WG	WIGAN WALLGATE LOCO
AM	MAIN	FL		3.14	MX	C	LONDON CAMDEN	MAIN	CARNFORTH
AM	MAIN	SL		4.19	MX	E	WARRINGTON WALTON OLD JUNCTION	MAIN	CARLISLE KINGMOOR
AM		GL		3.50	MX	G EB	WIGAN SPRINGS BRANCH	WG	WIGAN WALLGATE
AM	SBJn	SL		3.58	MO	H	SALFORD ORDSALL LANE	MAIN	PRESTON RIBBLE SIDINGS
AM	SBJn	SL	4.05	4.11	MX	H	SALFORD ORDSALL LANE	MAIN	CARLISLE KINGMOOR
AM	MAIN	SL		4.19	SO	E	CREWE S.S.NORTH	MAIN	FLEETWOOD WYRE DOCK
AM	MAIN	SL		4.34	MO	E	SHREWSBURY HARLESCOTT SIDINGS	MAIN	CARLISLE VIADUCT YARD
AM		SL		4.25	MX	J	WIGAN SPRINGS BRANCH	MAIN	CARNFORTH
AM		FL		4.50	TWFO	G EB	WIGAN SPRINGS BRANCH	MAIN	WIGAN RYLANDS SIDINGS
AM		GL		5.00	MX	J	WIGAN BAMFURLONG Jct & SIDINGS	WG	LIVERPOOL AINTREE
AM		GL	5.25	6.25		K	WIGAN BAMFURLONG Jct & SIDINGS	WG	WIGAN WALLGATE
AM		SL		5.52	SO	J	WIGAN SPRINGS BRANCH	MAIN	FLEETWOOD WYRE DOCK
AM	MAIN	SL		5.37	MX	E	BIRMINGHAM CURZON STREET	MAIN	PRESTON RIBBLE SIDINGS
AM	MAIN	FL		5.25	MX	D	BESCOT OLD YARD	MAIN	CARLISLE VIADUCT YARD
AM		SL		5.33	TWFO	J	5.33 FROM WIGAN RYLANDS SIDINGS	MAIN	FLEETWOOD WYRE DOCK
AM	WG		6.05	6.05	MX	K	WIGAN WALLGATE		WIGAN NORTH WESTERN
AM		GL		6.07	MO	J	WIGAN BAMFURLONG Jct & SIDINGS	WG	LIVERPOOL AINTREE
AM	MAIN	FL		6.00	MX	D	LONDON WILLESDEN	MAIN	CARLISLE VIADUCT YARD
AM	WG		6.10	6.10	MO	K	WIGAN WALLGATE		WIGAN N. W. CANAL SIDINGS
AM	MAIN	SL		6.14	MX	E	CREWE GRESTY LANE	MAIN	CARLISLE VIADUCT YARD
AM	MAIN	FL		6.20	MO	E	WARRINGTON WALTON OLD JUNCTION	MAIN	CARNFORTH
AM		GL		7.10	SO	H	WIGAN BAMFURLONG Jct & SIDINGS	WG	APPLEY BRIDGE LANCS
AM	MAIN	SL		6.52	MO	E	LONDON WILLESDEN	MAIN	CARLISLE VIADUCT YARD
AM	MAIN	SL	8.15	8.15	MX	F	WARRINGTON FROGHALL SIDINGS		WIGAN NORTH WESTERN
AM	MAIN	FL		7.27	MX	D	LONDON CAMDEN	MAIN	CARLISLE VIADUCT YARD
AM		SL		7.26	MO	F	WIGAN SPRINGS BRANCH	BHJn	BLACKBURN
AM		SL		7.34		J	WIGAN SPRINGS BRANCH	MAIN	FLEETWOOD WYRE DOCK
AM		SL		7.41	MX	H	WIGAN BAMFURLONG Jct & SIDINGS	BHJn	BLACKBURN
AM		FL		7.32	SO	J	WIGAN SPRINGS BRANCH	MAIN	WIGAN VICTORIA COLLIERY SIDINGS
AM		GL		7.35		J	WIGAN BAMFURLONG Jct & SIDINGS	WG	ORMSKIRK
AM	MAIN	FL		7.56	SO	C	WARRINGTON FROGHALL SIDINGS	MAIN	PRESTON RIBBLE SDGS
AM		FL		8.25		K	WIGAN BAMFURLONG Jct & SIDINGS	WG	SOUTHPORT
AM		FL		8.29	MX	G LE G	WIGAN SPRINGS BRANCH	BHJn	WIGAN ADLINGTON Jct
AM		FL		8.55		QJ	8.55 FROM WIGAN RYLANDS SIDINGS	MAIN	WIGAN VICTORIA COLLIERY SIDINGS
AM		FL		8.32		J	WIGAN Sp/ Br ENGINE/SHED SIDINGS	MAIN	PRESTON FARINGTON Jct
AM	MAIN	SL		9.33		H	CREWE S.S.NORTH	MAIN	CARLISLE LONDON RD YARD
AM		SL		10.09	MX	H	WIGAN SPRINGS BRANCH	MAIN	PRESTON RIBBLE SIDINGS
AM		SL	10.10	10.36		J	WIGAN BAMFURLONG Jct & SDGS	WG	WIGAN WALLGATE
AM		SL		10.34	SX	K	WIGAN SPRINGS BRANCH	BHJn	BLACKBURN
AM		SL	10.30	10.45	SO	K	WIGAN SPRINGS BRANCH	BHJn	BLACKBURN
AM	MAIN	FL		10.07	MO	G LE G	NORTHWICH HARTFORD SIDINGS	WG	WIGAN WALLGATE LOCO
AM	MAIN	SL		11.06	MX	H	WARRINGTON WALTON OLD JUNCTION	MAIN	CARNFORTH
AM	GOLJct	FL		10.40	MWFO	F	EARLESTOWN	MAIN	PRESTON FARINGTON Jct
AM		SL		11.08	MO	H	WIGAN SPRINGS BRANCH	MAIN	CARNFORTH
AM	MAIN	FL		11.37	SO	D	CREWE S.S.NORTH	MAIN	CARLISLE VIADUCT YARD
AM		FL		11.45	SX	G LE G	WIGAN SPRINGS BRANCH	MAIN	WIGAN RYLANDS SIDINGS
AM	GOLJct	SL	11.50	11.50		K	EARLESTOWN		WIGAN NORTH WESTERN
AM	MAIN	FL		11.56	SX	D	CREWE S.S.NORTH	MAIN	CARLISLE VIADUCT YARD
PM		FL		12.12	SX	G EB	WIGAN No 1	MAIN	WIGAN VICTORIA COLLIERY SIDINGS
PM		FL		12.25		J	12.25 FROM WIGAN RYLANDS SIDINGS	MAIN	FLEETWOOD WYRE DOCK
PM		FL		1.25		J Q	1.25 Ditto (NCB Loco)	MAIN	WIGAN VICTORIA COLL SDGS
PM	MAIN	FL		12.30		E	WARRINGTON WALTON OLD JUNCTION	MAIN	CARLISLE CANAL YARD
PM		FL		1.50		G LE G	WIGAN SPRINGS BRANCH LOCO	BHJn	ADLINGTON Jct (LANCS)
PM		SL	2.10	2.50		J	WIGAN BAMFURLONG Jct & SIDINGS	WG	WIGAN WALLGATE
PM		FL				J	1.20 FROM WIGAN RYLANDS SIDINGS	MAIN	PRESTON RIBBLE SIDINGS
PM		SL		2.18	SX	J	WIGAN SPRINGS BRANCH	MAIN	PRESTON FARINGTON Jct
PM		GL	2.40	2.42	SX	G LE G	WIGAN BAMFURLONG Jct & SIDINGS	WG	WIGAN WALLGATE LOCO
PM		GL		3.08		J	WIGAN BAMFURLONG Jct & SIDINGS	WG	LIVERPOOL AINTREE
PM	MAIN	SL	3.13	3.15	FO	F	LONDON BRENT E.S.	WG	LIVERPOOL AINTREE
PM		GL	3.25	3.29	SO	G LE G	WIGAN BAMFURLONG Jct & SIDINGS	WG	WIGAN WALLGATE LOCO
PM		GL	4.55	4.55	SO	G EB	WIGAN SPRINGS BRANCH		WIGAN NORTH WESTERN
PM		SL		5.30	SO	J	WIGAN SPRINGS BRANCH	MAIN	PRESTON FARINGTON Jct
PM	MAIN	SL	5.25	5.25	SX	G LE G	WARRINGTON DALLAM LOCO		WIGAN NORTH WESTERN
PM	MAIN	FL		5.56		D	CREWE GRESTY LANE	MAIN	CARLISLE KINGMOOR
PM	MAIN	FL		6.44	MSX	C	LONDON BROAD STREET	MAIN	GLASGOW BUCHANAN STREET

AM/PM	Route From	Line	Time Arr.	Time Dept.	Except.	Type	From	Route To	To
PM	MAIN	SL		7.00	SO	E	WARRINGTON DALLAM BRANCH SDGS	MAIN	PRESTON RIBBLE SIDINGSPM
PM	MAIN	SL	7.18		SX	J	WARRINGTON DALLAM BRANCH SDGS	MAIN	WIGAN RYLANDS SIDINGS
PM		SL	7.30		SX	J	WIGAN SPRINGS BRANCH	MAIN	PRESTON FARINGTON JUNCTION
PM		GL	7.32	7.33	SX	K	WIGAN CANAL SIDINGS	WG	WIGAN WALLGATE
PM	SBJn	FL		7.21	SO	E	MANCHESTER LIVERPOOL ROAD	MAIN	CARLISLE VIADUCT YARD
PM		GL		7.25	SO	J	WIGAN BAMFURLONG Jct & SIDINGS	WG	SOUTHPORT
PM		GL	7.35	7.35	SO	K	WIGAN BAMFURLONG Jct & SIDINGS		WIGAN NORTH WESTERN
PM		SL		7.43	SO	H	WIGAN SPRINGS BRANCH	MAIN	CARNFORTH
PM	SBJn	SL	7.50	8.05	SX	D	MANCHESTER LIVERPOOL ROAD	MAIN	CARLISLE VIADUCT YARD
PM	MAIN	FL		7.57	SX	C	LONDON CAMBDEN	MAIN	GLASGOW BUCHANAN STREET
PM	SBJn	FL		8.07	SO	E	MANCHESTER LIVERPOOL ROAD	MAIN	CARLISLE VIADUCT YARD
PM		SL	8.40	8.40	SX	K	WIGAN BAMFURLONG Jct & SIDINGS		WIGAN NORTH WESTERN
PM	MAIN	FL		8.16	SO	D	CREWE S.S.NORTH	MAIN	CARLISLE VIADUCT YARD
PM	MAIN	SL		8.16	SX	C	NORTHHAMPTON	MAIN	CARLISLE KINGMOOR
PM	MAIN	SL		8.46	SX	D	WARRINGTON FROGHALL SIDINGS	MAIN	CARLISLE VIADUCT YARD
PM		SL		8.50	SO	J	WIGAN SPRINGS BRANCH	MAIN	PRESTON FARINGTON Jct
PM		SL		9.13	SX	J	WIGAN SPRINGS BRANCH	MAIN	FLEETWOOD WYRE DOCK
PM	MAIN	SL		9.55	SO	E	SHREWSBURY HARLESCOTT SIDINGS	MAIN	CARLISLE VIADUCT YARD
PM		SL	10.40	10.40	SO	K	WIGAN INCE MOSS		WIGAN NORTH WESTERN
PM	MAIN	SL		10.19	SX	E	WARRINGTON WALTON OLD JUNCTION	MAIN	PRESTON RIBBLE SIDINGS
PM		SL		10.35	FSX	G LE G	WIGAN BAMFURLONG Jct & SIDINGS	MAIN	PRESTON - LOSTOCK HALL
PM		SL		10.50	SO	J	WIGAN SPRINGS BRANCH	MAIN	KIRKHAM NORTH Jct.LANCS
PM	SBJn	FL		11.03	SX	E	MANCHESTER LIVERPOOL ROAD	MAIN	CARNFORTH
PM		GL		10.40	SX	H	WIGAN BAMFURLONG Jct & SIDINGS	WG	SOUTHPORT
PM		GL		11.10	SO	J	WIGAN BAMFURLONG Jct & SIDINGS	WG	WIGAN WALLGATE
PM	MAIN	FL		11.26	SO	E	CREWE S.S.NORTH	MAIN	FLEETWOOD WYRE DOCK
AM	MAIN	FL	11.56	12.02		A	LONDON EUSTON	MAIN	PERTH
AM	MAIN	FL	12.07	12.20		A	LONDON EUSTON	MAIN	STRANRAER HARBOUR
AM	MAIN	FL		12.41		A	LONDON EUSTON	MAIN	GLASGOW CENTRAL & ABERDEEN
AM	MAIN	FL		12.15		A	WIGAN NORTH WESTERN	MAIN	PRESTON
AM	MAIN	FL		12.55		A	LONDON EUSTON	MAIN	GLASGOW CENTRAL
AM	MAIN	FL		1.02		A	LONDON EUSTON	MAIN	GLASGOW St.ENOCK
AM	MAIN	FL		1.24	SX	A	BIRMINGHAM NEW STREET	MAIN	GLASGOW BUCHANAN St.
AM	MAIN	FL		1.24	SO	A	COVENTRY	MAIN	GLASGOW BUCHANAN St.
AM	StHJn	SL	1.36	1.55		A	LIVERPOOL LIME STREET	MAIN	GLASGOW CENTRAL
AM	SBJn	FL	1.39	1.39		A	MO LEEDS CITY Sth. MX STALYBRIDGE		WIGAN NORTH WESTERN
AM	MAIN	FL		1.44		A	BIRMINGHAM NEW STREET	MAIN	GLASGOW CENTRAL
AM	MAIN	FL		2.01		A	LONDON EUSTON	MAIN	GLASGOW CENTRAL
AM	MAIN	FL	2.06	2.30	MX	C PCLS	CREWE	MAIN	PRESTON
AM	MAIN	FL		2.12	SO	A	LONDON EUSTON	MAIN	GLASGOW CENTRAL
AM	MAIN	FL		2.22	MSX	C PCLS	CREWE	MAIN	ABERDEEN
AM	SBJn	FL	2.41	2.41		A NEWS	MANCHESTER EXCHANGE		WIGAN NORTH WESTERN
AM	MAIN	FL	2.50	2.56		A	LONDON EUSTON	MAIN	PERTH
AM	MAIN	FL	3.00	3.06	MX	A	LONDON EUSTON	MAIN	WINDERMERE
AM		FL		3.21	MX	C PCLS	WIGAN NORTH WESTERN	MAIN	CARNFORTH
AM	MAIN	FL	3.20	3.27	A		LONDON EUSTON	MAIN	BLACKPOOL NORTH
AM	MAIN	FL		3.27	MO	A	LONDON EUSTON	MAIN	GLASGOW St.ENOCK
AM	MAIN	FL		3.40	MX	A	LONDON EUSTON	MAIN	GLASGOW St.ENOCK
AM		FL		3.50		A MAILS	WIGAN NORTH WESTERN	BHJn	BLACKBURN
AM	MAIN	FL		3.54		C PCLS	CREWE	MAIN	CARLISLE
AM	MAIN	FL		4.09	A		LONDON EUSTON	MAIN	GLASGOW CENTRAL
AM	MAIN	FL	4.22	4.43	MO	C PCLS	CREWE	MAIN	PRESTON
AM	MAIN	FL	4.22	4.43	MX	C PCLS	BIRMINGHAM NEW STREET	MAIN	CARLISLE
AM	MAIN	FL	4.39	4.57	MSX	C PCLS	LONDON MARYLEBONE GOODS	MAIN	PRESTON
AM		FL		5.20		B	WIGAN NORTH WESTERN	MAIN	PRESTON
AM		FL		5.48	MX	C PCLS	WIGAN NORTH WESTERN	BHJn	COLNE LANCS
AM	MAIN	FL	5.49	6.22	MX	C PCLS	LONDON WILLESDEN JUNCTION	MAIN	CARLISLE
AM		SL	6.15	6.15	SX	C ECS	WIGAN SPRINGS BRANCH		WIGAN NORTH WESTERN
AM	SBJn	SL	6.17	6.17	SO	C ECS	WIGAN PLATT BRIDGE		WIGAN NORTH WESTERN
AM	SBJn	FL	6.30	6.30	SX	C ECS	WIGAN PLATT BRIDGE		WIGAN NORTH WESTERN
AM		SL		6.33	SX	B	WIGAN NORTH WESTERN	BHJn	CHORLEY R.O.F. LANCS
AM	MAIN	SL	6.31	6.39		A	WARRINGTON BANK QUAY	MAIN	CARLISLE
AM	SBJn	FL	6.38	6.38	SX	B	MOTOR TYLDESLEY		WIGAN NORTH WESTERN
AM		FL	6.40	6.40	SO	C ECS	WIGAN SPRINGS BRANCH		WIGAN NORTH WESTERN
AM		FL		6.48	SX	B	WIGAN NORTH WESTERN	MAIN	LEYLAND LANCS
AM	SBJn	FL	6.55	7.04		B	MANCHESTER EXCHANGE	MAIN	PRESTON
AM	WG		6.56	6.56	SO	G LE P	WIGAN WALLGATE		WIGAN NORTH WESTERN
AM	MAIN	FL	7.00	7.20	MX	C PCLS	CREWE	MAIN	MORECAMBE PROMENADE
AM	StHJn	SL	7.01	7.10		B	LIVERPOOL LIME STREET	BHJn	BLACKBURN
AM	StHJn	SL	7.45	7.45		B	LIVERPOOL LIME STREET		WIGAN NORTH WESTERN
AM	MAIN	SL	7.52	8.02		B	WARRINGTON BANK QUAY	MAIN	MORECAMBE EUSTON ROAD
AM	SBJn	FL	7.52	7.52		B	MANCHESTER EXCHANGE		WIGAN NORTH WESTERN
AM	WG		7.56	7.56	MSX	G LE P	WIGAN WALLGATE		WIGAN NORTH WESTERN
AM	MAIN	SL	8.18	8.18		B	WARRINGTON BANK QUAY		WIGAN NORTH WESTERN

AM/PM	Route From	Line	Time Arr.	Time Dept.	Except.	Type	From	Route To	To
AM	StHJn	SL	8.44	8.44		B	LIVERPOOL LIME STREET		WIGAN NORTH WESTERN
AM	MAIN	FL		8.43	SO	A	BIRMINGHAM NEW STREET	MAIN	PRESTON (SCOTTISH TOURS)
AM	MAIN	FL		8.51	SO	A	BIRMINGHAM NEW STREET	MAIN	BLACKPOOL NORTH
AM	SBJn	FL	8.52	8.52	SX	B	TYLDESLEY		WIGAN NORTH WESTERN
AM	SBJn	FL	8.57	8.57		B	TYLDESLEY		WIGAN NORTH WESTERN
AM	SBJn	FL	9.05	9.10	SO	A	SALFORD CROSS LANE	MAIN	BARROW CENTRAL
AM	StHJn	SL	9.23	9.28	SX	B	LIVERPOOL LIME STREET	MAIN	PRESTON
AM	StHJn	SL	9.23	9.28	SO	B	LIVERPOOL LIME STREET	MAIN	BLACKPOOL NORTH
AM		FL		9.43	SO	G LE P	WIGAN NORTH WESTERN	MAIN	PRESTON
AM	MAIN	FL		9.49	SO	A	COVENTRY	MAIN	BLACKPOOL NORTH
AM	MAIN	SL	10.04	10.04		B	EARLESTOWN		WIGAN NORTH WESTERN
AM	MAIN	FL	10.09	10.15	SO	A	SALFORD CROSS LANE	MAIN	BLACKPOOL NORTH
AM	MAIN	FL	10.19	10.24	SO	A	WARRINGTON BANK QUAY	MAIN	CARLISLE
AM	StHJn	SL	10.22	10.22		B	LIVERPOOL LIME STREET		WIGAN NORTH WESTERN
AM	MAIN	FL	10.22	10.27	SX	A	CREWE MAIN	MAIN	PERTH
AM	MAIN	FL	10.26	10.31	SO	A	CREWE	MAIN	PERTH
AM	MAIN	FL	10.34	10.38		A	CREWE	MAIN	BLACKPOOL NORTH
AM	MAIN	FL		10.45	SO	A	STOKE-ON-TRENT	MAIN	BLACKPOOL NORTH
AM	MAIN	FL		11.03	SO	A	WALSALL	MAIN	BLACKPOOL NORTH
AM	MAIN	SL	11.16	11.25	SO	A	STOKE-ON-TRENT	MAIN	BLACKPOOL NORTH
AM	MAIN	FL		11.20	SO	A	COVENTRY	MAIN	BLACKPOOL NORTH
AM	MAIN	FL	11.26	11.31	SO	A	BIRMINGHAM NEW STREET	MAIN	BLACKPOOL NORTH
AM		FL	11.39	11.39		C PCLS	WIGAN SPRINGS BRANCH		WIGAN NORTH WESTERN
AM	MAIN	FL		11.36	SO	A	NORTHAMPTON CENTRAL	MAIN	MORECAMBE EUSTON ROAD
AM	SBJn	FL	11.48	11.48		B	MANCHESTER EXCHANGE		WIGAN NORTH WESTERN
AM	MAIN	FL	11.52	11.57	SO	A	CREWE	MAIN	WORKINGTON MAIN
PM	StHJn	SL	12.00	12.00		B	LIVERPOOL LIME STREET		WIGAN NORTH WESTERN
PM	MAIN	FL		12.02	SO	A	BLETCHLEY	MAIN	BLACKPOOL NORTH
PM	MAIN	FL	12.02	12.08	SX	A	LONDON EUSTON	MAIN	WINDERMERE
PM	MAIN	FL	12.07	12.13	SO	A	LONDON EUSTON	MAIN	WINDERMERE
PM	MAIN	FL	12.20	12.28	SO	A	BIRMINGHAM NEW STREET	MAIN	MORECAMBE EUSTON ROAD
PM	MAIN	SL	12.35	12.35		B	WARRINGTON BANK QUAY		WIGAN NORTH WESTERN
PM	MAIN	FL		12.24	SO	A	CARDIFF	MAIN	BLACKPOOL NORTH
PM		FL		12.45		B	WIGAN NORTH WESTERN	MAIN	PRESTON
PM	StHJn	SL	12.49	12.49	SO	B	LIVERPOOL LIME STREET		WIGAN NORTH WESTERN
PM	MAIN	FL	12.50	12.55	SX	A	CREWE	MAIN	BLACKPOOL CENTRAL
PM	WG		12.58	12.58		C PCLS	BURSCOUGH BRIDGE LANCS		WIGAN NORTH WESTERN
PM		FL		1.00	SO	B	WIGAN NORTH WESTERN	BHJn	BLACKBURN
PM		FL		1.05	SX	B	WIGAN NORTH WESTERN	BHJn	BLACKBURN
PM	MAIN	FL	1.05	1.11	SO	A	CREWE	MAIN	BLACKPOOL CENTRAL
PM	MAIN	FL		1.12	SX	A	LONDON EUSTON	MAIN	GLASGOW CENTRAL
PM	SBJn	FL	1.27	1.27	SO	B	MANCHESTER EXCHANGE		WIGAN NORTH WESTERN
PM	StHJn	SL	1.33	1.33	SX	B	LIVERPOOL LIME STREET		WIGAN NORTH WESTERN
PM	MAIN	FL		1.32	SX	A	BIRMINGHAM NEW STREET	MAIN	GLASGOW CENTRAL
PM		GL		1.45	SO	G LE P	WIGAN ARLEY MINES SIDINGS	WG	WIGAN WALLGATE LOCO
PM	MAIN	SL	1.50	1.50	SO		WARRINGTON BANK QUAY		WIGAN NORTH WESTERN
PM	MAIN	FL		1.36	SO	A	LONDON EUSTON	MAIN	GLASGOW CENTRAL
PM	MAIN	FL		1.41	SX	A	BIRMINGHAM NEW STREET	MAIN	EDINBURGH PRINCES St.
PM	MAIN	FL		1.42	SX	A	BIRMINGHAM NEW STREET	MAIN	GLASGOW CENTRAL
PM	MAIN	FL		1.52	SX	A	LONDON EUSTON	MAIN	GLASGOW CENTRAL
PM	MAIN	FL		1.56	SO	A	BIRMINGHAM NEW STREET	MAIN	EDINBURGH PRINCES St.
PM	MAIN	SL	2.01	2.42	SX	C PCLS	WARRINGTON BANK QUAY	MAIN	CARLISLE
PM	MAIN	FL		2.03	SO	A	LONDON EUSTON	MAIN	GLASGOW CENTRAL
PM	MAIN	FL		2.05	SXQ	A	LONDON EUSTON	MAIN	PERTH
PM	MAIN	FL		2.16	SO	A	LONDON EUSTON	MAIN	PERTH
PM	StHJn	SL	2.24	2.24		B	LIVERPOOL LIME STREET		WIGAN NORTH WESTERN
PM	MAIN	FL	2.27	2.32	SO	A	CREWE	MAIN	WINDERMERE
PM	SBJn	SL	2.33	2.33		B	MANCHESTER EXCHANGE		WIGAN NORTH WESTERN
PM	MAIN	FL		2.37	SO	A	LONDON EUSTON	MAIN	BLACKPOOL CENTRAL
PM	MAIN	FL	2.45	2.50		A	LONDON EUSTON	MAIN	CARLISLE
PM	MAIN	FL	3.02	3.09	SO	A	BLETCHLEY	MAIN	BLACKPOOL CENTRAL
PM	StHJn	SL	3.15	3.15		B	LIVERPOOL LIME STREET		WIGAN NORTH WESTERN
PM	MAIN	FL	3.20	3.26	SX	A	LONDON EUSTON	MAIN	BLACKPOOL CENTRAL
PM	MAIN	FL	3.25	3.31	SO	A	LONDON EUSTON	MAIN	BLACKPOOL CENTRAL
PM	MAIN	SL	3.39	3.39	SX	B	WARRINGTON BANK QUAY		WIGAN NORTH WESTERN
PM	MAIN	FL	3.40	3.46		A	LONDON EUSTON	MAIN	WORKINGTON MAIN
PM	MAIN	SL	3.52	3.52	SO	B	WARRINGTON BANK QUAY		WIGAN NORTH WESTERN
PM		FL		3.50	SX	G LE P	WIGAN NORTH WESTERN	MAIN	LOSTOCK HALL C'ge Sdg
PM	MAIN	FL	3.50	3.58	SX	A	LONDON EUSTON	MAIN	WORKINGTON
PM	MAIN	FL	3.54	4.00	SO	A	LONDON EUSTON	MAIN	WORKINGTON MAIN
PM	SBJn	FL	4.04	4.04	SO	B	MANCHESTER EXCHANGE		WIGAN NORTH WESTERN
PM	SBJn	FL	4.08	4.08	SX	B	MANCHESTER EXCHANGE		WIGAN NORTH WESTERN
PM	StHJn	SL	4.23	4.30		B	LIVERPOOL LIME STREET	MAIN	PRESTON
PM	SBJn	FL	4.36	4.38		A	MANCHESTER EXCHANGE	MAIN	BARROW CENTRAL

AM/PM	Route From	Line	Time Arr.	Time Dept.	Except.	Type	From	Route To	To
PM	SBJn	FL		4.51		A	MANCHESTER EXCHANGE	MAIN	PRESTON
PM	MAIN	FL		5.01		A	LONDON EUSTON	MAIN	GLASGOW CENTRAL
PM	MAIN	FL		5.07	SO	A	LONDON EUSTON	MAIN	GLASGOW CENTRAL
PM	SBJn	FL	5.11	5.11		B	MANCHESTER EXCHANGE		WIGAN NORTH WESTERN
PM	StHJn	SL	5.18	5.18		B	LIVERPOOL LIME STREET		WIGAN NORTH WESTERN
PM	MAIN	FL	5.16	5.22		A	LONDON EUSTON	MAIN	PERTH
PM	SBJn	FL	5.25	5.25	SO	C PCLS	WIGAN GOODS		WIGAN NORTH WESTERN
PM	MAIN	FL	5.28	5.32	SO	A	CREWE	MAIN	BLACKPOOL CENTRAL
PM		FL		5.26		B	WIGAN NORTH WESTERN	MAIN	PRESTON
PM	MAIN	FL	5.35	5.40	SX	A	CREWE	MAIN	BLACKPOOL CENTRAL
PM	MAIN	FL	5.45	5.50	SO	A	LONDON EUSTON	MAIN	BLACKPOOL CENTRAL
PM	MAIN	FL	5.35	5.40	SX	A	CREWE	MAIN	BLACKPOOL CENTRAL
PM	MAIN	FL	5.45	5.50	SO	A	LONDON EUSTON	MAIN	BLACKPOOL CENTRAL
PM	MAIN	SL	6.00	6.00		B	WARRINGTON BANK QUAY		WIGAN NORTH WESTERN
PM	SBJn	FL	6.05	6.05		B	MANCHESTER EXCHANGE		WIGAN NORTH WESTERN
PM		FL		6.05		B	WIGAN NORTH WESTERN	BHJn	BLACKBURN
PM		SL	6.14	6.14	SO	C ECS	WIGAN SPRINGS BRANCH		WIGAN NORTH WESTERN
PM		SL	6.16	6.16	SX	C ECS	WIGAN SPRINGS BRANCH		WIGAN NORTH WESTERN
PM	StHJn	SL	6.33	6.33		B	LIVERPOOL LIME STREET		WIGAN NORTH WESTERN
PM		FL		6.38	SX G LE P		WIGAN NORTH WESTERN	MAIN	PRESTON LOCO
PM	MAIN	SL	6.39	6.39	SX	B	WARRINGTON BANK QUAY		WIGAN NORTH WESTERN
PM	MAIN	FL	6.33	6.40	FSO	A	CREWE	MAIN	BARROW CENTRAL
PM		FL		6.46	FO G LE P		WIGAN NORTH WESTERN	MAIN	PRESTON LOCO
PM		FL		6.54		B	WIGAN NORTH WESTERN	MAIN	BLACKPOOL CENTRAL
PM	MAIN	FL	6.54	6.54	SX	G LE P	EARLESTOWN LANCS		WIGAN NORTH WESTERN
PM	SBJn	FL	7.03	7.03		B	MANCHESTER EXCHANGE		WIGAN NORTH WESTERN
PM	StHJn	SL	7.06	7.06		B	LIVERPOOL LIME STREET		WIGAN NORTH WESTERN
PM	MAIN	FL	7.09	7.14		A	CREWE	MAIN	CARLISLE
PM		FL		7.48		G LE P	WIGAN SPRINGS BRANCH LOCO	MAIN	PRESTON (to work 9.35pm Barrow)
PM	MAIN	SL	7.54	8.12		C PCLS	CREWE	MAIN	GLASGOW CENTRAL SX /CARLISLE SO
PM	MAIN	FL	8.09	8.09	SO	A	WARRINGTON BANK QUAY		WIGAN NORTH WESTERN
PM	StHJn	SL	8.19	8.23		B	LIVERPOOL LIME STREET	MAIN	PRESTON
PM	WG		8.34	8.34	SX	C PCLS	BURSOCOUGH BRIDGE LANCS		WIGAN NORTH WESTERN
PM	WG		8.34	8.34	SO	C PCLS	WIGAN WALLGATE		WIGAN NORTH WESTERN
PM	MAIN	FL		8.35	FSX	A	CREWE	MAIN	HEYSHAM LANCS
PM	MAIN	FL		8.38	FO	A	CREWE	MAIN	HEYSHAM LANCS
PM	MAIN	FL		8.57	SX	A	LONDON EUSTON	MAIN	BLACKPOOL CENTRAL
PM	MAIN	FL		9.0	SO	A	LONDON EUSTON	MAIN	BLACKPOOL CENTRAL
PM	StHJn	SL	9.14	9.14		B	LIVERPOOL LIME STREET		WIGAN NORTH WESTERN
PM	MAIN	FL	9.18	9.24	FSX	A	CREWE	MAIN	PRESTON
PM	MAIN	FL	9.20	9.26	FO	A	LONDON EUSTON	MAIN	PRESTON
PM	MAIN	FL	9.26	9.33	SO	A	CREWE	MAIN	PRESTON
PM	MAIN	FL	9.27	9.27	SX	C PCLS	PATRICROFT SALFORD		WIGAN NORTH WESTERN
PM	MAIN	SL	9.49	9.49		B	WARRINGTON BANK QUAY		WIGAN NORTH WESTERN
PM		FL		9.45		B	WIGAN NORTH WESTERN	BHJn	BLACKBURN
PM	MAIN	FL		9.51	FO	A	LONDON EUSTON	MAIN	HEYSHAM LANCS
PM	MAIN	FL		9.54	FSX	A	LONDON EUSTON	MAIN	HEYSHAM LANCS
PM	MAIN	FL		9.58	FO	A	LONDON EUSTON	MAIN	HEYSHAM LANCS
PM	MAIN	FL	10.07		SO	A	LONDON EUSTON	MAIN	HEYSHAM LANCS
PM		FL		10.15	SX	G LE P	WIGAN NORTH WESTERN	MAIN	PRESTON
PM	StHJn	SL	10.11	10.11		B	LIVERPOOL LIME STREET		WIGAN NORTH WESTERN
PM	SBJn	FL	10.15	10.15	SX	B	MANCHESTER EXCHANGE		WIGAN NORTH WESTERN
PM	SBJn	FL	10.19	10.19	SO	B	MANCHESTER EXCHANGE		WIGAN NORTH WESTERN
PM	MAIN	FL	10.24	10.29	SX	A	LONDON EUSTON	MAIN	PRESTON
PM	MAIN	FL		10.23	SO	A	LONDON EUSTON	MAIN	HEYSHAM LANCS
PM	SBJn	FL	10.35	10.35	SX	C PCLS	WIGAN GOODS		WIGAN NORTH WESTERN
PM	MAIN	FL		10.58	SO	A NEWS	LONDON EUSTON	MAIN	LAIRG ROSS & CROMARTY SCOTLAND
PM	MAIN	FL		11.10	SX	A	LONDON EUSTON	MAIN	INVERNESS
PM		WG	11.15	11.15	SX	C PCLS	WIGAN WALLGATE		WIGAN NORTH WESTERN
PM	SBJn	FL	11.16	11.21	SO	A	MANCHESTER EXCHANGE	MAIN	CARLISLE
PM	MAIN	FL		11.17	SX	A	LONDON EUSTON	MAIN	PERTH
PM	MAIN	FL	11.34	11.47	FO	A	LONDON EUSTON	MAIN	OBAN
PM	StHJn	SL	11.38	11.38		B	LIVERPOOL LIME STREET		WIGAN NORTH WESTERN
PM	MAIN	FL	11.34	11.47	FSX	A	LONDON EUSTON	MAIN	PERTH
AM	MAIN	FL	12.07	12.20		A	LONDON EUSTON	MAIN	STRANRAER HARBOUR
AM	MAIN	FL		12.41		A	LONDON EUSTON	MAIN	GLASGOW CENTRAL & ABERDEEN

WIGAN NORTH WESTERN TRAIN MOVEMENTS SUMMER MID 50s (SUNDAYS)
DOWN LINE

AM/PM	Route From	Line	Time Arr.	Time Dept.	Except.	Type	From	Route To	To
AM	MAIN	FL		12.24		F	CREWE S.S.NORTH	MAIN	PRESTON RIBBLE SIDINGS
AM		SL		12.14		J	WIGAN SPRINGS BRANCH	MAIN	CARNFORTH
AM		GL		12.28		J	WIGAN SPRINGS BRANCH	WG	WIGAN WALLGATE
AM		GL		12.35		H	WIGAN BAMFURLONG Jct & SIDINGS	WG	LIVERPOOL AINTREE
AM	MAIN	SL		2.25		H	WARRINGTON WALTON OLD JUNCTION	MAIN	CARLISLE VIADUCT YARD
AM	MAIN	FL		3.05		E	BESCOT OLD YARD	MAIN	CARLISLE VIADUCT YARD
AM	MAIN	SL		3.42		F	CREWE GRESTY LANE	MAIN	CARLISLE VIADUCT YARD
AM		GL		3.44		G EB	WIGAN BAMFURLONG Jct & SIDINGS	WG	WIGAN WALLGATE
AM	MAIN	SL		4.35		D	LONDON CAMDEN	MAIN	CARLISLE KINGMOOR
AM	MAIN	SL		7.58		H	BIRMINGHAM CURZON STREET	MAIN	PRESTON RIBBLE SIDINGS
AM	MAIN	FL		11.54		F	CREWE S.S.NORTH	MAIN	CARNFORTH
PM	MAIN	FL		5.03		E	WARRINGTON	MAIN	CARLISLE VIADUCT YARD
PM	MAIN	FL		5.49		D	CREWE GRESTY LANE	MAIN	CARLISLE VIADUCT YARD
PM	StHJn	SL		5.57		E	LIVERPOOL EDGE HILL	MAIN	CARLISLE VIADUCT YARD
PM	MAIN	FL		6.16		E	CREWE S.S.NORTH	MAIN	CARLISLE VIADUCT YARD
PM	MAIN	FL		6.44		D	CREWE S.S.NORTH	MAIN	CARLISLE VIADUCT YARD
PM	MAIN	SL		10.00		H	CREWE GRESTY LANE	MAIN	CARNFORTH
AM	MAIN	FL	11.56	12.02		A	LONDON EUSTON	MAIN	PERTH
AM	MAIN	FL	12.45	12.55		A	LONDON EUSTON (POSTAL)	MAIN	GLASGOW CENTRAL
AM	MAIN	FL		1.01		A	LONDON EUSTON	MAIN	GLASGOW CENTRAL
AM	MAIN	FL		1.10		A	LONDON EUSTON	MAIN	GLASGOW CENTRAL
AM	StHJn	SL	1.36	1.55		A	LIVERPOOL LIME STREET	MAIN	GLASGOW CENTRAL
AM	SBJn	FL	1.39	1.39		A	STALYBRIDGE		WIGAN NORTH WESTERN
AM	MAIN	FL		1.44		A	BIRMINGHAM NEW STREET	MAIN	GLASGOW CENTRAL
AM	MAIN	FL		2.01		A	LONDON EUSTON	MAIN	GLASGOW CENTRAL
AM	MAIN	FL	2.07	2.17		A NEWS	CREWE	MAIN	PRESTON
AM	MAIN	FL		2.23		A	LONDON EUSTON	MAIN	GLASGOW CENTRAL
AM	SBJn	FL	2.41	2.51		C PCLS	MANCHESTER EXCHANGE	MAIN	CARNFORTH
AM	MAIN	FL	3.17	3.24		A	LONDON EUSTON	MAIN	BLACKPOOL CENTRAL
AM	MAIN	FL		3.29		A	LONDON EUSTON	MAIN	GLASGOW CENTRAL
AM		FL	4.01	4.01		C PCLS	WIGAN SPRINGS BRANCH		WIGAN NORTH WESTERN
AM	MAIN	FL	4.06	4.29		C PCLS	LONDON EUSTON	MAIN	CARLISLE
AM	MAIN	FL	7.33	7.53		C PCLS	CREWE	MAIN	CARLISLE
AM	StHJn	SL	9.05	9.05		B	LIVERPOOL LIME STREET		WIGAN NORTH WESTERN
AM	SBJn	FL	9.10	9.10		B	MANCHESTER EXCHANGE		WIGAN NORTH WESTERN
AM	MAIN	SL	9.18	9.32		B	CREWE	MAIN	BLACKPOOL CENTRAL
PM	MAIN	FL		1.38		A	BIRMINGHAM NEW STREET	MAIN	GLASGOW CENTRAL
PM	MAIN	FL	2.19	2.54		C PCLS	LONDON EUSTON	MAIN	CARLISLE
PM	MAIN	FL		2.31		A	LONDON EUSTON	MAIN	GLASGOW CENTRAL
PM	MAIN	FL		2.44		A	LONDON EUSTON	MAIN	BLACKPOOL CENTRAL
PM	MAIN	FL	2.58	3.02		A	BIRMINGHAM NEW STREET	MAIN	BLACKPOOL CENTRAL
PM	SBJn	FL	3.20	3.20		B	MANCHESTER EXCHANGE		WIGAN NORTH WESTERN
PM		FL		3.45		C ECS	WIGAN NORTH WESTERN	MAIN	BLACKPOOL CENTRAL
PM	MAIN	FL	4.17	4.25		A	LONDON EUSTON	MAIN	CARLISLE
PM	MAIN	FL	5.19	5.19		G LE P	WARRINGTON BANK QUAY		WIGAN NORTH WESTERN
PM	MAIN	FL	5.35	5.39		A	LONDON EUSTON	MAIN	BLACKPOOL CENTRAL
PM	SBJn	FL	7.40	7.40		B	MANCHESTER EXCHANGE		WIGAN NORTH WESTERN
PM	MAIN	FL	7.47	7.54		A	LONDON EUSTON	MAIN	BLACKPOOL CENTRAL
PM	StHJn	SL	7.52	8.01		B	LIVERPOOL LIME STREET	MAIN	PRESTON
PM	MAIN	FL		8.26		A	LONDON EUSTON	MAIN	HEYSHAM
PM	MAIN	FL	8.55	9.00		A	LONDON EUSTON	MAIN	BLACKPOOL CENTRAL
PM	MAIN	FL	9.02	9.25		C PCLS	CREWE	MAIN	PRESTON
PM	MAIN	FL	10.18	10.18		C ECS	WARRINGTON BANK QUAY		WIGAN NORTH WESTERN
PM	MAIN	FL	10.25	10.30		A	LONDON EUSTON	MAIN	PRESTON
PM	StHJn	SL	10.43	10.43		B	LIVERPOOL LIME STREET		WIGAN NORTH WESTERN
PM	MAIN	FL		11.10		A	LONDON EUSTON	MAIN	INVERNESS
PM	SBJn	FL	11.44	11.51		A	MANCHESTER EXCHANGE	MAIN	GLASGOW CENTRAL

WIGAN NORTH WESTERN TRAIN MOVEMENTS SUMMER MID 50s (WEEK DAYS)
UP LINE

AM/PM	Route From	Line	Time Arr.	Dept.	Except.	Type	From	Route To	To
AM	WG	GL		12.18	MX	G LE G	WIGAN WALLGATE LOCO		WIGAN BAMFURLONG JCT & SIDINGS
AM	MAIN	FL		12.24	MX	D	CARLISLE UPPERBY	MAIN	CREWE GRESTY LANE
AM	MAIN	SL		12.52	MO	H	CARNFORTH	MAIN	CREWE BASFORD HALL
AM	MAIN	SL		12.38	MX	H	CARLISLE UPPERBY	MAIN	WARRINGTON WINWICK QUAY
AM	MAIN	SL		12.57	MX	H	PRESTON N.U.YARD	SBJn	PATRICROFT SALFORD
AM	MAIN	FLxGL		1.17	MX	E	CARNFORTH	SBJn	MANCHESTER LIVERPOOL ROAD
AM	WG	GL		1.36	MX	J	WIGAN WALLGATE		WIGAN BAMFURLONG Jct & SIDINGS
AM	MAIN	SLxGL		1.47	TO Q	E	CARLISLE UPPERBY	SBJn	CROSS LANE SALFORD
AM	MAIN	FLxSL		2.25	MX Q	D	PERTH	MAIN	MAIDEN LANE LONDON
AM	WG	GL		4.05	MX	G LE G	WIGAN WALLGATE LOCO		WIGAN BAMFURLONG Jct & SIDINGS
AM	WG	GL		4.33	MX	J	WIGAN WALLGATE		WIGAN BAMFURLONG Jct & SIDINGS
AM	WG	GL		4.58	MO	G LE G	WIGAN WALLGATE LOCO		WIGAN BAMFURLONG Jct & SIDINGS
AM	MAIN	FL		5.06	MO	H	CARNFORTH	MAIN	BUSHBURY WOLVERHAMPTON
AM	WG	GL		6.20		G LE G	WIGAN WALLGATE LOCO		WIGAN BAMFURLONG Jct & SIDINGS
AM	MAIN	FL		5.48		D	CARLISLE UPPERBY	SBJn	MANCHESTER LIVERPOOL ROAD
AM	WG	GL	5.30	5.35	TO	F	SIMONSWOOD Sdg KIRKBY	MAIN	THURROCK SIDINGS GRAYS LONDON
AM	BHJn	FLxSL	6.00	6.02	MO	J	HUNCOAT SIDINGS LANCS	MAIN	HARTFORD SIDINGS NORTHWICH
AM	MAIN	SLxGL		6.28	SO	D	CARLISLE UPPERBY	SBJn	MANCHESTER LIVERPOOL ROAD
AM	MAIN	FL		6.53		D	CARLISLE UPPERBY	MAIN	CREWE GRESTY LANE
AM	WG	GL	7.25	8.00		J	WIGAN WALLGATE		WIGAN BAMFURLONG SOUTH END
AM		SL		7.35		G EB	WIGAN NORTH WESTERN		WIGAN BAMFURLONG Jct & SIDINGS
AM		SL		9.15	SX	G LE G	WIGAN NORTH WESTERN		WIGAN SPRINGS BRANCH
AM		SL		9.29	MX	G LE G	WIGAN NORTH WESTERN	MAIN	WARRINGTON DALLAM BRANCH SIDINGS
AM	WG	GL		9.56	SO	G LE G	WIGAN WALLGATE LOCO		WIGAN SPRINGS BRANCH
AM		SL		10.50	SX	G LE G	WIGAN RYLANDS SIDINGS		WIGAN SPRINGS BRANCH LOCO
AM		SLxGL		11.36	SX	J	BLAINSCOUGH SIDINGS		WIGAN No1
AM	WG	GL		11.13		K	WIGAN WALLGATE		WIGAN BAMFURLONG SOUTH END
AM	BHJn	FLxGL		11.55	SO	G LE G	ADLINGTON Jct CHORLEY		WIGAN SPRINGS BRANCH LOCO
PM	MAIN	FL		12.22		H	CARLISLE UPPERBY	MAIN	CREWE GRESTY LANE
PM	WG	GL	12.33	12.35	SO	J	WIGAN PEMBERTON Jct		WIGAN BAMFURLONG Jct & SIDINGS
PM	MAIN	FL		12.44		J	CARNFORTH	MAIN	WARRINGTON EXTENSION SIDINGS
PM	WG	GL	1.41	1.45	SO	J	WIGAN PEMBERTON Jct		WIGAN BAMFURLONG Jct & SIDINGS
PM	WG	GL		2.04	SX	G LE G	WIGAN WALLGATE LOCO		WIGAN BAMFURLONG Jct & SIDINGS
PM	MAIN	FL		1.30	MWFO	F	PRESTON FARINGTON Jct	MAIN	SAINT HELENS
PM	WG	GL		2.13		J	WIGAN WALLGATE		WIGAN BAMFURLONG Jct & SIDINGS
PM		FLxSL		3.42	SX	K	WIGAN VICTORIA COLL Sdg	SBJn	WIGAN INCE MOSS
PM	WG	GL		3.28		G EB	WIGAN WALLGATE		WIGAN BAMFURLONG SOUTH END
PM	MAIN	FL		4.00	SX	C	FLEETWOOD WYRE DOCK	MAIN	BROAD STREET LONDON
PM	WG	GL		5.15	MO	G EB	WIGAN WALLGATE		WIGAN BAMFURLONG Jct SIDINGS
PM	MAIN	SL		4.49		H	CARLISLE UPPERBY	MAIN	WARRINGTON WINWICK QUAY
PM		GL		5.06	SO	K	WIGAN NORTH WESTERN		WIGAN BAMFURLONG Jct SIDINGS
PM	MAIN	FLxGL		5.26		H	CARLISLE UPPERBY SBJn		SALFORD ORDSALL LANE
PM	WG	GL		5.34	SO	F	SOUTHPORT GOODS MAIN		WARRINGTON EXTENSION SIDINGS
PM	WG	GL		5.37	SO	G LE G	WIGAN WALLGATE LOCO		WIGAN BAMFURLONG Jct & SIDINGS
PM		SL		6.15	SX	F	WIGAN NORTH WESTERN	MAIN	GOLBORNE
PM		FLxSL		6.17		J	WIGAN RYLANDS SIDINGS		WIGAN BAMFURLONG Jct & SIDINGS
PM	WG	GL		6.22	SO	G EB	WIGAN WALLGATE		WIGAN BAMFURLONG Jct & SIDINGS
PM	WG	GL		6.33	SX	F	SOUTHPORT GOODS	MAIN	WARRINGTON EXTENSION SIDINGS
PM	MAIN	FL		6.45	FSX	C	CARLISLE UPPERBY	MAIN	BROAD STREET LONDON
PM	MAIN	FL		7.01	SX	C	CARNFORTH	MAIN	WILLESDEN LONDON
PM	WG	GL		7.04	SX	G LE G	WIGAN WALLGATE LOCO		WIGAN BAMFURLONG Jct & SIDINGS
PM	BHJn	FL	7.15	7.15	FSX	C	BURNLEY CENTRAL LANCS		WIGAN NORTH WESTERN
PM		GL		8.00	FSX	G LE G	WIGAN NORTH WESTERN		WIGAN SPRINGS BRANCH LOCO
PM		FL		7.30	SO	G EB	WIGAN RYLAND'S SIDINGS		WIGAN SPRINGS BRANCH
PM	MAIN	FL	7.21	7.35	SO	C	FLEETWOOD WYRE DOCK	MAIN	BROAD STREET LONDON
PM	MAIN	SL		8.10	SX	G EB	PRESTON FARINGTON Jct		WIGAN SPRINGS BRANCH
PM	MAIN	FL		7.58	SX	C	CARLISLE UPPERBY	MAIN	WILLESDEN LONDON
PM		FL		8.20	FQ SX	G LE G	WIGAN NORTH WESTERN		WIGAN SPRINGS BRANCH
PM		FL		8.25	FQ SX	C	WIGAN NORTH WESTERN	MAIN	CHESTER
PM	MAIN	FL	8.16	8.35	FQ SX	C	FLEETWOOD WYRE DOCK	MAIN	BROAD STREET LONDON
PM	MAIN	SL		8.31	SO	D	CARLISLE UPPERBY	MAIN	WILLESDEN LONDON
PM		SL		8.50	SO	K	WIGAN NORTH WESTERN	SBJn	WIGAN INCE MOSS
PM	MAIN	FL		8.52	SX	D	BLACKPOOL TALBUT ROAD	MAIN	CREWE BASFORD HALL
PM	WG	GL		9.10	SX	J	WIGAN WALLGATE		WIGAN BAMFURLONG Jct & SIDINGS
PM		SL		10.00	SX	K	WIGAN NORTH WESTERN	SBJn	WIGAN INCE MOSS
PM		SL		11.00	SO	K	WIGAN NORTH WESTERN	SBJn	WIGAN INCE MOSS
PM	BHJn	FLxGL		11.15	SX	G LE G	ADLINGTON JUNCTION LANCS		WIGAN SPRINGS BRANCH LOCO
PM	WG	GL		11.34	SO	G LE G	WIGAN WALLGATE LOCO		WIGAN BAMFURLONG Jct & SIDINGS
PM		SLxFL		12.33	SO	J	WIGAN VICTORIA COLL Sdg		WIGAN BAMFURLONG Jct & SIDINGS
AM				12.10	MO	A MAILS	WIGAN NORTH WESTERN	StHJn	LIVERPOOL LIME STREET
AM	MAIN	FL		12.33	MX	C FISH	LAW JUNCTION LANARKSHIRE	MAIN	BIRMINGHAM NEW ST. LONDON BROAD ST.FO

AM/PM	Route From	Line	Time Arr.	Time Dept.	Except.	Type	From	Route To	To
AM	MAIN	FL	1.02	1.30	MX	C FISH	LAW JUNCTION LANARKSHIRE	SBJn	MANCHESTER OLDHAM ROAD
AM	MAIN	FL	1.23	1.42	MO	C MAILS	CARLISLE	MAIN	LONDON BROAD STREET
AM		SL		2.00		A MAILS	WIGAN NORTH WESTERN	StHJn	LIVERPOOL LIME STREET
AM		FL	2.00		MO	C FISH	WIGAN NORTH WESTERN	SBJn	MANCHESTER OLDHAM ROAD
AM	MAIN	FL	1.36	2.07	MX	C PCLS	PRESTON	MAIN	CREWE
AM	MAIN	FL		2.02	SO	A	GLASGOW CENTRAL	MAIN	LONDON EUSTON
AM	MAIN	FL	2.11	2.11		A PCLS	PRESTON		WIGAN NORTH WESTERN
AM	MAIN	FL		2.31		A	GLASGOW CENTRAL	MAIN	LONDON EUSTON
AM		GL		2.35	TWSO	C PCLS	WIGAN NORTH WESTERN		WIGAN SPRINGS BRANCH
AM	MAIN	FL	2.41	2.46	MO	A	PERTH	MAIN	LONDON EUSTON
AM	MAIN	FL	2.52	2.57	MX	A	GLASGOW CENTRAL	MAIN	LONDON EUSTON
AM	MAIN	FL		3.06		A	GLASGOW CENTRAL	MAIN	LONDON EUSTON
AM	MAIN	FL		3.16		A	PERTH	MAIN	LONDON EUSTON
AM	MAIN	FL		3.28		A	GLASGOW CENTRAL	MAIN	LONDON EUSTON
AM	MAIN	FL		3.50	MX	A	STRANRAER HARBOUR	MAIN	LONDON EUSTON
AM	MAIN	FL		4.04	MX	A	INVERNESS	MAIN	LONDON EUSTON
AM	MAIN	FL		4.10		A	GLASGOW CENTRAL	MAIN	BIRMINGHAM NEW STREET
AM	MAIN	FL		4.20	SO	A	EDINBURGH PRINCES STREET	MAIN	BIRMINGHAM NEW STREET
AM				5.17		C PCLS	WIGAN NORTH WESTERN	WG	WIGAN WALLGATE
AM	MAIN	FL	5.23	5.30		A	GLASGOW CENTRAL	StHJn	LIVERPOOL LIME STREET
AM		FL		5.40		A	WIGAN NORTH WESTERN	SBJn	MANCHESTER EXCHANGE
AM		FL		5.45		B	WIGAN NORTH WESTERN	SBJn	TYLDESLEY
AM	WG	GL		5.52	SX	G LE P	WIGAN WALLGATE LOCO	SBJn	WIGAN PLATT BRIDGE
AM		SL		6.16		B	WIGAN NORTH WESTERN	StHJn	LIVERPOOL LIME STREET
AM	MAIN	SL	6.08	6.17		B	PRESTON	MAIN	CREWE
AM		SL		6.39		B	WIGAN NORTH WESTERN	StHJn	LIVERPOOL LIME STREET
AM	MAIN	FL		6.39		C PCLS	GLASGOW CENTRAL	MAIN	LONDON WILLESDEN Jct CREWE SO
AM		FL		6.45		B	WIGAN NORTH WESTERN	SBJn	TYLDESLEY RAIL MOTOR SX
AM		FL		7.08		B	WIGAN NORTH WESTERN	MAIN	WARRINGTON B.Q SO LLANDUDNO
AM	MAIN	FL		7.15	MX	C FISH	CARLISLE	MAIN	CREWE
AM		FL		7.18	MX	C PCLS	WIGAN NORTH WESTERN	WG	WIGAN WALLGATE
AM	MAIN	FL	7.11	8.06	MX	C FISH	ABERDEEN	SBJn	MANCHESTER VICTORIA
AM	MAIN	SL	7.26	7.31		B	PRESTON	SBJn	MANCHESTER EXCHANGE
AM	MAIN	FL	7.34	7.37		A	MORECAMBE EUSTON ROAD	MAIN	CREWE
AM		SL		7.40		B	WIGAN NORTH WESTERN	StHJn	LIVERPOOL LIME STREET
AM		SL		8.02		B	WIGAN NORTH WESTERN	MAIN	EARLESTOWN LANCS
AM	MAIN	FL		8.11		A	HEYSHAM LANCS	MAIN	LONDON EUSTON
AM	BHJn	FL	8.28	8.28		B	BLACKBURN LANCS		WIGAN NORTH WESTERN
AM		SL		8.39		B	WIGAN NORTH WESTERN	MAIN	WARRINGTON BANK QUAY
AM	MAIN	FL	8.44	8.48	SO	A	PRESTON	MAIN	CREWE
AM	MAIN	FL	8.54	8.57	SX	A	BLACKPOOL CENTRAL	MAIN	CREWE
AM	MAIN	FL	8.59	9.03	SO	A	BLACKPOOL CENTRAL	MAIN	CREWE
AM		SL		9.03		B	WIGAN NORTH WESTERN	StHJn	LIVERPOOL LIME STREET
AM		FL		9.07		B	WIGAN NORTH WESTERN	SBJn	MANCHESTER EXCHANGE
AM	MAIN	FL		9.13		A	BLACKPOOL CENTRAL	MAIN	LONDON EUSTON
AM		FL		9.25	MX	C PCLS	WIGAN NORTH WESTERN	StHJn	LIVERPOOL LIME STREET
AM	MAIN	FL	9.55	9.57		A	WINDERMERE	SBJn	MANCHESTER EXCHANGE
AM	MAIN	FL		10.10	SO	A	BLACKPOOL NORTH	MAIN	CARDIFF
AM	MAIN	FL	10.25	10.30		B	CARLISLE	MAIN	CREWE
AM		SL		10.32		B	WIGAN NORTH WESTERN	StHJn	LIVERPOOL LIME STREET
AM	MAIN	FL		10.45	SO	A	MORECAMBE EUSTON ROAD	MAIN	BIRMINGHAM NEW STREET
AM	MAIN	FL	10.54	11.01	SO	A	MORECAMBE EUSTON ROAD	SBJn	MANCHESTER EXCHANGE
AM	MAIN	SL		10.58	SO	A	BLACKPOOL CENTRAL	MAIN	LONDON EUSTON
AM	MAIN	SL		11.12	SO	A	BLACKPOOL CENTRAL	MAIN	BLETCHLEY BUCKINGHAMSHIRE
AM	MAIN	FL		11.19	SO	A	CARLISLE	MAIN	BIRMINGHAM NEW STREET
AM	MAIN	FL		11.22	SX	A	BLACKPOOL CENTRAL	MAIN	LONDON EUSTON
AM	MAIN	FL		11.27	SO	A	WORKINGTON MAIN	MAIN	LONDON EUSTON
AM	MAIN	FL	11.40	11.46		A	CARLISLE	MAIN	LONDON EUSTON
AM	MAIN	FL	11.49	11.55	SO	A	BLACKPOOL NORTH	MAIN	CREWE
AM		SL		11.58	SX	B	WIGAN NORTH WESTERN	StHJn	LIVERPOOL LIME STREET
PM	MAIN	FL		12.03	SO	A	BLACKPOOL NORTH	SBJn	STOKE-ON-TRENT
PM		SL		12.10	SO	B	WIGAN NORTH WESTERN	StHJn	LIVERPOOL LIME STREET
PM	MAIN	FL		12.17	SO	A	COCKERMOUTH CUMBERLAND	MAIN	CREWE
PM		FL		12.20		B	WIGAN NORTH WESTERN	SBJn	MANCHESTER EXCHANGE
PM	MAIN	FL		12.26	SO	A	BLACKPOOL NORTH	MAIN	STECHFORD BIRMINGHAM
PM		SL		12.40		B	WIGAN NORTH WESTERN	MAIN	EARLESTOWN LANCS
PM	MAIN	FL		12.42	SO	A	BLACKPOOL NORTH	MAIN	COVENTRY
PM	MAIN	FL/SL	12.53	12.55	SO	A TO B	BLACKPOOL NORTH	MAIN	WARRINGTON BANK QUAY
PM	MAIN	SL	12.57	12.57		B	PRESTON		WIGAN NORTH WESTERN
PM	BHJn	FL	1.02	1.02		B	BLACKBURN LANCS		WIGAN NORTH WESTERN
PM	MAIN	FL		1.06	SO	A	WINDERMERE	MAIN	LONDON EUSTON
PM		SL		1.10	SO	B	WIGAN NORTH WESTERN	StHJn	LIVERPOOL LIME STREET
PM	MAIN	FL	1.11	1.16	SX	A	WINDERMERE	MAIN	LONDON EUSTON
PM	MAIN	SL		1.15	SO	A	BLACKPOOL CENTRAL	MAIN	LONDON EUSTON

AM/PM	Route From	Line	Time Arr.	Time Dept.	Except.	Type	From	Route To	To
PM		GL		1.20	SO	C PCLS	WIGAN NORTH WESTERN		SPRINGS BRANCH- ARLEY MINES SIDINGS
PM	MAIN	FL	1.22	1.26	SO	A	BLACKPOOL NORTH	MAIN	BIRMINGHAM NEW STREET
PM	MAIN	FL	1.35	1.38	SO	A	WINDERMERE	SBJn	MANCHESTER EXCHANGE
PM		SL		1.51		B	WIGAN NORTH WESTERN	StHJn	LIVERPOOL LIME STREET
PM	MAIN	SL	2.08	2.25	SX	C PCLS	CARLISLE	MAIN	CREWE
PM	MAIN	FL		2.00	SX	A	GLASGOW CENTRAL	MAIN	LONDON EUSTON
PM	MAIN	FL		2.07	SO	A	GLASGOW CENTRAL	MAIN	LONDON EUSTON
PM	MAIN	SL	2.30	2.30	SX	B	BLACKPOOL CENTRAL		WIGAN NORTH WESTERN
PM	MAIN	SL	2.30	2.37	SO	B	BLACKPOOL NORTH	SBJn	TYLDESLEY
PM	MAIN	FL		2.22		A	EDINBURGH PRINCES STREET	MAIN	BIRMINGHAM NEW STREET
PM	MAIN	FL		2.34		A	GLASGOW CENTRAL	MAIN	BIRMINGHAM NEW STREET
PM	MAIN	FL		2.47		A	GLASGOW CENTRAL	MAIN	LONDON EUSTON
PM	MAIN	SL		2.53	SO	A	BLACKPOOL NORTH	MAIN	SIOKE-ON-TRENT
PM	MAIN	FL		3.14	FSO	A	PERTH	MAIN	LONDON EUSTON
PM	MAIN	FL		3.25	FSX	A	PERTH	MAIN	LONDON EUSTON
PM	MAIN	FL		3.25	FSO	A	WORKINGTON MAIN	MAIN	LONDON EUSTON
PM		SL		3.38		B	WIGAN NORTH WESTERN	StHJn	LIVERPOOL LIME STREET
PM	MAIN	FL	3.52	3.57		A	BARROW Cent & MORECAMBE EUSTON Rd	MAIN	CREWE FX LONDON EUSTON FO
PM		FL		4.18		B	WIGAN NORTH WESTERN	SBJn	LEEDS CITY SOUTH
PM		SL		4.31		B	WIGAN NORTH WESTERN	StHJn	LIVERPOOL LIME STREET
PM	MAIN	SL		4.37	SO	A	BLACKPOOL NORTH	MAIN	WALSALL
PM		FL		4.53	SO	C ECS	WIGAN NORTH WESTERN	SBJn	TYLDESLEY
PM	MAIN	SL	4.58	5.08		B	PRESTON	StHJn	LIVERPOOL LIME STREET
PM	MAIN	FL	5.13	5.16		A	BLACKPOOL CENTRAL	SBJn	MANCHESTER EXCHANGE
PM	BHJn	FL	5.17	5.21	SX	B/C ECS	R.O.F.HALT CHORLEY LANCS		B WIGAN N.W. C ECS SPRINGS BRANCH
PM	BHJn	FL	5.38	5.38		B	BLACKBURN LANCS		WIGAN NORTH WESTERN
PM		SL		5.31		B	WIGAN NORTH WESTERN	MAIN	WARRINGTON BANK QUAY
PM	MAIN	SL	5.43	5.43	SX	B	LEYLAND LANCS		WIGAN NORTH WESTERN
PM	MAIN	FL		5.34		A	GLASGOW CENTRAL	MAIN	LONDON EUSTON
PM		FL		5.45		C ECS	WIGAN NORTH WESTERN	SBJn	WIGAN PLATT BRIDGE
PM	MAIN	SL	5.50	5.50	SX	B	PRESTON		WIGAN NORTH WESTERN
PM		SL		5.56	SX	B	WIGAN NORTH WESTERN	MAIN	WARRINGTON BANK QUAY
PM		FL		5.58		B	WIGAN NORTH WESTERN	SBJn	LEEDS CITY SOUTH
PM		SL		6.00		B	WIGAN NORTH WESTERN	StHJn	LIVERPOOL LIME STREET
PM	MAIN	FL		6.08		A	PERTH	MAIN	LONDON EUSTON
PM	MAIN	SL	6.22	6.22		B	PRESTON		WIGAN NORTH WESTERN
PM	MAIN	FL/GL	6.26	6.38	SO	C PCLS	HEYSHAM LANCS	MAIN	CREWE
PM	MAIN	FL	6.32	6.35		A	BLACKPOOL CENTRAL	MAIN	LONDON EUSTON
PM		SL		6.48		B	WIGAN NORTH WESTERN	MAIN	WARRINGTON BANK QUAY
PM	MAIN	FL	7.06	7.11	SO	A	BLACKPOOL NORTH	MAIN	STOKE-ON-TRENT
PM	MAIN	SL	7.44	7.53		B	PRESTON	StHJn	LIVERPOOL LIME STREET
PM		FL		8.05	SO	G LE P	WIGAN NORTH WESTERN	SBJn	MANCHESTER EXCHANGE
PM		FL		8.15	SX	B	WIGAN NORTH WESTERN	SBJn	MANCHESTER EXCHANGE
PM	MAIN	FL		8.26	SO	A	PRESTON	MAIN	BIRMINGHAM NEW STREET
PM	BHJn	FL	8.39	8.39		B	BLACKBURN LANCS		WIGAN NORTH WESTERN
PM		FL		9.00	SO	B	WIGAN NORTH WESTERN	SBJn	MANCHESTER EXCHANGE
PM		SL		9.05		B	WIGAN NORTH WESTERN	StHJn	LIVERPOOL LIME STREET
PM	MAIN	SL	8.46	9.10		B	PRESTON	MAIN	WARRINGTON BANK QUAY
PM	MAIN	FL	9.05	9.45	SX	C PCLS	KENDAL	MAIN	LONDON EUSTON
PM	MAIN	FL	9.19	9.24		A	GLASGOW CENTRAL	SBJn	MANCHESTER VICTORIA
PM	MAIN	FL		9.28	MWFO	C PCLS	PERTH	MAIN	LONDON WILLESDEN JUNCTION
PM	MAIN	FL	9.35	9.40	MFO	A	BLACKPOOL NORTH	MAIN	CREWE
PM	MAIN	FL	10.06	10.13		A	CARLISLE	MAIN	CREWE
PM		SL		10.30	SO	B	WIGAN NORTH WESTERN	MAIN	EARLESTOWN LANCS
PM		FL		10.30		B	WIGAN NORTH WESTERN	SBJn	MANCHESTER EXCHANGE
PM		SL		10.35		B	WIGAN NORTH WESTERN	StHJn	LIVERPOOL LIME STREET
PM	MAIN	SL	10.37	10.37		B	PRESTON		WIGAN NORTH WESTERN
PM	MAIN	FL		10.42	FSX	C PCLS	PERTH	MAIN	LONDON BROAD STREET
PM	MAIN	SL		10.49	FO	A	BARROW CENTRAL	MAIN	LONDON EUSTON
PM	MAIN	FL		10.42	FO	A	GLASGOW SAINT ENOCH	MAIN	PLYMOUTH
PM	MAIN	FL		11.06		A	WINDERMERE	MAIN	LONDON EUSTON
PM	MAIN	FL		11.32		A POSTAL	GLASGOW CENTRAL	MAIN	LONDON EUSTON
PM	MAIN	FL		11.45		A	GLASGOW CENTRAL	MAIN	LONDON EUSTON
AM	MAIN	FL	12.06	12.12	MX	A	PRESTON	StHJn	LIVERPOOL LIME STREET

WIGAN NORTH WESTERN TRAIN MOVEMENTS SUMMER MID 50s (SUNDAYS)
UP LINE

AM/PM	Route From	Line	Time Arr.	Dept.	Except.	Type	From	Route To	To
AM	MAIN	SL	12.13	12.19		A	PRESTON	StHJn	LIVERPOOL LIME STREET
AM	MAIN	SL		12.38		H	CARLISLE UPPERBY	MAIN	WARRINGTON WINWICK QUAY
AM	WG	GL		1.03		J	WIGAN WALLGATE		WIGAN SPRINGS BRANCH
AM	MAIN	FL		1.12		C	CARLISLE UPPERBY	MAIN	LONDON BROAD STREET
AM	MAIN	FL/GL		1.25		E	CARNFORTH	SBJn	SALFORD PATRICROFT
AM	MAIN	FL		1.35		E	CARLISLE UPPERBY	MAIN	CREWE BASFORD HALL
AM	WG	GL		4.28		J	WIGAN WALLGATE		WIGAN BAMFURLONG Jct & SIDINGS
AM	MAIN	FL		5.51		H	GARSTANG & CATTERALL LANCS	SBJn	WIGAN INCE MOSS
AM	MAIN	FL		6.32		H	BURTON & HOLM WESTMORLAND	MAIN	WARRINGTON
AM	MAIN	FL		6.42		E	CARLISLE UPPERBY	MAIN	WARRINGTON
AM	MAIN	FL		7.22		E	CARLISLE UPPERBY	MAIN	CREWE GRESTY LANE
AM	MAIN	FL/SL		8.05		E	CARLISLE UPPERBY	SBJn	WIGAN INCE MOSS
AM	MAIN	SL		8.28		E	CARLISLE UPPERBY		WIGAN SPRINGS BRANCH
AM	MAIN	FL		8.53		E	CARLISLE UPPERBY		WIGAN SPRINGS BRANCH
AM	MAIN	FL		9.32		H	CARLISLE UPPERBY	MAIN	WARRINGTON WINWICK QUAY
AM	MAIN	FL		11.00		H	CARLISLE UPPERBY	MAIN	CREWE GRESTY LANE
PM	MAIN	FL		6.28		C Q	CARLISLE UPPERBY	MAIN	LONDON BROAD STREET
PM	MAIN	FL		9.04		H	CARLISLE UPPERBY	SBJn	WIGAN INCE MOSS
PM	MAIN	SL		9.41		H	CARLISLE UPPERBY	MAIN	WARRINGTON
PM	MAIN	FL		9.34		D	CARLISLE UPPERBY	MAIN	CREWE GRESTY LANE
PM	MAIN	SL		11.14		E	CARLISLE UPPERBY	MAIN	BUSHBURY WOLVERHAMPTON
AM		SL		2.10		A	WIGAN NORTH WESTERN	St.HJn	LIVERPOOOL LIME STREET
AM	MAIN	FL		2.31		A	GLASGOW CENTRAL	MAIN	LONDON EUSTON
AM	MAIN	FL	3.17	3.22		A	PERTH	MAIN	LONDON EUSTON
AM	MAIN	FL		3.29		A	GLASGOW CENTRAL	MAIN	LONDON EUSTON
AM	MAIN	FL		3.36		A	GLASGOW CENTRAL	MAIN	LONDON EUSTON
AM	MAIN	FL/GL		3.40		G LE P	PRESTON	MAIN	WARRINGTON DALLAM LOCO
AM	MAIN	FL		3.50		A	STRANRAER HARBOUR	MAIN	LONDON EUSTON
AM	MAIN	FL		4.04		A	INVERNESS	MAIN	LONDON EUSTON
AM	MAIN	FL		4.10		A	GLASGOW CENTRAL	MAIN	BIRMINGHAM NEW STREET
AM	MAIN	FL	5.23	5.30		A	GLASGOW CENTRAL	St.HJn	LIVERPOOL LIME STREET
AM	MAIN	FL		5.40		A	WIGAN NORTH WESTERN	SBJn	MANCHESTER EXCHANGE
AM	MAIN	FL	6.16	6.57		C FISH	ABERDEEN	SBJn	MANCHESTER OLDHAM ROAD
AM	MAIN	FL		7.08		C FISH	ABERDEEN	MAIN	CREWE
AM	MAIN	FL		7.35		A	HEYSHAM	MAIN	LONDON EUSTON
AM		FL		8.10		C PCLS	WIGAN NORTH WESTERN	St.HJn	LIVERPOOL LIME STREET
AM	MAIN	FL		8.20		A	HEYSHAM	MAIN	LONDON EUSTON
AM	MAIN	SL	8.47			B	PRESTON		WIGAN NORTH WESTERN
AM	MAIN	FL	9.04	9.10		B	BLACKPOOL CENTRAL	MAIN	LONDON EUSTON
AM		FL/SL		9.27		B	WIGAN NORTH WESTERN	MAIN	CREWE
AM		SL		9.35		B	WIGAN NORTH WESTERN	St.HJn	LIVERPOOL LIME STREET
AM		FL		9.43		B	WIGAN NORTH WESTERN	SBJn	MANCHESTER ECHANGE
PM	MAIN	FL	12.26	12.35		C PCLS	HEYSHAM	MAIN	CREWE
PM		FL		12.45		C PCLS	WIGAN NORTH WESTERN		WIGAN SPRINGS BRANCH
PM	MAIN	FL	1.19	1.24		A	BLACKPOOL NORTH	MAIN	LONDON EUSTON
PM	MAIN	FL	1.35	1.40		A	WORKINGTON	MAIN	LONDON EUSTON
PM		FL		1.58		B	WIGAN NORTH WESTERN	SBJn	MANCHESTER EXCHANGE
PM	MAIN	FL		2.43		A	GLASGOW CENTRAL	MAIN	BIRMINGHAM NEW STREET
PM	MAIN	FL		3.20		A	GLASGOW CENTRAL	MAIN	LONDON EUSTON
PM	MAIN	FL	3.32	3.36		A	BLACKPOOL CENTRAL	MAIN	BIRMINGHAM NEW STREET
PM	MAIN	FL		3.59		A	GLASGOW CENTRAL	MAIN	LONDON EUSTON
PM	MAIN	FL	4.06	4.11		A	BARROW CENTRAL	MAIN	LONDON EUSTON
PM	MAIN	FL	4.14	4.19		A	BLACKPOOL CENTRAL	MAIN	LONDON EUSTON
PM	MAIN	FL		6.36		C PCLS	CARLISLE	MAIN	LONDON EUSTON
PM	MAIN	SL	6.50	6.55		B	BLACKPOOL CENTRAL	St.HJn	LIVERPOOL LIME STREET
PM		FL		6.57		B	WIGAN NORTH WESTERN	SBJn	MANCHESTER EXCHANGE
PM		FL		7.12		B	WIGAN NORTH WESTERN	MAIN	WARRINGTON BANK QUAY
PM	MAIN	FL	8.55	9.00		A	BLACKPOOL CENTRAL	MAIN	WARRINGTON BANK QUAY
PM	MAIN	FL	10.43	10.48		A	BLACKPOOL CENTRAL	MAIN	BIRMINGHAM NEW STREET
PM	MAIN	FL		11.05		A	BLACKPOOL CENTRAL	MAIN	LONDON EUSTON
PM	MAIN	FL		11.32		A POSTAL	GLASGOW CENTRAL	MAIN	LONDON EUSTON
PM	MAIN	FL	11.46	11.51		A	GLASGOW CENTRAL	MAIN	LONDON EUSTON

II. THE NEW SPRINGS BRANCH

As has been previously stated, the Wigan Branch Railway Act of 1830 had also included for the construction of a branch line from a junction with the Parkside-Wigan line at Springs Branch, to run in a north-easterly direction to New Springs.

In December 1830, the Board of Directors instructed their engineer, Vignoles, to furnish an estimate of the cost of constructing a single line of railway from "Ince Mill to New Springs" and, "furnishing the same to be worked without machinery, or, alternatively, with a self acting plane and such machinery as might be expedient." Further, in January 1831, the Board had decided to proceed with the construction of the line to New Springs "if the funds of the company would admit it." The following month it was decided to make the New Springs Branch, for the present, "a single line of rails as far as the Hindley turnpike road, (now the A577 Manchester Road, Ince.) but to take land for a double line all the way to New Springs hereafter."

It was at this same meeting that the distance between running lines, the "way," was first "fixed" at 6ft. However, at the next board meeting in March a change of heart occurred, and perhaps with Huskisson's accident at Parkside in mind, it was decided to increase the distance between rails to 6ft - 6in.

It may be that some preliminary work on the New Springs route had begun but the company's funds, or lack of them, were beginning to have an adverse effect. One Edward Wilson, Director, protested strongly against construction of the New Springs line "being gone on with," on the grounds that the company's finances, even with the full borrowing powers allowed by the Act, "would not admit of it without getting into debt," which he thought was not justifiable. Edward Wilson had enough like-minded supporters to win the argument and a committee was appointed to examine the matter further.

It is evident that the confidence of the investing public putting their money into railway schemes was not to be taken for granted, particularly when additional capital needed to be raised, and the ways and means in which to do so. It was certainly a concern of the Board that the coal owners whose mines lay alongside or near to the projected route, and who had canvassed for the New Springs line to be built, would not give any cast-iron guarantees of freight traffic to the company.

The Board of the Wigan Branch Railway met twice in

Plate 139. Fowler 0-6-0 No.44867 takes the Springs Branch line towards Bridge Hole about 1958 with a train of wooden bodied wagons.   *B.Nichols.*

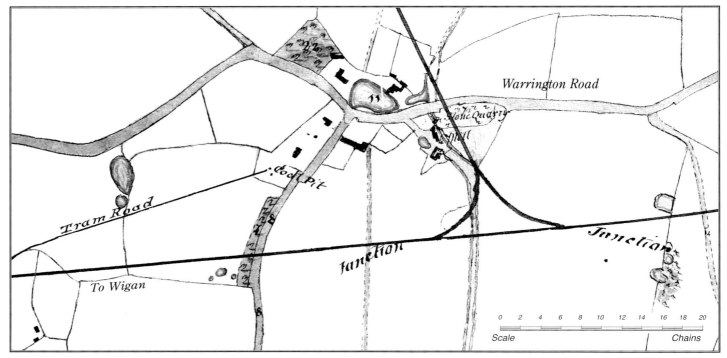

Fig 21. The 1829 line plan of the Springs Branch clearly shows that both north and south facing junctions were intended and the omission of the north curve was undoubtedly an economy measure and, in the event, the construction of the branch was not implemented until 1836, after the formation of the North Union Railway. Although C.B.Vignoles signature appears on the plan it would appear that one John Mather carried out much of the survey. It will be noted when compared with *Fig 22,* that the branch as built passes south of the quarry. The tramway shown in the left foreground made a connection with the Leeds-Liverpool Canal at Westwood, just below lock 21, from pits adjacent to Westwood Lane owned by H&E. Hilton c1838. By 1840, a siding to the North Union Railway had been built. These are the pits later taken over by Pearson & Knowles and known as Crow Orchard Colliery. *See page 84.*

April 1831 and, after much debate, finally decided on the 6ft 'way.' The question of constructing the New Springs line, or not, was deferred for three months. In conducting negotiations for the purchase of land for the branch, the Treasurer was authorised to offer a certain amount "per Cheshire acre." (10,240 sq yards).

It is interesting to note that the following rule was made with regard to the attendance of Directors at Board Meetings, viz: "That the Treasurer do pay each Director one sovereign for each attendance, but not to pay any Director who shall not be present within *ten minutes* of the time appointed for the meeting." Punctuality, therefore, was considered a virtue by the Board and they intended to enforce it and no one, not even a Director, was going to be allowed to to drain income from the cash-strapped company.

It was not until 1836, after the Wigan Branch Railway had amalgamated with the Wigan & Preston Railway to become the North Union, that Vignoles was authorised to set out the New Springs line and he provided estimates of £19,324 for double track, £13,270 for single track and £14,105 for single track but including in this the infrastructure, i.e. bridges, crossings and land to accommodate double track at a later stage. In fact, the third option was constructed for £6,900 with part of the route at gradients of 1:132, 1:30 and 1:880 respectively.

The rails were 'T' section weighing 45lbs per yard in 15ft lengths with 3ft bearings. On embankments, 9ft x 10in x 5in sleepers were used. In cuttings and level track stone blocks 4ft sq x 1ft thick were used (1 cubic ft). Ballast consisted of sand with an upper layer of stone 4in thick. The length of the line was 2m 54 chains and was opened for traffic on 31st October 1838.

Initially, there were some horse working arrangements over the flat crossings and other parts of the branch but generally it was worked by steam locomotives.

The reminiscences of G.P.Neele some years later record that the branch was "worked on a system solely guided by the knowledge of the local superintendent, (then a Mr. Hill) under whose control all the coal traffic and all the brakesmen working coal trains to the south were placed."

On 16th January 1845, authorisation for the line to be doubled was granted and by mid 1845 the section between Springs Branch and Manchester Road Ince, had been completed, work continuing toward Kirkless. However, where the line crossed the Lancaster Canal it remained as single track for some yards, opening out to double track again after Withington Lane.

Plate 140. (Below). The main running lines of the New Springs Branch are prominent in this view at Bridge Hole on 31st October 1994. On the extreme left a single line gave access to Brewery Sidings whilst on the extreme right access was gained, from Engine Shed Crossing, to Springs Branch Shed. When EWS began their operations here these lines would become filled with redundant locomotives awaiting scrapping or salvage, just as they had towards the end of the steam era in the 1960s. *Author.*

Plate 141. The 1880s were a period of expansion for the railways around Springs Branch necessitating the rebuilding of bridges to accommodate extra running lines and in this respect business went both ways. The former mining company of Pearson & Knowles had amalgamated with Dallam Forge, Warrington, in 1874, and being long established railway users at least received some work in return as evidenced by the bridge plate on Warrington Road bridge, as seen above. *Author.*

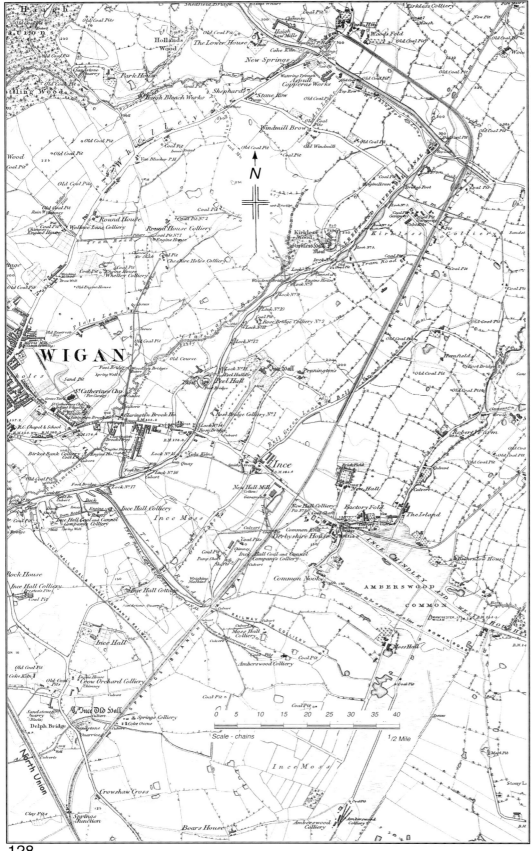

Fig 22. The New Springs Branch is shown in its entirety from the mid 1840s survey. When built, the line crossed a number of colliery tramways which had been in existence since the late eighteenth or early part of the nineteenth centurys and some of these had already made provision for connections with the Springs Branch.

The branch is shown here as single track, the first section to be doubled not completed until 1845. The Springs Colliery connection is shown at bottom left on the east side of the branch, just below those of the Ince Hall Coal & Cannel Company on the west side.

It will be noted that at this period, north of the Ince & Hindley Turnpike Road, only one mining concern - that of the Earl of Crawford & Balcarres, made a direct connection to the Springs Branch, end-on, close to the Lancaster Canal near his Haigh Saw Mill.

Plate 142. One of the BR Standard Class '4s' No.76075 is seen withdrawn, in Brewery Sidings on 12th November 1967. *John Sloane.*

Plate 143. Ex-LMS 2-6-0 No.46432 is seen being propelled into Brewery Sidings as the steam era draws to a close. *Gerry Bent.*

Plate 144. Class '40' No.40 058 had been withdrawn from service shortly before photographed in Brewery Sidings on 24th April 1984. *Author.*

Plate 145. Brake vans were in use on Britain's railways until the 1980s when a change of rules allowed freight trains to be used without them. This particular vehicle, No.B954781, has only recently been overhauled when seen on Engine Shed Sidings on 24th April 1984, and may be of interest to modellers having formerly been in use on the Bickershaw (Abram North Sidings) - Springs Branch - Fiddlers Ferry Circuit. Behind, in Brewery Sidings, a line of withdrawn Class '25s' await their fate. *Author.*

Plate 146. Nature encroaches on 160 years of railway activity on the New Springs Branch as retired Signalman Bill Paxford stands at 'Shuffle Junction' in October 1994 where, as a young man, he worked traffic over this once busy crossing. In late 1998 this section of track between Engine Shed Sidings (Bridge Hole) and Ince Hall was lifted and the New Springs Branch now terminates on the far (west) side of Warrington Road bridge, seen in the background. *Author.*

The township of Ince, to the south of Wigan, was littered with coal mines, some of which had been worked in the eighteenth century. A number of these had their own horse-drawn colliery tramways and the arrival of the Leeds-Liverpool Canal on the scene in 1816 had given an extra impetus to mining in the area and, in the following ten or twenty years, colliery tramways were extended to loading basins on the canal.

When constructed, the Springs Branch would cut across some of these tramways and where this happened the mine owners were provided with flat crossings by the North Union. Some of these same mining companies would make connections with the Springs Branch, followed in later years by other mining and industrial concerns.

It was not until the 1890s that the signalling arrangements on the New Springs line were completed for, as industry along the route expanded, likewise the signal installations themselves were installed as necessary. These were located at Engine Shed Crossing, Ince Hall, Manchester Road Level Crossing at Ince; at Belle Green Lane Level Crossing; at Kirkless Hall Junction and at Hindley Sidings. Initially, Engine Shed Crossing was known as Springs Branch Shunting Cabin, dating from 1885 and having 24 levers. In the 1922, and subsequent appendices, the cabin is not listed but the distance to Engine Shed Crossing remains the same at 317 yards from Springs Branch No.2. The location generally became known as 'Bridge Hole', but 'Crack' was another name used particularly by the footplate crews on account of a defect in the bridge itself.

By the 1940s' the signalman employed at Bridge Hole had only two signals, for the Up and Down lines situated on the west side of Warrington Road, and a cross-over road under his control. The small cabin was situated on the west side of Warrington Road bridge and was a three turn job, the cabin also used by the Springs Branch Shunters and the Yard Foreman. Bridge Hole Sidings were under the latters supervision. The shunter was responsible for working traffic to/from the various works which were connected to the New Springs Branch. A single stroke bell was Bridge Holes contact with Springs Branch No.2 cabin.

At Bridge Hole, a road from Engine Shed Crossing, logically called 'Shed Road' gave access to Springs Branch Shed, running alongside No.1 shed, without the need to run the length of the shed yard. Brewery Sidings were situated on the north-west side of the New Springs running lines, adjacent to Cemetery Road. The Yard Foreman had control of these sidings, access to which was gained by reversal.

As previously stated, Engine Shed Crossing was under the control of the signalman who had his own nickname for this location of 'Shuffle Junction'. This name arose because of a foot stirrup fitted to the bottom of the point lever, foot held, or shuffled, which eased the effort required by the signalman when constantly working these hand points for the numerous shunting movements carried out at this location, a process hard to visualise today when one views the scene. The cross-over road was situated on the east side of Warrington Road bridge in close proximity to the Wigan Wagon Works outlet. Here the signalman would spend most of his time, out in the open working this crossing.

Ince Hall signal box had control of two signals and the Moss Hall Colliery cross-over. A single stroke bell was Ince Hall's contact with Manchester Road cabin. Trains travelling on the 'Down' line to Kirkless would be

Plate 147. An '8F', No.48117, and 'Crab' No.42954, are prominent in this view at Engine Shed Sidings about 1967. The adjacent Brewery Sidings are packed with redundant vans of various types. Because of overcrowding in the sheds, engines were often prepared for the road on these sidings. *Gerry Bent.*

Plate 148. Type '2' No.25 248 arrives on the Springs Branch with trip 85 from Warrington, sand for the CWS Glassworks at Platt Bridge, on 5th March 1974. St Mary's church still stands, but for how long? *Tom Sutch.*

Plate 149. The view from Warrington Road overbridge as a pair of Class '20s' draw forward with loaded vans from the Roburite works at Gathurst in February 1988 and are seen at Engine Shed Crossing, or 'Shuffle Junction'. In the distance is the Gullick Dobson Works occupying the former Ince Forge site. Also of interest is the embankment of the abandoned Lancashire & Yorkshire Railway's Pemberton Loop line which passed by the works. *Bob McClellan.*

Plate 150 (opposite). In the 1990s the track continued for a few hundred yards towards Ince to allow for the storage of MGR wagons then in use on the Bickershaw to Fiddlers Ferry circuit. On 11th February 1992 Class '20s' Nos 20 081//016 are returning to Springs Branch after dropping of the empties from Fiddlers Ferry. *Author.*

offered by Ince Hall to Manchester Road who would then offer the train to Belle Green box. If the train was accepted by by the latter, only then would the Manchester Road signalman close the crossing gates to road traffic allowing the train to proceed.

In the 1950s the only booked working direct into Bridge Hole was a Copley Hill-Springs Branch train. A Springs Branch crew would work an Ince Moss-Patricroft train and return from Patricroft with the ex-Copley Hill train, arriving at Bridge Hole about 4am. However, shunting and trip movements at Bridge Hole ensured the shunter and signalman were kept busy.

The signal box at Manchester Road, Ince, a London & North Western Type '4' had been commissioned on 17th August 1883 but there would have been some means of controlling this crossing before its installation, probably by use of a Flag Man. Belle Green Lane Crossing is another candidate for a simple flag arrangement before a signal cabin opened here in August 1884, another Type '4' box with 14 working levers. It is not clear if Kirkless Hall Junction had a telegraph box dating from 1869/70 prior to the opening of a new cabin there in October 1897 with 13 working levers. This box was closed 1939/40 as a result of the recession which decimated the industry sited alongside the Springs Branch here. It was replaced by a ground frame for working traffic to/from the Lancashire Union connection at Rose Bridge Junction.

Hindley Sidings Cabin was, until 1922, known as California Crossing on account of the mineral railway connections with the Springs Branch from California Pits at Pennington Green, north of Hindley. The 1922 and the 1931 appendices, put the cabin it at 445 yards from Kirkless Hall Junction. The same appendix gives a line distance between Hindley Sidings and Springs Branch No.2 as 2 miles 78 yards. This is slightly at odds with later appendices which give an additional line distance of + 18 yards. However, as the junction at Springs Branch saw successive alterations between 1880 and 1895 this is hardly surprising and it may also be that with the replacement of older signal cabins with new ones further errors have crept into the equation.

Line distances from the 1931 appendix:
Springs Branch No.2 to
Engine Shed Sidings............317 yards
Moss Hall Crossing ....911 yards
Ince Hall Ironworks Sdgs....195 yards
Manchester Road Crossing..532 yards
Belle Green Lane Crossing..607 yards
Kirkless Hall Junction..........392 yards
Kirkless Hall Sidings...........199 yards
Hindley Sidings....................445 yards

Notes

Kirkless Hall Junction to Rose Bridge Junction was 389 yards with block on Down line for freight trains.

Manchester Road Crossing. Running catch points 420 yards in rear of Belle Green Down signal. 1:36 gradient.

Propelling of wagons to Albion Ironworks from Springs Branch No.2 allowed.

Wigan Coal & Iron Co. engines must carry one white light over left hand buffer.

The survey of connections on the Springs Branch is made more complicated by the fact that a number of collieries had the same or similar name as in 'Ince Hall Colliery' or 'Ince Hall Coal Co.' and some never had a connection with the Springs Branch at all. Furthermore, in later years when a particular colliery was taken over it would also have a similar name, or if closed completely, the site was often taken over by engineering or other works.

Moving along the branch from the main lines the the first connection with the branch is that of Pearson & Knowles who had sunk their Springs Colliery on the east side of the branch in 1840. They worked their coal trains to Preston and had a number of other mines in the Wigan area as mentioned in Chapter 1. They also had a foundry in Liverpool where the locomotive *LIVER*, an 0-6-0 with 4ft -7in diameter wheels was constructed in 1844. A number of successful trails were carried out between Wigan and Boar's Head using this engine which hauled 260 tons, unassisted, up the 1 in 100 incline in February 1845. *LIVER* was involved in an accident at Boar's Head in 1850 when working from Preston to their colliery on the Springs Branch.

Springs Colliery closed about 1870 but Pearson & Knowles had established engineering shops and wagon repair facilities on the same site. In the early years of the twentieth century the site was taken over by T.Burnett & Co. who leased some of the existing buildings for a wagon works, using Pearson & Knowles' original connection with the Springs Branch* under a new agreement with the London & North Western as from December 1905. In 1937 the firm were given notice to quit the site and the private sidings agreement terminated by the LMS.

The Wigan Wagon Co. set up their works alongside the Springs Colliery site in 1873/4. It was extended in 1884 and a new internal railway system built. The Wigan Wagon Cos. traffic had also been worked in over the Pearson & Knowles connection but in 1896 a new connection was put in south of the original. The Wigan Wagon Company was taken over by Wagon Repairs Ltd. about 1945, surviving until 1965 when the sidings agreement was terminated and most of the site cleared, although some buildings remained until 197

For over forty years the site of Springs Colliery and the wagon works companies remained derelict but in 2006 house building commenced on the site and in a year or two it will be difficult to perceive the activity that once occured here.

* For Ordnance Survey see *Fig 15*, page 84.

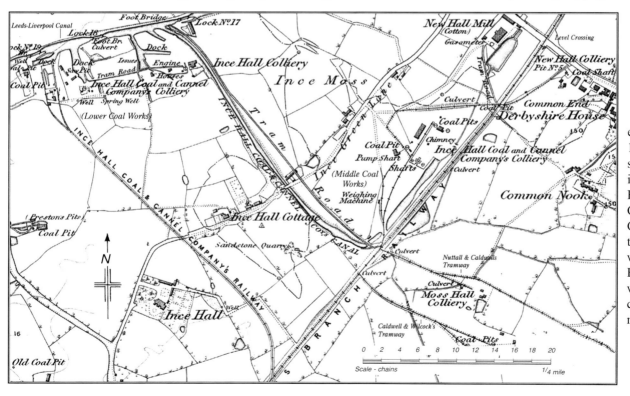

Fig 23. An extract from the 1840s survey shows the workings of the Ince Hall Coal & Cannel Company and their connection with the Springs Branch, together with the new canal arm in more detail.

INCE HALL COAL & CANNEL COMPANY

Messrs John Lancaster, James Hodgkinson and James King had obtained mining rights for an area of land between the Leeds-Liverpool Canal and Ince Green Lane, previously worked from the 1820s by one Richard Swarbrick. Known as James King & Company of the Ince Hall Coal & Cannel Company, the firm built a side basin alongside the canal near lock 19 and constructed a standard gauge railway just over 1/2 mile in length to join with the Springs Branch by a south-west facing curve This was in operation by the time the first series Ordnance Survey was completed in 1845/6. Further mines were sunk in the same area in later years becoming known as 'Lower Coal Works'.

William Lancaster, brother to John, also had mining interests in a partnership known as John Swindells & Company, or the Ince Union Coal & Cannel Company. These mines were to become 'Middle Coal Works'. In January 1847, Swindells & Co. had taken over James King & Co., and in 1848 a joint stock formed under the title of the Ince Hall Coal & Cannel Company.

Preceeding the workings of the Ince Hall Coal & Cannel Co., and the Springs Branch, a tramway had existed, pre 1829, and is shown on the deposited plans of that year for the Springs Branch. The tramway ran from a point near lock 17 on the Leeds-Liverpool Canal to Moss Hall Colliery, owned by Nuttall and Caldwell, sited east of the Springs Branch, and a flat crossing was provided by the North Union to facilitate the colliery working to the canal. In 1845 a short standard gauge connecting branch was put in allowing transfer of coal from narrow gauge to standard gauge wagons.

A second tramway approximately 100 yards south of the above also crossed the Springs Branch on the level from another group of Moss Hall Collieries owned by Caldwell and Wilcocks. This tramway also ran to the Leeds-Liverpool Canal. However, it was to close north of the Springs Branch about 1845. The latters mines are believed to have been taken over by Nuttall and Caldwell and it is known that the two firms were closely connected. The remaining part of this tramway is shown east of the Springs Branch line on the first series Ordnance Survey.

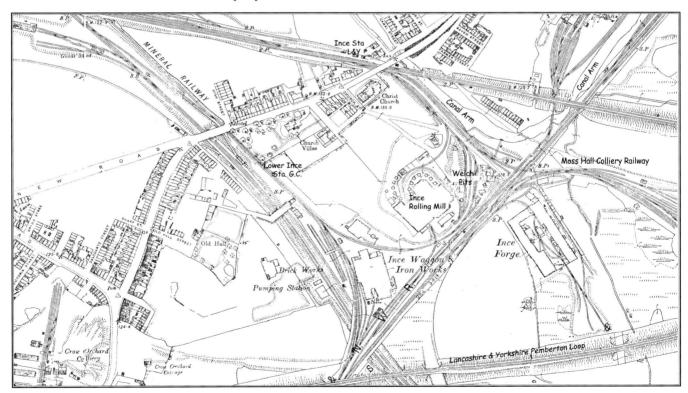

Fig 24. By the time the second Ordnance Survey was carried out in the late 1880s considerable expansion had occured in the area with the construction of Ince Wagon Works and Ince Forge. Additional industrial railways had been laid and the Lancashire & Yorkshire, and Wigan Junction railways now criss-crossed in the same vicinity. The Welch Pits are situated alongside the Ince Rolling Mill. *N.B. this is X2 scale of* **Fig 23.**

Returning to the Ince Hall Coal & Cannel Cos. interests, a lengthy arm of the Leeds-Liverpool Canal was cut from the main canal between locks 17 and 18, running south-east toward the Springs Branch, taking the ground previously occupied by Caldwell & Wilcocks tramway, and completed in 1845/6. As the canal arm approached the Springs Branch it turned north-east to reach the Ince Halls Cos. Middle Works. This new canal arm cut across Nuttall and Caldwells tramway, the northern portion of which was abandoned. However, still crossing the Springs Branch on the level, the southern part was converted to standard gauge and a new standard gauge railway built which was to run alongside the recently opened canal arm to reach the Lancashire & Yorkshire Railway at Ince Station which had opened in 1848. This is the Moss Hall Colliery's private railway as in **Plate 165.**

The Ince Hall Coal & Cannel Company had two locomotives, *Colonel* and *Black Diamond.* Both were 2-4-0 tender engines with 5ft-0in driving wheels. The Company were working their own trains to Preston, and to Liverpool via Parkside Junction. In 1848, Trevithick, the Grand Junction Railway Engineer, had reported that the Ince Hall Coal & Cannel Company were not using their own locomotive for deliveries of coal to Crewe as per their contract. Exactly whose engine they were using is not known but it seems likely they had 'borrowed' one from another of the colliery companies using the Springs Branch.

In May 1871, the Ince Hall Coal & Cannel Company became a Limited Liability Company and their sphere of operations was extended with the sinking of new shafts at East Cannel Pits, north of Manchester Road, Ince. Connections were made with the Springs Branch at the northern and southern extent of their sidings in 1873. However, by 1878, these were no longer in use as a tubway had been constructed to connect with Middle Coal Works where all the coal from the East Cannel pits was screened. In 1884 the Company was declared bankrupt on a petition from one of its lessors. Much of the Company's workings and property were taken over by Charles Gidlow Jackson, including the Middle Coal Works and East Cannel Pits

INCE WAGGON WORKS

Richard Olive's Ince Wagon Works was situated adjacent to the Ince Hall Coal & Cannel Cos. line from Lower Coal Works, and Olive's Works was reached over the Ince Hall connection from the Springs Branch. Richard Olive was declared bankrupt in 1881 and the premises taken over by the Ince Wagon & Ironworks Company Ltd. in 1883. The latter company took over the railway from its connection with the Springs Branch to the Lower Coal Works in 1892 to maintain a connection with the Wigan Junction Railway which had opened to Darlington St. Wigan in January 1884.

In January 1901, the Ince Wagon & Iron Company purchased an 0-4-0 tank locomotive via Mitchells of Bolton, from William Ramsden's Shakerley Collieries at Tyldesley. Over the next 25 years a number of ex-colliery locomotives arrived at the works and others sold on as surplus to requirements.

One W.R.Davis acquired a controlling interest in the company in 1919. Davis, who had other works in various parts of the country, was declared bankrupt in 1932. The works was taken over by the Central Wagon Company Ltd in 1933, who carried out much needed improvements at the works. New agreements were signed in respect of sidings at Lower Ince with the LNER in 1943 (this was for the old Wigan Junction Railway connection) and BR in 1948. The works finally closed in 1980 and some redevelopment has taken place in recent years but at the time of writing much derelict land remains.

THE WELCH PITS

In the same vicinity as Ince Hall Rolling Mills were the Welch Pits on the west side of Springs Branch. Dating from the early 1860s, these pits were worked by one Robert James who traded as the Ince Hall Coal Company or the Ince Hall Company. Welch Pits had a sidings connection with the Lancashire & Yorkshire at Ince Station from 1862. On the Springs Branch there were two connections at 743 yards and 1,236 yards from Springs Branch Junction.

Robert James' activitys did not last long as he was bankrupt in 1866 and his Welch Pits taken over by Crompton & Shawcross who also had pits at Amberswood and Strangeways as referred to in Chapter 1.

It is believed that from about 1885 Crompton & Shawcross were only using the Springs Branch connections from the Welch Pits which, from the same period became known as the Ince Hall Pemberton Pits. After a period of inaction in the 1890s, these pits were to close completely in 1901 and the sidings connection at 743 yards removed; that at 1236 yards was used by Church Iron Works.

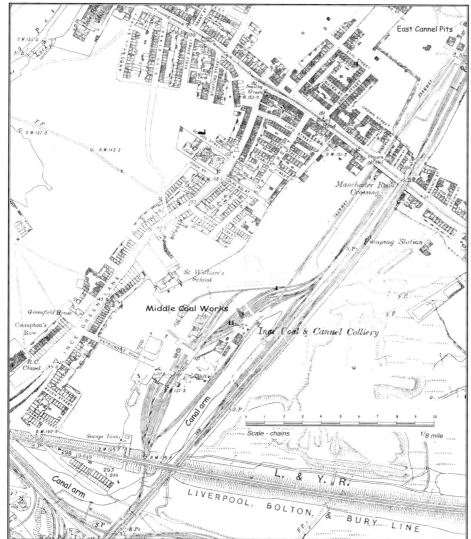

Fig 25. Middle Coal Works in the 1880s. The 'Pumping Station' marks the site of William Gidlows No.5 colliery. East Cannel Pits, north of Manchester Road are shown, as is the tramway or tubway which ran under the road to Middle Coal Works for a number of years. The canal arm from the Leeds - Liverpool is believed to have been infilled about 1900 after a burst.

Plate 151. (below). The redundant trackbed of the Springs Branch towards Central Wagon and Thompsons is seen in April 1995, although not much of either of those two works remained at this period. A Metro Cammell DMU passes on the former Lancashire & Yorkshire route from Wigan Wallgate to Crows Nest Junction. The bridge on the left passed over the lines into the Middle Coal Works of the Ince Hall Coal & Cannel Co. when it was first built and, in later years, the same lines as used by Ince Wagon Works, Ince Wagon & Iron Works Co., and Thompsons/Central Wagon Co. The centre bridge spanned the canal arm from the Leeds - Liverpool Canal near locks 17 and 18, completed in 1845/6. In the immediate foreground would have been the Moss Hall Colliery tramway which closed about 1956 *(See also* **Plate 165***)* The fence on the right marks the boundary of the Joy Mining Co. on the site previously occupied by Ince Forge, Gullicks and Longwall Roof Supports.

Author.

Plate 152. One of the 0-6-0 diesel shunters No.D3184, is seen on the branch near to Central Wagon on 4th June 1969. Compare this with *Plate 151*, previous page.
John Sloane.

Plate 153. During the late 1980s much reclamation work took place on derelict land at Ince and Amberswood erasing the scars of 150 years of mining and industrial activity, this photograph being taken from new landscaping alongside Seaman Road, off the A577 Manchester Road at Amberswood. The 2x2 car Metro Cammell units working the 09.50 Manchester Victoria - Southport are passing Gullick Dobson's works on the approach to Wigan Wallgate, running right to left across picture. This is the site once occupied by Ince Forge who had set up operations in 1856, dealing principally in equipment for the mining industry, then in full flow around Wigan. Over the next century, connections with mining ensured that the owners prospered as the need for coal grew ever greater. Gullick Dobson operated from the site from the 1950s when there was still a healthy mining industry in Lancashire generally, and a good export business. In the mid 1990s the firm became Longwall Roof Supports Ltd., and more recently Joy Mining Ltd. It is worthy of note that the Moss Hall Colliery Railway once passed beneath the very spot on which I stood to take this photo on 15th May 1992. *Author.*

INCE HALL ROLLING MILLS

The Ince Hall Rolling Mills opened on 1st January 1872 on a site adjacent to the Ince Hall Coal & Cannel Cos railway and the Springs Branch. Apparently they used the same connection to the Springs Branch as did the nearby Welch Pits. By 1878 there were 24 furnaces and 4 rolling mills here. Unfortunately, the company was soon in financial trouble and the works purchased by the Wigan Rolling Mills Company in 1881 but was closed again around 1890.

In 1900, after laying dormant for some ten years, the premises were taken over by the Salford firm of W&J. Ellison, nail manufacturers, and the name change to Church Ironworks, but the company was in liquidation by 1906.

The Church Ironworks Company Ltd was registered by a Mr J. Wood in 1909 and a new agreement signed with the London & North Western Railway in 1915 in respect of their connection at 1236 yards from Springs Branch Junction. In the 1920s, the works came under the control of Monks, Hall & Company Ltd of Warrington.

The Church Ironworks was voluntarily liquidated in 1936, closing in 1937 and the site taken over by Ince-in-Makerfield Urban District Council for housing development. The former works connection was latterly used for the delivery of building materials.

INCE FORGE

Ince Forge was situated south of the Ince Moss Colliery railway, on the east side of the Springs Branch, opening about 1856. The firm dealt in heavy engineering equipment, much of it for the mining industry. They aslo constructed a number of mainline and colliery locomotives, including some 2-4-0 broad gauge saddle tanks for the South Devon Railway. In 1875, 'kits' for three more 2-4-0s were supplied, intended for assembly at the South Devon's Newton Abbott workshops. In the event, they were assembled as standard gauge 2-4-0s at Swindon on amalgamation of the South Devon Railway with the Great Western.

Ince Forge became a Limited Company in 1900. The works also had a connection with the Lancashire & Yorkshire Railway by way of the Moss Hall Colliery's railway who worked their traffic to Ince. However, in the 1920s this arrangement ceased and all traffic from Ince Forge was worked out via the Springs Branch.

In 1943 the firm became a subsidiary of William Park (Forgemasters) Ltd, whose origins date from 1790 when William Park was in partnership with James Diggle. In the 1950s Gullick Dobson Ltd operated from the site having been absorbed by William Park. Gullick Dodson supplied mining equipment to the NCB and overseas. On a personal note, in the 1990s, I was contracted to make a model of their successors hydraulic roof supports which were being supplied to the South Bulga Colliery in Australia by Longwall Roof Supports Ltd. The site is now operated by Joy Mining Ltd.

Plate 154. Engineering work is still carried out on the former Ince Forge site, although no longer rail connected. Their hydraulic roof support systems are familiar to mining companies world-wide and coming from a mining family it was with some satisfaction that I was engaged to construct a scale model of the full-size version seen here.

Author.

CENTRAL WAGON COMPANY AND THOMPSON'S YARD

In the early years of the nineteenth century William Gidlow, uncle to Charles Gidlow Jackson, had a number of pits on a site near Manchester Road, Ince. When the Springs Branch was constructed it cut across Gidlow's existing tramway which served his No.5 pit, situated on the east side of the Springs Branch. On the west side of the branch a standard gauge siding served his New Hall Pit.

From the 1840s, the site on the western side was occupied by the Middle Coal Works of the Ince Hall Coal & Cannel Co. After the latters demise the site was taken over by Charles Gidlow Jackson who was trading as Ince Coal & Cannel Company.

He also took over the Ince Hall & Cannel Coals No.2 pit, formerly William Gidlows No.5 pit. The latter was known to be still operating in the 1870s but by the time the second Ordnance Survey was carried out it is shown only as a pumping station and the tramway to it which had crossed the Springs Branch on the level, and an associated siding, were lifted.

Charles Gidlow had also taken over the East Cannel Pits north of Manchester Road *(also see page 136)*. The southern connection from East Cannel Pits with the Springs Branch was reinstated in 1889, and the northern connection in 1893. Gidlow Jackson was working spoil trains over the Springs Branch from East Cannel Pits to Middle Coal Works for use as infil on land east of the Springs Branch and a new connection provided for this purpose at 1,643 yards from Springs Branch Junction.

Gidlow Jackson's collieries were closed in 1899 and the sites and equipment put up for sale. The East Cannel Pits were taken over by Thomas & William Latham and under an agreement dated 26th March 1900 they had permission to run over the Springs Branch between Rose Bridge Sidings and the "Belle Green End of their Ince Sidings". This undoubtedly refers to the northern connection at East Cannel Pits. On 12th January 1904, Latham Brothers sent in an application to the Officers Meeting at Euston for permission to work their trains "to cover the Manchester Road crossing end of the Ince Sidings and are prepared to pay an additional £5 per annum for the privilege". This seems to infer that the southern connection at East Cannel Pits with the Springs Branch had also been reinstated. The application was granted.

For a few years, the Bolton firm of Thomas Mitchell who dealt in second hand machinery and locomotives, used the Middle Coal Works site by which time all the mines on the site had closed.

The Chorley Wagon Company seems to have arrived on the scene in 1907, using the same connection, 1643 yards from Springs Branch Junction as that used by Charles Gidlow Jackson did to reach his No.5 pit on the east side of the branch.

The Central Wagon Company Ltd. was registered in 1911, taking acquisition of the Chorley Wagon Company and setting about a complete reorganisation of the site with new workshops, extending the premises right up to Manchester Road. A new connection was provided by the London & North Western at 1,479 yards from Springs Branch Junction in October 1913. Developments were also to take place on the western side of the branch about 1918 when Central Wagon leased additional land to extend their works. As from March 1917, Central Wagon were allowed to use the sidings connection at 1,456 yards along the branch, that as originally used by Ince Hall Coal & Cannel Company as a secondary access to Middle Coal Works and Gidlow Jackson's Ince Coal & Cannel Company. The relative Sidings Schedule states that the points at this location had been spiked " Out of Use" in 1900 after Gidlow Jackson's operations ceased the year before.

New agreements were made with the LMS in 1923 and most of the new workshops referred to earlier had been constructed in the late 1920s and early 1930s. After the end of W.W.II., Central Wagon Company's works on both sides of the Springs Branch were reconstructed and in 1962, further land acquired from BR as by then the Springs Branch had been cut back to terminate south of Manchester Road. More land became available in the 1960s when part of Thompson's Yard was cleared.

The wagon building business was profitable enough during the 1960s, and the scrapping of thousands of wagons per year continued throughout the same period, but the declining demand for new wagons as BR's freight business began to fade away in the 1970s was a bitter blow considering all the investment carried out, rail traffic to Central Wagon ceasing in 1973.

Thompson & Company leased the southern part of the

former Middle Coal Works about 1900 and the firm used the former Ince Hall Coal & Cannel Company's No.1, or southern connection, with the Springs Branch. The old engine shed at this location was taken over by Thompsons, as was an office block built for Gidlow Jackson's in 1884. The engine shed was still extant in 1968.

Thompson & Company were into scrap metal, machinery and locomotives purchased from local collieries; some for scrap and others to be rebuilt and sold on. The firm had become a subsidiary company of Central Wagon and new workshops were constructed here. Between 1959 and 1966, a steady stream of mainline steam locomotives arrived and were cut up, mostly ex-LMS types but also a number of ex- GWR and LNER engines. Only one 'Pacific' was cut up here, No.46243 *City Of Lancaster,* one 'Royal Scot" No.46129 *The Scottish Horse,* and a single 'Patriot', No.45522 *Prestatyn.*

The yard was to close in 1983 and put up for sale in 1985.

The following list of engines cut up at Thompson's Yard is compiled from a number of sources but may not be the complete total:-

Ex-L&Y 2-4-2T No.50712.

Ex-LMS 4-4-0 Nos. 40586, 40674, 40684 & 41158.

Ex-GW 0-6-0PT Nos.3723, 5744, 5761, 5766, 5779, 5789, 5793, 7753, 7762, 8715, 8727, 8750, 8788, 8797, 9753.

Ex-LMS 0-6-0T Nos.47228, 47257, 47291, 47301, 47350, 47352, 47361, 47375, 47387, 47416, 47440, 47461, 47470, 47477, 47514, 47528, 47537, 47549, 47575, 47584, 47585, 47586.

Ex-L&Y 0-6-0ST (former Barton-Wright Class 23) Nos:- 51316, 51404, 51408, 51413, 51415, 51423, 51457, 51458, 51497, 51512.

Ex-LNER Class J94 (former M.o.S.) 0-6-0ST No.68068

Ex-GW 0-6-0 No. 3208.

Ex-S&D 0-6-0 No. 43211

Ex-MR (Johnson) 0-6-0 Nos. 43271, 43335, 43339, 43387, 43388, 43398, 43422, 43502, 43538, 43558, 43580, 43619, 43630, 43674, 43711, 43753.

Ex-MR (Fowler) 0-6-0 Nos. 43890, 43910, 43925, 43961, 43976, 43984, 44000, 44007, 44014.

Ex-LMS 0-6-0 Nos.44117, 44119, 44186, 44225, 44240, 44280, 44291, 44293, 44361, 44438, 44464, 44471, 44479, 44549.

Ex-L&Y 0-6-0 Nos.52183, 52269, 52271, 52431, 52443.

Ex-LMS 2-6-0 (Hughes 'Crab') Nos.42707, 42708, 42734, 42751, 42757, 42761, 42772, 42776, 42778, 42788, 42817, 42820, 42826, 42840, 42842, 42851, 42855, 42858, 42888, 42892, 42901, 42904, 42932, 42937, 42941, 42943.

Ex-LMS 2-6-0 (Stanier Mogul) Nos.42951, 42952, 42956.

Ex-LMS 2-6-0 (Ivatt) No.43031.

Ex-LNER 2-6-0 Nos.61817, 61880, 61886, 61890, 61915, 61942, 61954, 61963.

Ex-BR 2-6-0 Nos. 77011, 78002.

Ex-LMS (Fowler) 2-6-2T Nos.40003, 40004, 40007, 40015, 40017, 40018, 40021, 40052, 40055, 40056, 40059, 40061, 40068.

Ex LMS (Stanier) 2-6-2T Nos.40091, 40103, 40127, 40134, 40141, 40143, 40163, 40166, 40174, 40192, 40194, 40199, 40208.

Ex-LMS (Ivatt) 2-6-2T No. 41205.

Ex-BR 2-6-2T Nos. 84010, 84015, 84016, 84028.

Ex-LMS 2-6-4T (Fowler) Nos. 42077, 42155, 42280, 42309, 42369, 42378, 42386, 42423, 42424.

Ex-LMS 2-6-4T (Stanier) Nos.42428, 42471, 42475, 42479, 42481, 42549, 42558, 42565, 42569, 42570, 42572, 42635, 42637, 42640, 42670.

Ex-LMS 2-6-4T (Fairburn) No. 42696.

Ex-BR 2-6-4T No.80050.

Ex-GW 2-6-4 'Hall' Class Nos. 4950, 4976,

Ex-GW 4-6-0 'Castle' Class No.5015.

Ex-LMS 4-6-0 Nos.45108, 45313, 45414.

Ex-LMS 4-6-0 'Patriot' Class No.45522.

Ex-LMS 4-6-0 'Jubilee' Class Nos.45583, 45592, 45601, 45623, 45631, 45657, 45681, 45710.

Ex-LMS 4-6-0 'Royal Scot' Class No.46129.

Ex-LNER 4-6-0 Class 'B1' Nos. 61041, 61044, 61052, 61054, 61056, 61066, 61096, 61144, 61149, 61152, 61171, 61182, 61251, 61254, 61280, 61286, 61363.

Ex-LNW 0-8-0 Nos.48915, 48942, 49007, 49119, 49160, 49191, 49209, 49268, 49421.

Ex-LMS 0-8-0 (Fowler) Nos. 49505, 49511, 49582, 49592, 49616, 49640, 49662, 49667, 49668.

Ex-GW 2-8-0 No.3829.

Ex-LMS 2-8-0 Nos.48050, 48771.

Ex-LNER 2-8-0 Nos.63923, 63930, 63933, 63948, 63961, 63966, 63971.

Ex-WD 2-8-0 Nos.90109, 90140, 90147, 90157, 90173, 90212, 90219, 90245, 90257, 90359, 90374, 90375, 90388, 90416, 90425, 90495, 90526, 90552, 90559, 90566, 90574, 90592, 90595, 90599, 90608, 90667, 90712, 90721, 90724.

Plate 155. The only ex-LMS 'Pacific' to be cut up at Central Wagon, No.46243 *City of Lancaster,* is seen with plates removed in June 1965.
David Hill.

Plate 156. On 30th January 1965, ex-LMS 'Jinty' No.47549 proudly displays its final destination whilst awaiting the cutters torch. It is backed up against a Fowler tender and, alongside a Midland 0-6-0 on the cabside of which is written "Central Wagon Co, Private Sidings, Springs Branch, Wigan."
Peter Eckersley.

Plate 157. A line of Horwich built, Hughes 2-6-0 'Crabs,' including Nos.42504 & 42728, are seen at in Thompson's Yard on 25th July 1965. *Tony Oldfield.*

Plate 158. 'Jubilee' class 4-6-0 No.45710 *Irresistible's* withdrawal has obviously pulled at someone's heart-strings having its smokebox inscribed "Goodbye Old Pal" and remarkably still has its nameplate in situ on 30th January 1965. These were the days when a nameplate could be bought for its scrap value - typically £3 to £5 - and not the thousands it cost today. *Peter Eckersley.*

Plate 159. Ex-GWR 'Hall' Class No.4976 *Warfield Hall,* seen at Central Wagon shortly after arrival when photographed in June 1965. *David Hill.*

Plate 160. Amidst the clutter of the scrapyard, Fowler Class '4' 2-6-4T No.42369 seems relatively intact in this view on 25th July 1965. Over on the left is ex-GWR No.5105 *Kingswear Castle.* *Tony Oldfield.*

Plate 161. Seen at Central Wagon on 1st July 1965 are a pair of ex-LNER Class B1s with No.61056 nearest, and No.61144.
Tom Heavyside.

Plate 162. The L.M.S. Ivatt, taper-boilered 2-6-2 Class '2s' were introduced in 1946 and were quite a nippy little engine, some being equipped with push-pull apparatus for working local passenger services. A number of these engines were shedded at Plodder Lane from 1948 until replaced by the B.R. version of the same engine. No.41205 is seen at Central Wagon on 30th January 1965.
Peter Eckersley.

Plate 163. One of the ex-LMS 'Jintys' No.47470 awaits its turn for attention outside Thompson's Yard in November 1962. Refer also to *Plates 151 & 152* for location. *G.Kaye.*

Plate 164. This is literally the end of the line on the New Springs Branch after it had been cut back to the west side of the A577 in 1958 and was used to store condemned locomotives purchased for scrap by Central Wagon Co. Class 'B1' 4-6-0 No.61041 is seen on 13th September 1963 awaiting the cutters attention. The locomotive has suffered some collision damage prior to arriving here. *Dr.J.G.Blears.*

Plate 165. The 'signal box,' if one can call it that, at Ince Hall level crossing in the early 1950s has obviously seen better days, and what possible protection could this dilapidated cabin give to any railwayman needing to work the four lever frame here? Alongside is a long-lived example of London & North Western lower quadrant signalling.

On the 'Down' line, one of the ex-Lancashire & Yorkshire 0-6-0s is about to propell axles into Thompson's Yard which is out of sight on the left. The Lancashire & Yorkshire's Railway between Hindley and Wigan Wallgate runs across the picture and beyond the overbridge Central Wagon Works can be seen. The Moss Hall Colliery railway in the foreground connected with the Lancashire & Yorkshire Railway at Ince station. *W.S.Garth.*

ROSE BRIDGE COLLIERY

Rose Bridge Colliery has its beginnings in the 1830s and was situated north of Manchester Road, Ince. In the early years all its produce went out via the Leeds-Liverpool Canal. A connection with the Springs Branch, just north of Belle Green Lane crossing, is thought to have been made in 1858 when new shafts were being sunk. When the plans for the Lancshire Union Railway first appear in 1864 the Company's owners, Case & Morris, opposed the plans but were persuaded to withdraw their objections on the basis that a link would be put in to the Lancashire Union line by the London & North Western who would transport their coal to Widnes, Runcorn and Garston for 1s 2d per ton. In the event, this link was never constructed but the London & North Western hauled their coals over the Springs Branch for the rate agreed previously.

The company were trading as Rose Bridge & Douglas Bank Collieries from 1875 and only posessed one small 0-4-0 saddel tank named *INCE*, much too small for main-line use.

The pits at Rose Bridge were acquired by Thomas & William Latham in 1894 who, as stated previously, were working their own trains from Rose Bridge to the Manchester Road crossing at Ince. It seems, however, that the tolls for use of the Springs Branch by the Latham Brothers were not paid after 1909 on the advice of their solicitor who claimed that use of the Springs Branch by private engines was free of tolls as per Section 96 of the North Union Act of 1834. Outstanding debts due to the London & North Western were not persued. In the event, both of the Latham Brothers died between November 1910 and November 1911, and Rose Bridge and East Cannel Pits closed.

Plate 166. The Hindley Turnpike Road, referred to in the text, is more commonly known today as the A577 (Manchester Road, Ince). This view of the level crossing dates from 26th July 1956 showing the offices of Central Wagon Co. alongside. The line was singled beyond Manchester Road in 1943. An interesting clerestory roofed coach lurks in the company's yard. *B.R.*

Plate 167. Our second view of the level crossing at Manchester Road as viewed toward Ince Bar is from the same period. Central wagon Offices are on the left with the ex-London & North Western type '4' signal box, commissioned on 17th August 1883, controlling the crossing, centre of picture behind the lamp post. Note also the traffic free environment of the day. *B.R.*

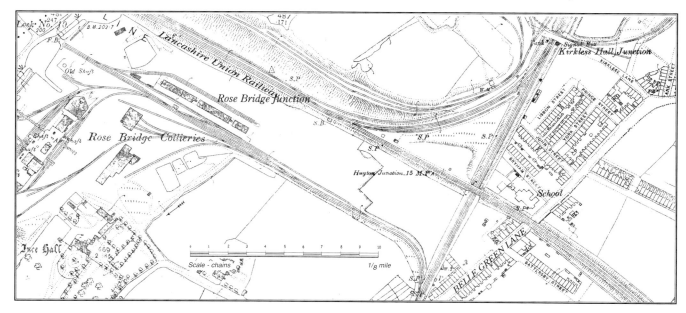

Fig 26. Rose Bridge Colliery and its connections with the Springs Branch c1890. Note that the Lancashire Union Railway crosses the Springs Branch in close proximity to the colliery and a proposal to make a connection between the Lancashire Union line and Rose Bridge Colliery was rejected. Length of curve - Rose Bridge Junction to Kirkless Hall Junction = 389 yards.

Plate 168. Belle Green Lane crossing and the former London & North Western signal cabin are seen on 26th July 1956 as viewed in the 'Down' direction toward Kirkless. In the left background the former Lancashire Union Railway's overbridge crosses the New Springs line, and just off centre, crosses Belle Green Lane. The Rose Bridge Colliery connection forked off to the left just beyond the gates. The signal cabin here open in August 1884 and had 14 working levers. *B.R.*

Plate 169. A second view at Belle Green Lane crossing on the same day. North of Belle Green Lane, sidings were installed c1943/4 for use by U.S. Forces, a nearby building being used for storage of equipment. *B.R.*

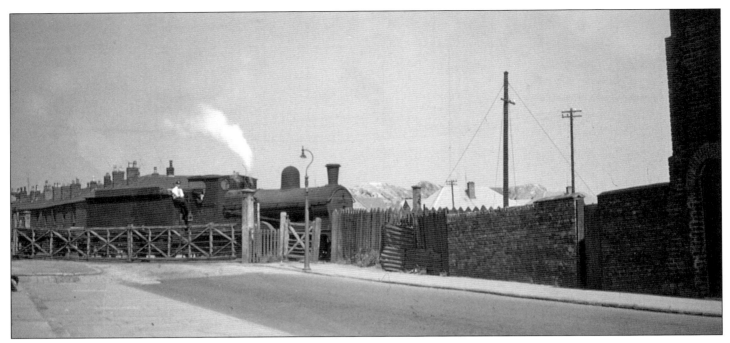

Plate 170. This photograph at Belle Green Lane is taken between 1952 and 1958, after the arrival of the Class 'J10s' at Springs Branch from Lower Ince, but before the track was cut back to Manchester Road, Ince in 1958. The 'J10' No.65156, is heading towards Kirkless Works with at least one low sided wagon in tow. *Harold Hunt.*

Plate 171. The view North-East towards Kirkless dates from 1953. The bridge in view is Kirkless Lane and the photographer is standing beneath the Lancashire Union overbridge seen in the far left of *Plate 168.* Just in front of Kirkless Lane bridge, alongside the lifted Up line, had been Kirkless Hall Signal Box and opposite, Kirkless Hall Junction came in from Rose Bridge Junction *see Fig 27.* This curve had closed c1938. However, it was to re-open on 13th May 1958 in order to give access to Kirkless Engine Shed by colliery locomotives until 15th May 1965. This section of the Springs Branch from Manchester Road Crossing to Kirkless Hall Junction was closed in 1958, having been singled in 1943. *Harold Hunt.*

KIRKLESS

Ralph Thickness, one of the promoters of the Wigan Branch Railway, had acquired an interest in collieries at Kirkless from about 1810, where cannel mining had been in evidence from the mid-eighteenth century. Further pits were sunk by Thickness to seams at shallow depth and these pits and colliery tramways are shown on the deposited plans for the Wigan Branch Railway's Springs Branch of 1829. It is therefore presumed that these tramways date from the late eighteenth and early nineteenth centurys. When the Springs Branch was constructed these tramways were to cross it on the level.

Mining leases for deeper seams in the same area were granted to the Kirkless Hall Coal Company in 1845 and two new pits were sunk between the Leeds-Liverpool Canal and the Springs Branch, connected to the latter by standard gauge sidings. However, Ralph Thickness continued to work the shallower seams at Kirkless until his death in 1854.

In 1792, the Lancaster Canal Company obtained an Act to construct a canal from Kendal to Westhoughton (east of Wigan). However, the canal was built only as far as Kirkless. In 1816 the Leeds-Liverpool Canal made a connection here at what became known as Top Lock.

Fig 27. Again, the 1829 line plan of the Springs Branch, showing its close proximity to the Lancaster Canal at its northern end. There are three tramroads in the vicinity at this period, two south of the Lancaster Canal running to wharves on the Leeds - Liverpool Canal, one of which, belonging to Ralph Thickness, has a distinct 'junction' midway along its length, and a very short tramroad to the Lancaster Canal midway along the section as shown here. It is apparent, however, when comparing this plan with the later mid 1840s Ordnance Survey, *(see Fig 28 page 152)* that the line of the Springs Branch was altered in view of the obstruction posed by the Lancaster Canal extension of 1835. Its eventual path will pass to the right of the tramway 'junction' from that as shown here following a much straighter course north of Belle Green Lane, thus moving the railway east, away from the Leeds - Liverpool Canal, and the point at which it changes direction by 90⁰ moved north to maintain an easier crossing over the Lancaster Canal. This, in turn, also gave a greater distance from the bank of the canal to the railway, which in itself was fortunate for those industries which would later arrive on the scene and set up heavy industry, a feature of the Kirkless area for decades.

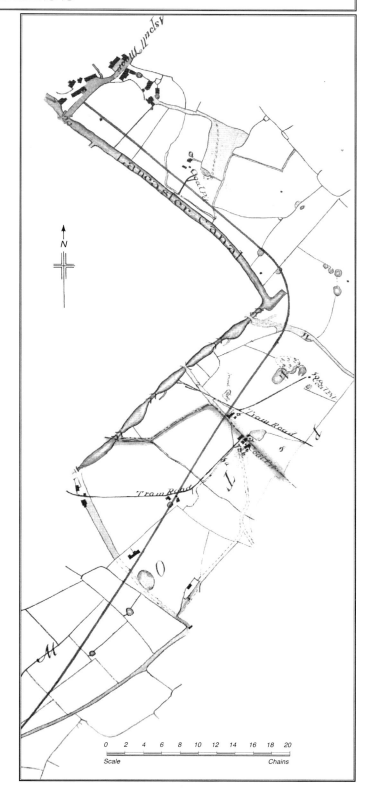

Negotiations also took place between the Lancaster Canal Co. and the Duke of Bridgewater for a link canal to run from Westhoughton to the Duke's canal at Worsley. This proposal was successfully opposed in 1794 by Henrietta Maria Atherton, of Atherton Hall, over whose estate the canal would be cut. In the event, the Duke built his own canal from Worsley to Leigh, opening in 1799. The Leeds-Liverpool would eventually meet this end-on at Leigh by construction of a branch from their canal at Wigan, this the Leeds- Liverpool Canal, Leigh Branch, opening in 1820.

In 1835, the Lancaster Canal Co. decided to extend their canal by a short distance from Top Lock, mainly to cause inconvenience to the North Union Railway who were now about to commence construction of the Springs Branch and, as a by-product of this act of single mindedness, also causing considerable grief to Ralph Thickness by undermining and then removing part of his tramway and flooding the excavation in February 1836, thus extending the canal by a short distance adjacent to Withington Lane.

Thickness took the canal company to court but lost his case on the grounds that the 1792 Act did not stipulate a time limit on construction and the Lancaster Canal Company were within their rights to carry out this extension.

An examination of the relevant Ordnance Survey seems to indicate that the tramway in question was that at the top end of the Springs Branch where the latter changed course by 90º. The tramway is not shown on the 1829 Springs Branch line plan but is shown on the 1st series Ordnance Survey c1845, which it crossed on the level to terminate at what was the end of the Lancaster Canal before its extension in 1835. It seems reasonable to conclude, therefore, that this tramway was constructed between 1829 and 1835, and thus fell foul of the Lancaster Canal Company's devious scheme.

Ralph Thickness also had other mines which the Springs Branch was to cross at Kirkless. These date from the 1820s, served by a loading wharf on the Leeds-Liverpool Canal between locks 2 and 3.

After the death of Ralph Thickness in 1854, the tramway concerned in the court case, and the mines it served, were worked by one William Barton and a short standard gauge siding was constructed alongside the Springs Branch allowing transhipment from the narrow gauge tramway. In the 1870s the pits were taken over firstly by J. Parry in 1873, then by R. Parry in 1876.

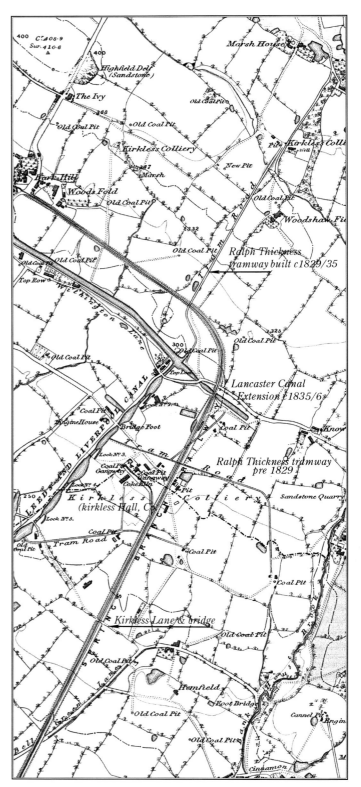

Fig 28. Tramways at Kirkless c1845 and the beginings of the Kirkless Hall Coal Company's operations between the Springs Branch and the Leeds-Liverpool Canal. Kirkless Lane bridge is indicated and is seen in *Plate171*.

An agreement between R. Parry and the London & North Western Traffic Committee of March 1877 authorised a connection with this siding and the Springs Branch. It is presumed that the colliery tramway had been converted to standard gauge by this period and the level crossing to the Lancaster Canal lifted, as it is not shown on the second Ordnance Survey of the 1880s. *(See **Fig 31** Page 160).*

Following the death of R. Parry, the surviving partner, a Mr Poulson, continued to trade as R. Parry & Company until 1886 when he sold out to the Kirkless Colliery Company Limited. The new owners lasted about ten years and despite some reorganisation the pits were no longer proffitable and ceased working in 1896. The following year the firm's former sidings alongside the Springs Branch were lifted except for those on London & North Western property which were retained.

From the mid 1840s the Kirkless Hall Coal Company began to expand their operations considerably and having already made connections at 1 mile 547yards with the Springs Branch from those mines situated between the branch and the Leeds-Liverpool Canal, now turned their attention to the east side of the branch. In the 1850s a line of standard gauge colliery railway $1/2$ mile in length to California Pit, a new working at Pennington Green north of Hindley, connected with the Springs Branch at 1 mile 1738 yards. Another crossing put in here later at 2 miles 78 yards became the California Crossing/Hindley Sidings of respective appendices. Over the coming years new connections were installed or relocated as traffic or new works demanded.

In 1854, the Kirkless Hall Coal Company had taken over the leases of Hindley Deep Pits and began a process of modernisation of these, constructing a new line of standard gauge railway to replace an earlier tramway. New connections with the Springs Branch, and the Lancashire & Yorkshire Railway west of Hindley Station were provided.

The Company were working their own trains over the main lines by this period and one of their engines, *Vesta*, was involved in at least two accidents, the first at the North Union's Wigan Station in 1850, and the second on the Springs Branch in 1851. Another of their locomotives was in collision with a London bound train at Springs Branch Junction in January 1854. A further accident involved a Kirkless Hall Company engine colliding with a Lancashire & Yorkshire train at Castleton a month later.

In 1858 the Kirkless Hall Coal Company had decided to become involved in iron making and changed its name to the Kirkless Hall Iron & Coal Company. They had considerable quantities of small coals for which there was little demand, but useful as good quality coke. In the late nineteenth - early twentieth centurys, small coals were also sent to Kirkless from collieries in the Westleigh coalfield - Priestners and Parsonage, the latter sunk in 1914. From Westleigh, colliery engines worked these trains along the colliery railway to Daisy Hill, onto the Lancashire & Yorkshire line, and via Hindley No.2 Junction, gained access towards Kirkless. As no deposits of iron ore existed locally this had to be transported by rail from Furness in North Lancashire.

The ironworks as constructed, lay between the Springs Branch and the Leeds-Liverpool Canal and by 1860 four blast furnaces were in operation with connections at 1 mile 418 yards and 1 mile 464 yards, both on the western side of the Springs Branch.

Trains between Kirkless and Rylands Sidings seem to have started about 1860, after the Kirkless Hall Coal & Iron Co. had taken over collieries at Standish. Five return trips per day are shown in the July 1861 W.T.T. between Hindley, Lancashire & Yorkshire Junction, and Rylands Sidings, so evidently theses trains were using the recently constructed colliery railway as mentioned above to work via the junction at Hindley to reach Wigan. By using the Hindley Junction, the Kirkless Hall Coal & Iron Co. also ran their trains to Bolton and Bury.

A later working over the Lancashire & Yorkshire lines began about 1870 when the Hewlett Pits at Hart Common were opened. These pits were situated in a triangle of land between the Lancashire & Yorkshire's Crow's Nest - Lostock Junction route and the later 1888 Crow's Nest - Atherton route.

A light engine ran every day from Kirkless engine shed over the line to Hindley Junction, then main line via Hindley Station, to shunt at the colliery sidings and returning by the same route in the evening. This practice continued until the Hewlett Pits closed in December 1930.

In 1865 the Kirkless Hall Coal & Iron Company amalgamated with the collieries of the Earl of Balcarres, the collieries of the Standish & Shevington Coal & Cannel Company, and A. Hewletts collieries at Broomfield & Langtree, to become the Wigan Coal & Iron Company Ltd, formed on 2nd December 1865. This company was, arguably, the most dominant in its field in South Lancashire and would continue to be so for the next 60 or so years. Included in its portfolio were those collieries of the Westleigh coalfield formerly the property of the Kirkless Hall Coal Company,

At Kirkless, with the expansion of the ironworks and its associated industries, a network of industrial railways made further connections with the North Union, Lancashire & Yorkshire and Lancashire Union Railways.

A new four-road engine shed to hold twelve engines was constructed at Kirkless, connecting with the Springs Branch on its eastern side at 1 mile 466 yards, together with with workshops for locomotive servicing, general repairs and construction of locomotives. It is a well known fact that the London & North Western Design Office at Crewe provided the necessary information to Mr C.M.Percy of Kirkless Hall Coal Company in 1864 allowing, with some modification for industrial use, construction of a number of 0-6-0 Saddle Tank engines with 14in cylinders, the first of which *Bessumer,* emerged from Kirkless Works in 1865.

Another four engines of the same design followed, three built at Kirkless in 1866/7, and one, *Achilles*, by the contractor Hudswell, Clarke & Rodgers in 1880. An upgrading of the design with 16in cylinders and a longer wheelbase, the first of which was *Vesta* appeared in 1868, and in total ten engines were so built, three by outside contractors. The last was *Wantage,* which emerged from Kirkless Works in 1898. One of this batch, *Kirkless,* was built at Nasmyth-Wilsons at Patricroft.

This was not quite the end of locomotive construction at Kirkless, for, in 1900, a modified 16'in cylinder design was produced, the last one *Siemens*, appeared in 1912. It is of some credit to the design and construction of all of the Kirkless locomotives that a number were in service for over eighty years with the Wigan Coal & Iron Company and their successors the Wigan Coal Corporation and the National Coal Board.

Further expansion at Kirkless occurred from about 1870 onwards and with the advent of the Lancashire Union Railway, additional connections made at Round House Junction and, Rose Bridge Junction - Kirkless Hall Junction on the Springs Branch. Steel Manufacturing began at Kirkless in 1888, so that by this period the area between the Lancashire Union's lines and the Lancaster Canal was a maize of industry served by numerous sidings and mainline connections.

In 1902 modernisation of the coking plant at Kirkless took place and at the same time a tarmacadam plant and a concrete paving flag works opened using waste materials from the iron and steel works. In the 1920s a fertilizer plant was in operation using blast furnace slag. Traffic for this plant was worked over the Springs Branch by Wigan Coal & Iron Company locomotives but departures went out via Rose Bridge Junction.

Plate 172. Ex-Wigan Coal & Iron Company locomotive *Wantage* undergoing overhaul at Kirkless Works on 17th June 1958. If the photograph is any sort of yardstick, all concerned seem to be doing a fine job on a locomotive which has already seen 60 years of service.
The late Cyril Golding.

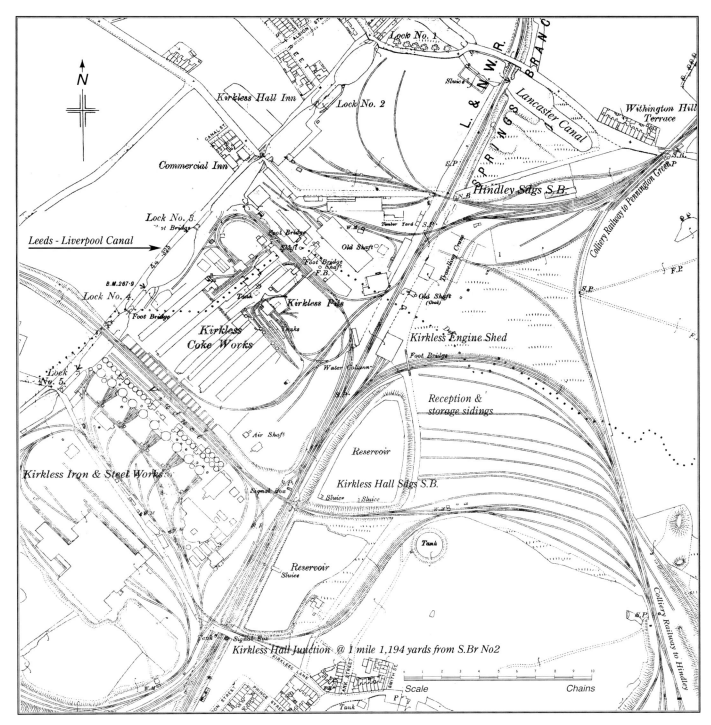

Fig 29. Expansions in the Kirkless area up to the late 1880s have taken up all the land between the Leeds - Liverpool Canal and the Springs Branch, and also an equal amount on the east side. Further developments and improvements would take place here in the early years of the twentieth century followed by a rapid decline in the 1920s and 30s. High level lines constructed by the Wigan Coal & Iron Company from their Iron & Steel and Coke Works, crossed over the Springs Branch near Kirkless Hall Junction and Kirkless Hall Sidings Signal Box respectively. The waste products from these plants was then easily transportable to the tips and the storage sidings on the east side. Here a tarmacadam plant and a flag works would later be built. Note also Hindley Sidings (California Sidings) cabin at approximately 2 miles 78 yards.

Plate 173. Former Wigan Coal & Iron Co. 0-6-0ST *Lindsay,* built in 1887, is seen at Kirkless Works on 13th May 1962 having just been overhauled. This is the only engine of the former Wigan Coal & Iron Co. to find its way into preservation.
Peter Eckersley.

During W.W.I there were over twenty light engine movements and about a dozen trains per day running between Kirkless Works and California (Hindley) Sidings, working over the Springs Branch for some 300 yards. Again, authorisation for these workings came from the North Union Act of 1834, Section 95, relating to the Kirkless Hall Coal & Iron Co. As from 1st January 1871, the London & North Western had made a charge of £100 per annum for such use of its tracks.

The 1920s were a period of rapid decline for the Wigan Coal & Iron Company as the recession took a severe toll of its industries. " A land fit for heroes" certainly did not materialise in the years after W.W.I. as thousands of able bodied men all over the country found themselves out of work with little or no financial support, many on the absolute poverty line.

Most of the collieries served by the Springs Branch had closed by the mid 1920s and the Government urged upon the mining industry the need for change as a countermeasure to offset the severe effects of recession. Therefore, using the powers of the Mining Acts passed in 1926, the Wigan Coal & Iron Company amalgamated with the Pearson & Knowles Coal & Iron Co. Ltd., the Moss Hall Coal Co. Ltd., and the Wigan Junction Colliery Co. Ltd., to form the Wigan Coal Corporation, effective from 1st August 1930. The collieries of Cross Tetley & Co. were taken over by the Wigan Coal Corporation in 1934 after the former had gone into receivership.

The various steel and iron concerns of the above were incorporated into the Lancashire Steel Corporation at Irlam and the Dallam Forge at Warrington. Kirkless iron and steel works were closed.

The route from Hindley Sidings to the former Lancashire & Yorkshire lines at Hindley No.2 Junction was out of use by the late 1930s but re-opened about 1942. Henry Parkinson, late of Leigh, who was an engine driver at Parsonage Colliery, remembered working light engines from the latter, via the connections at Daisy Hill and Hindley No.2, to Kirkless Works c1949/50, just before the colliery lines to Hindley Sidings were finally closed.

With the closure of these colliery lines it was now only possible to access Kirkless Works for engine overhauls via the Springs Branch. A conductor was necessary, and often, a brake van and pilot engine for the colliery locomotive. This continued until the Rose Bridge Junction - Kirkless Hall Junction curve reopened in 1958.

The workshops at Kirkless had remained in use as the main repair facility for the Wigan Coal Corporation until taken over at nationalisation of the mines in 1947, becoming the property of the National Coal Board. Locomotives continued to be repaired and overhauled here until 1962.

It was not unknown at this period for ex-Wigan Coal & Iron locomotives to find their way to areas outside their normal circuit, as at Bedford (Wood End) Colliery, Leigh, or Chanters Colliery at Atherton, which were designated as Wigan area collieries at the time.

Some of the buildings at Kirkless were used as storage for machinery until the late 1980s.

Plate 174. Also seen in Kirkless works on 2nd March 1957 undergoing overhaul is *Crawford*. As built in 1883, *Crawford* had shorter saddle tanks which terminated behind the chimney. However, in later years it would recieve the tanks from *Emperor* as seen here and ran in this form until scrapped at Gibfield Colliery, Atherton in 1964.
The late Cyril Golding.

Plate 175. The end is nigh for ex-Wigan Coal & Iron locomotive *Kirkless,* seen in the process of being dismantled at Kirkless Works on 16th September 1956. Some of the parts will be used on other locomotives. This engine was one of a batch of ten built with 16in cylinders and longer wheelbase, this particular example by Nasmyth-Wilson at Patricroft in 1892. *The late Cyril Golding.*

Plate 176. The *Kirkless Hall Inn* is situated south of lock No.2 and is viewed here in the 1950s. In the background is Woodshaw Tip the dumping ground for spoil from Marsh House Washery and from other parts of the Kirkless complex, at first by locomotive haulage but later by ariel roadways. It remains to this day as a testament to the industry of yesteryear and looks much better for all the greenery that grows upon it. *Harold Hunt.*

Plate 177. One of the 'Austerity' built 0-6-0STs *Fred*, is seen at Kirkless on 11th November 1961 looking in pretty poor shape, yet it was, apparently, sent to Walkden Yard on the 21st inst. from whence it returned to Bickershaw Colliery in May 1962. *Peter Eckersley.*

ALBION IRONWORKS

The Albion Ironworks was situated in the narrow strip of land between the Lancaster Canal and the Springs Branch, where the latter changed direction to a north-westerly course on land previously used by Ralph Thickness' tramway to the Lancaster Canal. Siding connections to Albion Ironworks were provided in October 1870.

By 1881, the company was in some financial difficulty and the works put up for sale. It was eventually acquired by the Wigan Coal & Iron Co., and leased to Monks Hall & Co Ltd. of Warrington. The lease was given up in 1923 but the works continued to be operated by the Wigan Coal & Iron Co until closure in 1930. It may have been the intention to re-open the works at a later date, or let it out for another purpose as the sidings agreements for the works were not terminated with the L.M.S. until 1933.

THE EARL OF CRAWFORD AND BALCARRES RAILWAYS

The Earl of Crawford & Balcarres had constructed a tramway from his Wall Hey and Moor pits at Haigh and Aspull to a wharf on the Lancaster Canal in the 1830s to a gauge of 4ft. When the springs branch opened in 1838 a standard gauge railway was built from this tramway at the canal end to make an end-on connection with the Springs Branch at Bark Hill. In 1839/40 the tramway to Wall Hey and Moor pits was converted to standard gauge, and the line being steeply graded, was probably rope worked, loaded wagons descending hauling the empties up the incline. The short connecting spur to the Springs branch was worked by North Union locomotives which then transported the traffic along the Springs Branch to the main line and beyond. However, in 1842, the Earl entered into an agreement with Richard Blundell of Amberswood Colliery* to haul up to 100 tons of the Earl's coal per day to Liverpool. As has already been noted, Richard Blundell was working his own trains to Liverpool from Amberswood via Parkside Junction.

By 1844, the Earl had at least four of his own locomotives, built at his Haigh Foundry. In 1843 he had applied to the Liverpool & Manchester Railway to work his own trains over their line in the same fashion as did Blundell. The request was rejected in September 1843 by Mr Booth, the Secretary, on the grounds that the Liverpool & Manchester did not want any more private engines working over their route. This probably arose out of concern at the number of accidents involving privately worked colliery trains.

An extension of the Earl's private railway meant that by the 1850s he was already working his own traffic to Preston, Salford and Rochdale via Grimeford Siding on the Waterhouse Branch where it made a connection with the Bolton-Preston route. In the late 1850s the colliery railway would be extended in the opposite direction over the Lancaster Canal to the Lindsay Pits which were then being sunk. Further extensions occurred in 1862 to Haigh Foundry and Brock Mill Forge.

In 1865, the Earl amalgamated with the Kirkless Hall Coal & Iron Company and other Wigan colliery concerns to become a part of the Wigan Coal & Iron Company. Two of the latters Kirkless built locomotives were named after the Earl, namely, *Crawford*, built in 1883 and *Balcarres* built in 1892. A previous locomotive also named *Balcarres* had collided with a Lancaster & Preston train in Fishergate Tunnel at Preston in 1849. Another accident at Bolton Trinity Street in October 1851 involved the Earl's locomotive *Countess* whilst hauling a train from his Haigh Colliery.

* See Page 70 Chapter I

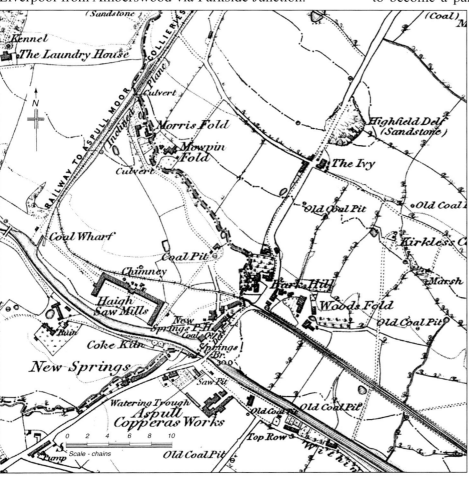

Fig 30. The Earl of Crawford & Balcarres' private railway to his Wall Hey and Moor pits at Aspull is shown linked to the Springs Branch end-on in the 1840s survey. It is likely that although the line to Aspull was built as narrow gauge it had been converted to standard gauge by 1840. In the 1850s and 60s extensions to his railway would take it over the Lancaster Canal to serve his Lindsay Pits and Haigh Foundry.

The Springs Branch terminates on the eastern side of Bark Hill. On the second Ordnance Survey it is given as "Springs Branch Junction".

Plate 178. Top Lock in October 2007 as taken from Withington Lane Bridge looking North-West. The Leeds Liverpool Canal comes in from the left to meet, what was, the Lancaster Canal, and it is from this junction of the two canals that the extension eastwards was built in 1835 to thwart the North Union's Springs Branch, forcing them to build an over-bridge. The canal extension, which extends along Withington Lane for another 300 yards or so, is almost totally choked with weeds. It is ironic that in later years the canals became the property of the very railway it intended to impede. *Author.*

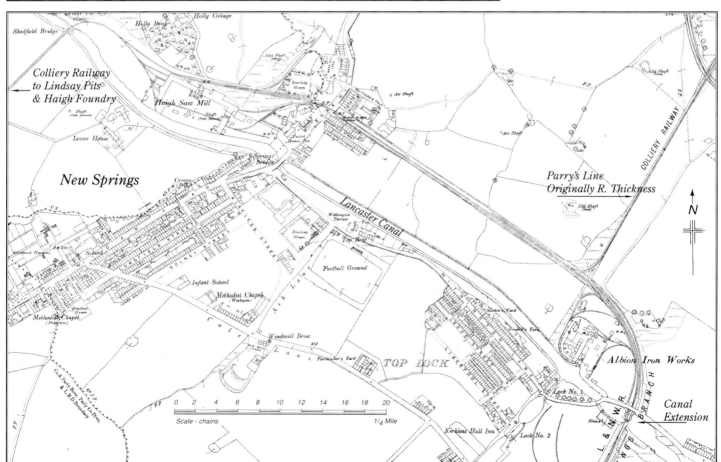

Fig 31. End of the Springs Branch c1892. By the time the second series Ordnance Survey was carried out the Earl of Crawford & Balcarres' railway to Aspull via the inclined plane at the canal end had been abandoned and the Moor pits at Aspull reached over further extensions of the Wigan Coal & Iron railway system. However, as can be seen, additional lines have been laid from the end of the Springs Branch to Haigh Saw Mills, and also to Haigh Foundry and Lindsay Pit south of the Lancaster Canal, which could also be reached from the Lancashire Union's line.

Plate 179. Coal barge Margaret Waddington is seen tied up on the Lancaster Canal c1953. Alongside, right, the line of fencing marks the then still visible trackbed of the Springs Branch as it ran North-West to meet the Earl of Balcarres Railways at Bark Hill, seen in the background, crossing the Whelley - Aspull road on the level. *Harold Hunt.*

The peaceful, almost idyllic setting at Top Lock today belies its industrial past. Within the space of one-hundred and fifty years, major industries, their transport needs and services, which often had acrimonious relationships between the providers, arrived, flourished and departed the scene, mostly without trace. There is little physical evidence of the iron & steel works, the coking plants and the mining activity which once occupied the banks of the Leeds - Liverpool and Lancaster Canals, complete with the maize of railway lines which spread in all directions rather like the tentacles of some voracious creature of the deep.

The London & North Western Railway leased the northern section of the Lancaster Canal in 1864, whilst the southern section was leased to the Leeds - Liverpool Canal Co. However, in 1885 the London & North Western purchased the Lancaster Canal in its entirety and if ever there was a case of chickens coming home to roost - this is it, for the thorn in the side of the Wigan Branch Railway and its successors over the years, the forebearer of bad relationships, had surely been the Lancaster Canal Company.

We are, though, fortunate that the canal system hereabouts has survived to provide the recreational needs of the twenty-first century. Perhaps it was, after all, only a matter of time before the Springs Branch would succumb to piecemeal closure. The depression of the 1920s had an immediate effect and the top end of the route from Kirkless Workshops to New Springs closed in the mid-1930s. North of Manchester Road, Ince, the line was singled in 1943, closing between Belle Green Lane and Kirkless Hall Junction in 1958. At this date Kirkless Hall Junction to Rose Bridge Junction, having closed in 1938, was re-opened allowing colliery (now N.C.B.) locomotives access to Kirkless Workshops as by this period access had only been possible by way of Springs Branch Junction. Manchester Road to Belle Green Lane is believed to have closed in April 1958. The reduction of mining operations in the Wigan area led to the closure of Kirkless workshops, and the remaining section of the Springs Branch here between Kirkless Hall Junction and the workshops closed on 15th May 1965.

For a while the remainder of the route from Springs Branch Junction to Central Wagon was kept busy. New freight vehicles were being constructed as thousands of older wagons were scrapped and, as the 1960s arrived, an increasing number of steam locomotives would traverse these ancient metals to make their final journey, and their ultimate appointment with the cutters torch.

Rail traffic to Central wagon ceased in 1973 and more track was lifted. The double line of rails from Springs Branch towards Ince was retained for MGR Wagon storage. However, in 1992, the closure of Bickershaw and Parkside Collieries would make this need redundant. In late 1998, this track, northward from Bridge Hole, was also lifted and the New Springs Branch, the gestation period of which caused the Wigan Branch Railway such a financial headache, was no more.

SPRINGS BRANCH SHEDS

The early history of an engine shed at Springs Branch may well be lost with the passing of time. However, The SLS Journal of January 1959 reported that an engine shed is said to have been built by the Liverpool & Manchester Railway at Wigan in 1832. As the Liverpool & Manchester were working the passenger trains over the Wigan Branch Railway from its opening in September 1832, this may well be the case, and if so, was, in all probability, situated at the Wigan Branch Railway terminus at Chapel Lane.

The North Union Secretary was, on 7th September 1838, authorised "to remove the engine shed at Wigan to a more convenient location to the south side of the (Leeds-Liverpool) canal."

The Wigan Branch Railway crossed the Leeds-Liverpool Canal at Westwood, south of Chapel Lane and the date of the instruction, coming when it did, suggests that some difficulties were foreseen in continuing to use the Wigan engine shed at its present location once the line to Preston opened the following month. The grid reference given in the SLS report - SD584051 corresponds to where Do-it-All is today - the site of Chapel Lane Station in 1832!

A shed at Springs Branch is reported to have opened prior to 1847, being brick built with two through roads. Other facilities included a turntable which was located in the triangle between the New Springs lines and the main running lines and this is shown on the line plan of the North Union Railway c1864. On 9th December 1858, a shed was ordered to be built at Springs Branch and in the following May Ramsbottom, Chief Locomotive Superintendent, complained to the operating department of the London & North Western Railway that "no provision is made for a *large* engine turntable without which the shed cannot be used with advantage by the goods engines."

Plate 180. Springs Branch Sheds, a view dating from about 1912, well stocked with London & North Western locomotives of the era. The Ramsbottom, or No.1 shed of 1869 with the hipped roof on the left and the Webb northlight pattern No.2 shed of 1882 on the right. No.2 shed would later receive modified smoke vents. There seems to be evidence of track alterations in progress on the extreme right with what appears to be a pit road being infilled with rubble, alongside of which are wagons pushed under the coaling stage on a raised platform.
A.G.Ellis.

Plate 181. This 1965 view at Springs Branch shows the complete change in appearance of the two sheds. On the left, No1 shed as rebuilt by the L.M.S. in 1946, and No.2 shed on the right which was re-roofed by BR in 1955. No.2 shed had only another twelve months to go before it was demolished to make way for the new diesel depot, whilst No.1 shed would last for almost another twenty years before it would succumb to the demolition gang. Some of the track looks in dire need of attention. *Brian Magilton.*

Evidently, little or no progress was made, for in October1864, Ramsbottom again referred to the inadequate facilities existing at Springs Branch and that additional shed accommodation was urgently required, similar, he said "to the one now in progress at Ordsall Lane" which was to hold 24 engines. The present shed, it seemed, held only six engines when at least sixteen were in steam daily. The London & North Western Committee recommended enlargement at Springs Branch and a 'temporary' wooden structure was erected in 1864 located south of the two road (pre-1847) shed, which, complained Ramsbottom, "was worthless." In June 1867, the Committee, perhaps having a guilt complex about their inaction, made a more rational decision and presented a plan, under the stewardship of a Mr. Worthington, for a new steam shed on or near the site of the 'temporary' shed at Springs Branch, estimated at £12,500. Alterations to this scheme at the planning stage were to include a 64,000 gallon water tank.

By late 1868 the shed was still not complete and Ramsbottom recommended that the shed, planned to hold 24 locomotives "should be for forty now." He goes on to say that "The original brick engine shed holds six (engines) only, is inconvenient and the present wooden shed is useless. There are twenty-five engines in steam and often ten extra at Springs Branch." The Committee Members were unhappy about the extra £4,500 that would be required to enlarge the shed being built and referred the proposal to a 'Special Committee' who gave their approval to the extra works required in December 1868.

The new shed, in the traditional building style with hipped roofs, opened the following year and had eight roads and, as it transpired, inadequate ventilation which was later rectified. This shed became known as 'No.1' shed and the two earlier sheds mentioned previously were demolished..

However, some ten years later the allocation of locomotives at Springs Branch had increased to eighty or more as a result of the rapidly expanding coal trade. Therefore, in 1881, Locomotive Superintendent Webb sought approval for another new shed to be built alongside the 1869 building, apparently with more immediate success than his predecessor Ramsbottom had done. This second shed, also with eight roads, became known as No.2 shed and was built in the northlight style, much favoured in the use of industrial buildings, opening in 1882.

By the 1920s there were more than 100 locomotives at Springs Branch. In 1935 the shed was coded 10A under L.M.S. auspices, the principal shed in the area which included Patricroft, Plodder Lane, Preston and Sutton Oak (Lower Ince was added as a sub-shed in early B.R. days) The L.M.S set about a process of modernisation at many installations on the system and in 1935 new coal and ash plants were installed at Springs Branch, and in 1937, a new 100,000 gallon water tank.

C1945/6, the LMS rebuilt No.1 shed in the reinforced concrete column-brick panel style, a pattern of construction much favoured by the LMS in the 1930s & 1940s when many sheds on the system were reconstructed in the drive for efficiency. During the rebuilding, No.1 shed was reduced to a six road, dead-end shed.

In 1955, B.R. re-roofed No.2 shed in the corrugated sheeting style, as were many more sheds now under 'New Management.' By the early 1950s, the allocation of engines at Springs Branch had dropped to around 65, not only reflecting the downturn in the Wigan coalfield as the coal seams became exhausted, but also the improvement in locomotives as more modern designs came on-stream and the older, less standard engines, went to the scrap yard.

Some of the ex-L&NW 'G2' 0-8-0s remained alongside the newer L.M.S Class '5s' together with the odd ex-L&Y 2Fs/3Fs and 2-6-4Ts for local passenger diagrams. On the nearby, former Great Central route to Wigan, the shed at Lower Ince had closed in 1952 and its allocation of 'J10s' were transferred to Springs Branch.

As from February 1958, Springs Branch was coded 8F, as a sub-shed of Edge Hill, with the number of locomotives here remaining around the mid-sixty mark through to the 1960s. With the demise of steam traction in favour of diesel and electric motive power numbers began to be reduced and/or replaced by diesel engines of the 'New Order.'

In 1966 work began on the construction of a new diesel shed on the site of No.2 shed and this opened the following year. It had been realised that an old steam shed was not the best place to service and maintain this new technology which was altogether more fussy in terms of its working parts.

Plate 182. 'Patriot' Class 4-6-0 No.5514 *Holyhead,* is seen inside Springs Branch No.2 shed about 1935 having some smokebox and middle cylinder attention.
Authors Collection.

Springs Branch shed closed to steam as from 4th December 1967 and a new chapter in the operation of the railway had begun. No.1 shed remained in use for stabling and storage, eventually to be demolished in 1984.

In the 1970s, the majority of workings from Springs Branch were coal trains- from Parkside Colliery, a new mine only opened in the early 1960s, transported directly to Fiddlers Ferry Power Station, and from Howe Bridge West Sidings on the remaining section of the route via Tyldesley to Manchester. (Most of this route had closed on 3rd May 1969). This traffic was, at this period, still worked to Howe Bridge by colliery locomotive from Parsonage Colliery, Leigh, for onward transport by BR to Ince Moss Sidings. This trip would also include a pick-up at Abram North Sidings where coal from Bickershaw Colliery had been shunted by N.C.B. locomotives. Coal trains from Golborne Colliery also continued to be worked by Springs Branch locomotives at this time.

However, in August 1974, underground connections between Parsonage, Bickershaw and Golborne Collieries resulted in all rail-borne coal being wound at Bickershaw and worked up to Abram North Sidings by N.C.B engines. Another change occurred in 1984 when a new, 300 tonne, automatic discharge bunker was erected at Bickershaw and the whole of the remaining branch line from Springs Branch, Manchester Lines Junction to Bickershaw Colliery was re-laid using welded rail, together with some easing of the gradient at Bickershaw. These works were completed during the 1984/5 miners strike at a cost of some £8,000,000.

As a result of these changes, twelve pairs of Class '20' locomotives were allocated to Springs Branch Depot for direct colliery to power station workings, each train topped and tailed hauling 45 'Merry-go-Round' hopper wagons, all bound for Fiddlers Ferry, between Warrington and Widnes. The leading pair of '20s' would detach at Springs Branch, two locomotives regarded as being sufficient on the easier gradients to work out and back. As the new Class '60s' came on stream in the early 1990s these could also be seen on the MGR workings from Bickershaw.

The death knell for Springs Branch Depot came in 1992

Plate 183. The L.M.S. designed 2-6-4 tank engines were first introduced in 1927 under the auspices of Henry Fowler as parallel boilered engines. In 1934 W.A.Stanier continued the development with a taper boiler, three cylinder design for L.T.&S., and a two cylinder version in 1935 for the L.M.S. It is the latter type, represented by No.42465, which is seen outside No.2 shed at Springs Branch about 1954.
G. Mellor.

with the closure of Bickershaw, Parkside and Parsonage Collieries, and the loss of coal traffic from these pits. As a result, the depot was downgraded to a permanent way and overhead line maintenance depot, the class '20s' transferred to Warrington Arpley.

With the 'sectorisation' of British Rail the depot had been taken over by Transrail. However, the Privatisation Act of 1993 saw the former BR freight companies sold off, mostly to the American operator, Wisconsin Central. This company set up their U.K.operations as E.W.S - English Welsh & Scottish Railways - and immediately set about identifying the requirement for a new fleet of modern locomotives, the result of which was the purchase of engines from General Motors plant at La Grange in North America. As these engines entered traffic, designated as Class '66s', wholesale withdrawl of existing, ex-B.R. designs began, many of which were well beyond their expected lifespan.

This was somewhat of a reprieve for Springs Branch and although the shed had officially closed on 4th May 1997, the depot was quickly taken over, reopening as a component recovery depot by EWS and a steady stream of withdrawn locomotives began to arrive, many of which were transported by road as the shambolic nature of the Privatisation Act took hold of the railway hierachy.

By late 2005 this work had ceased and it only remained for the shells of cannibalised, gutless locomotives to be removed and these could be seen on a regular basis on low loaders going by road destined for the scrap yard. In 2003 offices at the depot were leased by First Engineering Group and a number of firms continue to occupy the offices at the rear of the former diesel shed, including EWS. Some P.W. activities are still carried out, notably the seasonal weed-killing trains which operate with Class '37' locomotives and in recent months a small number of locomotives have been repaired here.

Plate 184. A rare visitor in the shape of 'K.3/2' No.61867, seen alongside No.2 shed in the mid 1950s. First introduced in 1920 as 'K3/1s', the 'K3/2s' were a Gresley development of the former, built to L.N.E.R loading gauge. In later years the Great Northern Railway built locomotives were modified to 'K3/2' class. *G. Mellor.*

Plate 186. (opposite). Stanier Class '5' No.45140 has drawn its train out of Springs Branch Yard and is reversing from Cromptons Sidings onto the Up Goods Loop with the breakdown crane and a couple of antiquated former London & North Western coaches which serve as mess and tool vans. The L.M.S. replacement of Ramsbottoms shed is on the left with the re-roofed No.2 shed on the right. *Dr. J.G.Blears.*

Plate 185. The mainstay of the London & North Western Railway's freight engines was the Class 'G2/2A' 0-8-0 first introduced in 1912, of which many were rebuilt in later years with G2 boilers and Belpaire firebox as in this example. No.48942 is seen outside Springs Branch No.1 shed about 1954.
G. Mellor.

Plate 187. The 'J10s' were transferred to Springs Branch from Lower Ince shed following the latters closure in March 1952, shortly after the withdrawl of the St. Helens-Lowton-St.-Marys passenger service which ceased on 1st March. Nos.65192 & 65197 are seen shortly after arrival at Springs Branch. They would continue to work the early morning workmen's trains to Irlam and general passenger trains to Manchester Central for a few years until replaced by ex-LMS designs.
Eddie Bellass.

Plate 188. A typical atmospheric scene at Springs Branch shed with 'Patriot' Class 4-6-0 No.45503 *The Royal Leicestershire Regiment* coaled and watered ready for its next turn of duty, stands alongside one of the ex-Great Central's 'JI0' Class No.65159.
G. Mellor.

Plate 189. Coronation 'Pacific' No.46257 *City of Salford* at Springs branch on 11th September 1964 carrying the 'Britain's Railway Queen' headboard. This was one of two locomotives, and the final member of its class, to receive modifications by Ivatt before entering service in 1947, the other being No.46256 *Sir William A. Stanier.* They were easily identifiable by the shortened cab sides and different trailing bogies; but who, I wonder, was 'Britain's Railway Queen'?
Tony Oldfield.

Plate 190. A number of the Metrovic built Type '2' Co-Bos were shedded at Spring Branch but they were not one of BRs most successful designs. Having been introduced in 1958, by September 1969 all the class had been withdrawn for scrap. This picture was taken earlier that year. *Gerry Bent.*

Plate 191. On 22nd June 1969 a pair of Type '2' diesels Nos.D5208 & D5201 are seen outside No.1 shed in B.R. green livery with the half front yellow warning panel which had been introduced by B.R. in the mid-1960s, amidst concerns over high-speed, almost silent running by modern locomotives, after the introduction of electric services between Manchester and Crewe. Later, this yellow panel would be applied to both ends in full on all diesel and electric locomotives. *Gerry Bent.*

Plates 192 & 193. The arrival on shed at Springs Branch in 1954 of new Class '9F' No.92010 has obvoiusly struck a chord with the shed staff and the engine gets the 'once-over' from all concerned. Crowding into the cab, left, are Percy Gaskell in the drivers seat, with Duncan Whillaby, Jack Draper and Isworth Mitchell standing, whilst Alan Edwards sits on the footplate. *G. Mellor.*

In the view below, Brian Carter leans on the buffers whilst apprentice fitter Kevin Lewis sits on the frame.

The '9Fs' were undoubtedly fine locomotives and unquestionably the best of the BR Standard designs, equally at home on freight, the express remit for their being, or passenger services whenever the need required. This particular engine was one of a batch of five, Nos. 92010/14, built at Crewe between September - October 1954 and allocated to the Eastern Region. The locomotive is coupled to a BR1F tender holding 5,625 gallons of water and 7 tons of coal which weighed in at 55.5 tons when fully laden and, together with the engine, weighed in at approximately141 tons. Many of the class had very short working lives due to the mistaken policy that removal of the steam locomotive from BR would be the panacea to cure all their problems. As a result, locomotives with years of productive service left in them were unmercifully scrapped.
G.Mellor.

Plate 194. Stanier 'Mogul' No.42954 is seen at Springs Branch in 1964. These 2-6-0 engines were introduced in 1933, a total of only 40 being built.

John Sloane.

Plate 195. As in many sheds the facilities were often basic and this view of the booking-on point at Springs Branch c1974, no exception. It presents an altogether gloomy insight of the grimy surroundings at these locations which had been built in the previous century. The three nearest camera left to right are- Tommy Mullin, Vince Monks and Fred Rutter. The mess room on the left was, originally, the General Office. *Tom Sutch.*

Plate 196. The jackshaft drive 0-6-0 shunters, first introduced by the LMS in 1939, were built at Derby Works. No.12020 is seen at Springs Branch on 8th July 1967.

John Sloane.

Plate 197. A pair of Stanier Class '5s' Nos.45415 and 44918 nearest camera, are seen near the coaling plant in 1963. *Brian Magilton.*

Plate 198. 'Royal Scot' Class No.46168 *The Girl Guide* is seen in the shed yard in May 1964, having worked the R.O.F. works train earlier in the day.

Tom Sutch.

Plate 199. One of the BR Standard, Caprotti fitted Class '5s' No. 73131 is seen near the new diesel shed in 1968, alongside 'Britannia' No.70011 *Hotspur.*

John Sloane.

Plate 200. One of the Class '2' diesels, D5023, is seen near the coal plant on 5th August 1967. These locomotives were first introduced in 1958, this example being one of the BR/BTH batch. Under the TOPS renumbering scheme they would become Class '24s'. The axles in the foreground tempt a sardonic comment but I'll refrain. *John Sloane.*

Plate 201. Class '8F' No.48675 may have worked its last train when seen in Engine Shed Sidings on 15th February 1968. These fine Stanier designed 2-8-0 freight engines were first introduced in 1935, this particular engine being one of a batch built at Brighton in 1944. A number of the class were sent overseas during W.W.II, particularly to the Middle East, and some survived into the 1980s on the Turkish railway system. Others were lost at sea due to enemy action.
John Sloane.

British Rail held an open day at Springs Branch in August 1970. Amongst the literature issued for the event was a shed plan which shows the existing fuelling point and the proposed new position which eventually came to pass.

All documents courtesy of Alf Yates.

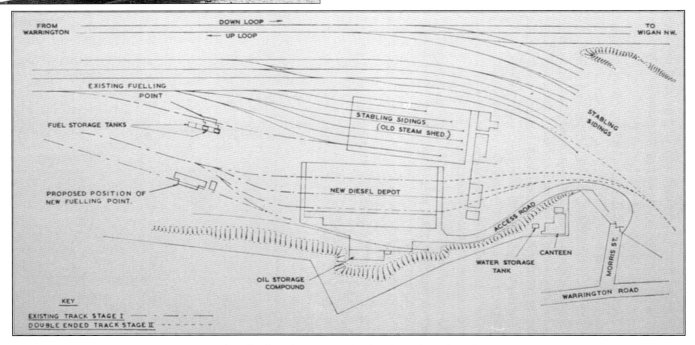

Fig 32. Springs Branch c1970. Note that the line from Crow Orchard Coal Yard, and the junction it makes with the Springs Branch, is still in situ.

Plate 202. In the 1970s Class '50s' were often to be seen on shed at Springs Branch. On 28th November 1975 No.50 041 stands outside the old No.1 shed and if the headcode is anything to go by may have been working an engineers train. *Tom Sutch.*

Plate 203. 'Peak' class locomotives were infrequent visitors to Springs Branch. On 25th November 1978 Class '45' No.45 063 shares the road with a class '40'. *Tom Sutch.*

Plate 204. A panoramic view of Springs Branch sheds taken in June 1975 is obviously on a weekday when few locomotives were on shed. Stabled over on the right is the overhead electric line stock, complete with a cable drum on a lowflat with brake van attached, and to the left of these is the fuelling point. At the far end behind the offices, canteen and stores block, a class '40' lurks. There seems to be a predominance of Class '25' locomotives in the diesel shed, two outside and at least two inside. In the centre are the fuel storage tanks alongside which are yet two more '25s' and an '08' shunter. The LMS re-built No.1 shed plays host to some old surburban coaching stock in the first road, the breakdown crane in the third, another '25' in the fifth and a couple of 16ton wagons in the sixth. Beyond the sheds a rake of MkI coaching stock occupies a road in Brewery Sidings, whilst on Engine Shed Sidings are at least two brake vans, a fuel tank - probably empty, and a Class '20'. Westwood Power Station chimneys stand tall on the left and St. Marys Church, right.

Tom Sutch.

Plate 205. The most recent arrivals at Springs Branch Shed in the 1990s were the BR Class '60s' and a number of these were noted on Merry-go-Round workings to Fiddlers Ferry from Bickershaw Colliery. On 8th November 1995, No.60 058 *John Howard*, comes off shed as the driver makes his way to the opposite cab. There appears to be a fair mixture of locomotives on shed and in the sidings namely Classes '08', '20', '31', '37', '56' & '60'. *Author.*

Plate 206 The BR diesel-mechanical Class '03' 0-6-0 shunters were hardly an outstanding success. All the class were built in 1961, with the exception on Nos. 2370/1, and by 1968 half had gone for scrap, including No.2376 seen here at Springs Branch on 5th August 1967.
John Sloane.

Plate 207. In the 1980s, a number of Class '40s' were given departmental numbering. Former 40 060 is seen in its new guise as No. 97 405 at the fuelling point on 18th August 1985 and, in addition, has its original pre-TOPS No.260 at the opposite end.
Author.

Plate 208. For a time a number of Class '56s' were sheded at Springs Branch. No.56 025, in coal sector livery, manoeuvres towards the shed in the company of No.56 004 on 25th October 1990.
Author.

Plate 209. The occasional A.C.Electric arrived on shed from time to time, usually after failing. On 24th November 1982, Class '86' No.86 325 is seen in the company of Class '47' No.47 489 behind which is Class '40' No. 40 015 inside the shed. *Tom Heavyside.*

Plate 210. The planned introduction of passenger services by A.C.Electrics over the northern sections of the WCML with the Summer Timetable of 1974 necessitated crew training, therefore, Class '87' No.87 013 was duly dispatched to Springs Branch for such purposes, seen in virtually new condition on shed earlier that year. *Tom Sutch.*

Plate 212. (overleaf). ScotRail liveried Class '47' No.47 704 *Dunedin* is seen inside Springs Branch shed on Sunday 28th April 1985, having failed on the morning Liverpool -Glasgow/Edinburgh train. *Author.*

Plate 211. The Class '40s' and '47s' worked the coal trains from Bickershaw for a number of years before the arrival of the Class '20s' en-block, and the new Class '60s' at Springs Branch. On a misty 15th November 1983, No.40 082 departs for Abram North Sidings near Bickershaw with a train of MGR empties after running round on the Goods Loops. In the foreground the mangled track is the result of a derailment of a Bickershaw-Fiddlers Ferry train some months previous. When eventually relaid the overhead equipment would be removed. *See* **Plate 205,** *page 177.* *Author.*

Plates 213 & 214. It's a certainty that not many 'Westerns' made it to Springs Branch. The occasion for D1062s arrival on shed is the forthcoming Liverpool & Manchester 150 celebrations when locomotives from all over the country arrived in the North-West to take part in the Rainhill Cavalcade on three consecutive days, 24th, 25th & 26th May 1980, the Bank Holiday weekend.

The days preceding the celebrations were a joy to behold as locomotives made their way to the stabling point at Bold Colliery Sidings. At every vantage point enthusiasts gathered to see some quite unique survivors of the steam age in addition to more modern traction.

In the above shot, D1062 *Western Courier* is seen arriving at Springs Branch and later, left, being shunted into the diesel shed. The driver is Tommy Crook. *Tom Sutch.*

Plate 215. A graffiti-ridden Class '37' No.37 298 is seen at Springs Branch on 29th October 2005 all ready to be dispatched by road for one last journey and oblivion. Many of these 'last journeys' were to Booth's scrapyard at Rotherham and the approved route being Warrington Road Ince, Liverpool Road - *Bird it'h Hand* -Hindley -A577-Leigh Road, Hindley Green-Wigan Road-Twist Lane Leigh-A579-A580 East Lancs Road-M6 south to Rotherham via the M1. *Alan Hart.*

English Welsh & Scottish Railway used Springs Branch as a component & recovery depot after its closure as an engine shed. Redundant locomotives were either sold off as scrap after any reusable components had been salvaged or, in a small number of cases, sold into preservation. By late 2005 this work had ceased.

Plate 216. A view of the EWS' Component Recovery Depot from across the main running lines on 29th May 1999. Classes '37', '47' & '56' are lined up for attention. Some components stripped from these locomotives would be sent to Crewe for re-use.
Author.

Plate 217. A single Class '73' would arrive at Springs Branch for scrapping, No.73 132, and is seen in the company of a Class '08' shunter and a Class '47' on 4th March 2004.
Alan Hart.

Plate 218. Class '37s' predominate in this line-up at Springs Branch on 14th July 2003. The wheelsets alongside are, presumably, destined for Crewe. *Alan Hart.*

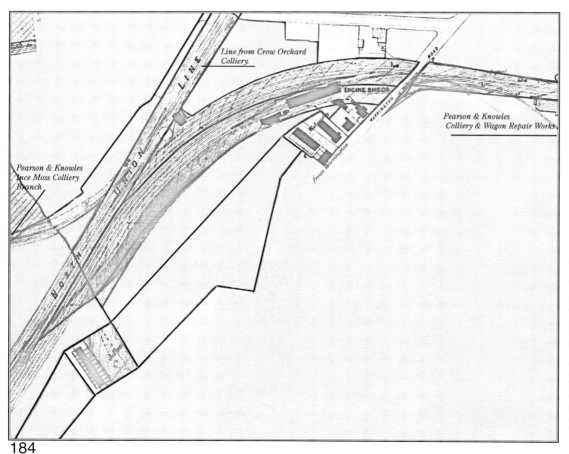

Fig 33. The 1865 line plan of the North Union Railway shows the c1847 shed at the top end of Springs Branch Yard with a water column and coal stage adjacent. The innermost line which gives access to the shed, splits into two through roads, joining again at Bridge Hole and there are already a number of sidings for the stabling of coal traffic. The two outermost lines are those of the Springs Branch itself and east of Warrington Road bridge, the connection to Pearson & Knowles Collieries and Wagon Works. Of further interest is the locomotive turntable situated in the triangle of the Up Main and Down Springs Branch lines. The Crow Orchard Colliery line joins the Up Main here.

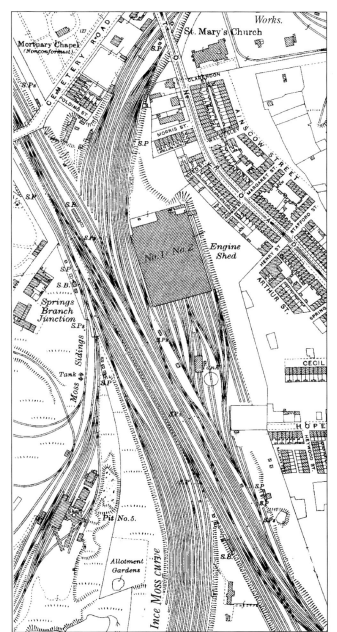

Fig 34. It is rather difficult to visualize that in 1832 a single line of railway passed through the Springs Branch area. This section from an early twentieth century updated Ordnance Survey, is based on that carried out between 1888 and 1892 showing the system of railways at their zenith, a complete transformation occurring in some seventy years or so. Beginning with the opening of the Springs Branch itself in 1838, the main running lines have been quadrupled, an additional pair of goods lines installed and the routes from St. Helens and Manchester make junctions here. There are five stubb end sidings - Brewery Sidings, which run round from Bridge Hole, following the curvature of the Up and Down Springs Branch lines and likewise, Engine Shed Sidings nearest the sheds. The sheds themselves have eight roads per shed. On the left, a series of sidings- Ince Moss and Springs Branch North Sidings are adjacent to the St. Helens route lines. The coaling stage is now sited centrally, south of the sheds with a water tank over.

The first engine shed at Springs Branch, believed to have been constructed about 1847, was sited where Engine Shed Sidings now are, south of Bridge Hole, opposite Morris Street. A second two-road 'temporary' shed was erected in 1864, south of the 1847 shed, both of which were referred to by Ramsbottom, the Chief Locomotive Superintendent at the time as "inadequate".

Between 1880 and 1894, successive track, sidings and junction alterations were carried out at Springs Branch but the plan shown here essentially remained the same until the LMS modernised the shed layout in the 1930s.

Fig 35. The shed plan, below, of Springs Branch dates from the LMS period in the mid-1930s the most noticeable difference being the re-siting of the turntable alongside shed No.2 and the new coaling plant. No.1 shed was reduced to six roads when rebuilt by the LMS c1945/6.

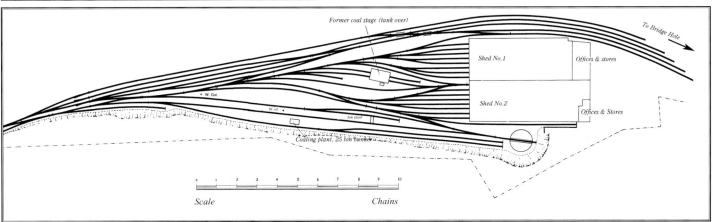

Plate 219. Only one AC Electric was to be cut up at Springs Branch, No.86 603. It is seen in Engine Shed Sidings devoid of its bogies in July 2005.
Alan Hart.

Plate 220. Once the stripping of components from withdrawn locomotives was completed a final journey was undertaken by road for delivery to various scrap metal merchants, this particular example to Booths at Rotherham. Class '37' No. 37 370 is seen near the junction of Wigan Road and Nel Pan Lane, Leigh, on 19th August 2005.
Author.

III. THE PLATT BRIDGE JUNCTION RAILWAY AND, THE BAMFURLONG JUNCTIONS RAILWAY.

The Platt Bridge Junction Railway was authorised by an Act of 16th July 1883 which granted the London & North Western Railway permission to construct a railway 1 mile 7 chains in length from a junction with the North Union at Bamfurlong to meet with the Lancashire Union Railway at Amberswood West Junction, the contract being awarded to J.D.Newell for £12,930 on 13th May 1885. The same act also contained powers for the widening of the North Union Railway between Golborne and Springs Branch, a distance of 4 miles 48 chains. Construction of the latter began in July 1886 and has often been quoted as completed on 29th October 1888. However, this may not have been the case.

The Bamfurlong Junction Railways Act of 8th July 1887, provided for burrowing lines beneath the main running lines, including the re-routing of the Down Platt Bridge line from its original connection on the east side, relocated to the west side, running alongside the new Up and Down goods lines which gave access to Springs Branch Sidings and Sheds, and the Whelley lines at Platt Bridge Junction. The relocated 'Down' Whelley is given as completed by October 1889.

The Ordnance Survey of 1892 for Bamfurlong shows the Up Fast line as incomplete and terminating as a stub end on the south side of the newly constructed underpass bridge and the former Down Whelley connection still in situ which implies work was still in progress at Bamfurlong when the survey was carried out.

Further Acts of 1890 authorised the widening of tracks between Springs Branch and Wigan, this contract awarded to J.Wilson & Sons whose tender of £13,184. 10s was accepted on February 17th 1892, the work being completed in 1894. Construction of Bamfurlong Sorting Sidings, allowed under the same Act, was completed by 1895. An update of the Ordnance Survey issued in 1905 shows Bamfurlong, its Junctions and Sidings in their final form. See *Fig.15*, page 65

Fig 36. The as yet, incompleted arrangements at Bamfurlong c1892 with the Platt Bridge Junction's Down connection still in situ although the new Down line appears to have been completed. The new 'Up Fast' line terminates near the underpass bridge and it may be that it was not in operation until the widening between Springs Branch and Wigan, and alterations to junctions for the Springs Branch itself were completed.

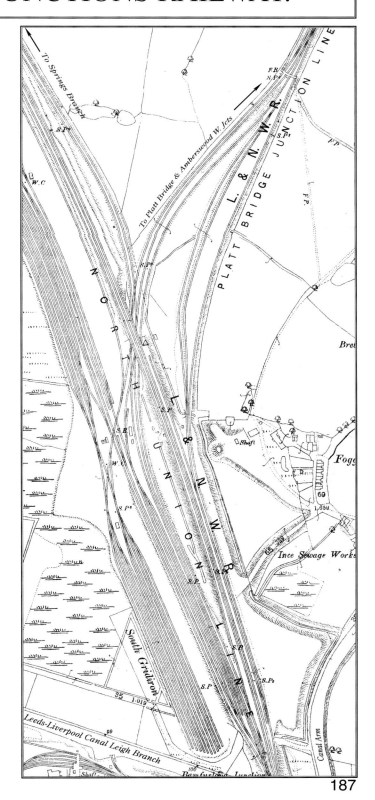

Plate 221. The scene at Bamfurlong Junction on 10th May 1966 as Stanier Class '5' No.45442 on a through freight with at least four fitted vans, slowly makes its way up the gradient from Bamfurlong Sorting Sidings to join the WCML Up Slow line junction which was sited on the bridge carrying the railway over the Leeds-Liverpool Canal (Leigh Branch). Over on the right the curvature of the fence line indicates the location of a long redundant arm of the canal which was used by the Strangeways Hall Coal Co. This was accessed by their private railway from mines at Strangeways Hall, Amberswood. First constructed as a tramway between 1848 & 1850, it was later reconstructed as a standard gauge, locomotive worked branch and a connection made with the North Union Railway north of the canal. See **Fig 14** *page 63*. *W.D.Cooper.*

The original Platt Bridge Junction 'Down' line became a siding and connected with the 'Up' line near Bamfurlong 'Flying Junction' and together with an adjacent siding became known as Bamfurlong Screens. In W.W.II additional sidings were built here to cope with war traffic.

Banking engines were stabled at Bamfurlong Sidings to assist heavy freight trains routed over the Whelley line to Standish Junction. Some freights for East Lancashire would reverse at De Trafford Junction allowing the banker to be detached, the train thence proceeding via Hindley No.2 Junction and Lancashire & Yorkshire metals to reach its destination.

The same 1883 Act that authorised The Platt Bridge Junction Railway, also provided powers for the Hindley Junctions Railway from the London & North Western's Tyldesley-Wigan route at Bickershaw, to meet with the Lancashire Union at Amberswood East, running alongside and completely independent of the Manchester, Sheffield & Lincolnshire Railways Wigan Junction Railway which ran from Glazebrook to Strangeways at Amberswood, and at this period was being extended to its first terminus at Darlington St., Wigan.

In the event, the Act as passed obliged the London & North Western to make connections with the Wigan Junction Railway south of Hindley & Platt Bridge Station, at Strangeways East Junction, with a south to east curve in the Up direction and a burrowing junction under the Tyldesley route in the Down direction. The North Western were allowed running powers over the

Plate 222. A pair of Class '20s' Nos.20 008/135 proceed towards Springs Branch from Bamfurlong Junction and are about to pass beneath the WCML on 9th April 1986. *Author.*

Plate 223. Bamfurlong South Sidings are in the background as 'Jubilee' Class 4-6-0 No.45629 *Straits Settlements* is seen on the Down Through Road to Platt Bridge from Bamfurlong Junction in the Winter of 1965/6. Right is Bamfurlong Sorting Sidings cabin. The locomotive seems to have a few steam leaks which at this late stage in the steam era would not be rectified.

Tom Sutch.

Wigan Junction lines and by way of Strangeways West - Amberswood West Junctions, completed by the Manchester, Sheffield & Lincolnshire in 1882, and Strangeways West - Amberswood East, make connection with the Lancashire Union Railway. The works of the Hindley Junctions Railway were completed in 1886 and, it is believed, Strangeways West - Amberswood East Junctions were completed in the same year.

In 1955 The Co-operative Wholesale Society built a glass works alongside the Platt Bridge lines and a sidings connection with the Up Through line controlled by a ground frame, the agreement with British Railways dating from 19th April 1958.

Through lines between Bamfurlong Junction and Platt Bridge were closed on 2nd October 1972 and the pointwork at Bamfurlong (Flying) Junction taken out on 15th January 1973. Part of the Up line was retained to serve the glass works siding and a new ground frame gave a connection off the Whelley Goods lines near the site of the former Platt Bridge Junction. In 1976, the Goods lines were also taken out except for a short section off the Up line between the glass works ground frame and the junction with the low level goods lines from Springs Branch. Trains now had to make a double reversal to reach the works, traffic consisting of sand deliveries from Oakmere in Staffordshire. These ceased in July 1986 and the sidings agreement terminated.

Plate 224. Ex London & North Western Class 'G2/G2A' No.49154, has an unidentified ex-W.D. 2-8-0 in tow on the Down Goods Loop about 1960 on the approach to Springs Branch from Bamfurlong Junction, the W.D. having suffered some damage to its cab roof. Over on the left a train makes its way along the Platt Bridge Junction route towards Amberswood West Junction. *Jim Carter.*

Plate 225. B.R.Standard 'Pacific' No.70054, formerly *Dornoch Firth*, is seen heading toward Bamfurlong on the Up Goods Loop in July 1966. Again, Fir Tree House cabin is visible, centre top, and, just in view under the Lancashire Union line bridge, a glimpse of Bamfurlong North End Sidings and West Loop.

This particular Britannia was the last member of the final batch to be built, Nos.70045-70054. These were paired with the high sided, BR1D, tender which increased coal capacity to 9 tons, and water to 4,725 gallons. They were also equipped with coal a pusher which is seen to advantage in this going away shot.

Alex Mann.

Plate 226. Stanier Class '5' No.44684, on the approach to 'Flying Junction' and seen on the Platt Bridge Up line, has worked over the Whelley route with a through freight in the Winter of 1965/6. The cabin in the distance, far left, is Ince Moss. *Tom Sutch.*

Plate 227. 'Royal Scot' Class No.46157 *The Royal Artilleryman* working an unfitted freight, is signalled for the Up Slow at Bamfurlong Junction and is about to pass under bridge No.28 which carries the W.C.M.L. over the low level lines at Bamfurlong. The train has worked south over the Whelley route from Standish Junction on 27th September 1962. On the left are the goods lines from Springs Branch and in the background are the Tyldesley lines from Springs Branch, Manchester Lines Junction to Eccles. *W.D.Cooper.*

Plate 228. '8F' No. 48193 approaches 'Flying Junction' after working an engineers train over the Whelley route in 1965. Hardly flying though, more like plodding.
Tom Sutch.

Plate 229. The late, low autumn sunshine casts a shadow on ex-WD No.90173, acting as banker, seen waiting for its next job on the Up Loop line from Platt Bridge. Behind the locomotive is the Down Through Road and on the nearside, the Down Loop. There are at least two sidings at Bamfurlong Screens, far right, containing wagons. In the background the 1950s built CWS glassworks, like the railways that served it, now demolished. Platt Bridge Junction S.B. is visible on the embankment of the Tyldesley route in the distance.
Tom Sutch.

Plate 230. A grimy, unidentified BR Standard Class '4' 4-6-0 approaches the low level junctions with the Platt Bridge route from Springs Branch in late 1965 and has an ensemble consisting of an ex-LMS jackshaft drive, 0-6-0 shunter, a 16 ton all steel wagon containing the shunters coupling rods and a guards van. En-route to Crewe, perhaps - a fine place for sick engines! *Tom Sutch.*

Plate 231. Having worked south over Whelley, '4F' 0-6-0 No.44347 approaches on the Up Loop line from Platt Bridge with a freight for Bamfurlong Sidings in 1965. W.D. No.90173 follows on behind, not banking, just saving the block. *Tom Sutch.*

Plate 232. Class 4F 0-6-0 No.44121 banks another member of the same class towards Platt Bridge with a northbound coal train from Bamfurlong Sidings, this a Springs Branch turn. The train is photographed from the signal gantry seen in *Plate 231* located between the Up Loop and Down Through Road. *Jim Carter.*

Plate 233. Class '31' No.31 305 has arrived at the CWS sidings with a load of sand, trip worked from Springs Branch on 2nd May 1986. With the closure of the Platt Bridge lines as a through route a section of the Up line was retained, access to the CWS worked by a ground frame. The sand for the works came from Oakmere until July 1986, at which time the sidings agreement was terminated. The works was demolished in the 1990s. *Tom Sutch.*

Plate 234. Stanier Class '5' No.45195 passes under the Wigan-Tyldesley-Eccles route at Platt Bridge with a freight train from Bamfurlong Sidings in August 1964. Platt Bridge Signal Cabin was unusual in that it controlled traffic on two separate routes, the Tyldseley lines alongside which it was sited, including Platt Bridge Junction for connections with the former Lancashire Union Railway at Fir Tree House Junction, and the Platt Bridge Junction - Amberswood route at lower level. *Eddie Bellass.*

Situated between the Up Whelley line and the Up & Down Goods lines at Platt Bridge were Bamfurlong Screens, which originally had been constructed as sidings for coal dispatches. Here, southbound freights were often re-marshalled and again, particularly during W.W.II., it was a very busy location. Bamfurlong-Bescot, and Bamfurlong-Hinksey Yard trains departed from here. The latter train included whisky vans worked from Scotland via Carlisle for the armed forces, often a target for theft. Other trains worked to Southampton and a number of destinations in southern England.

Driver Alan Grundy recalls coaching stock being stored in the sidings in the 1950s and the request would come through from a particular station, or from control, that stock was needed to form a relief excursion as 150-200 passengers were stranded and not able to board the scheduled train because of unanticipated demand. An engine and crew would be dispatched from Springs Branch to Bamfurlong Screens to collect the stock required as quickly as possible.

Wouldn't happen today of course, no spare stock, and one only has to witness the gross overcrowding on the daily peak services from Wigan Wallgate to Manchester, and return, to realise what a state the railways are in!

Plate 236. (overleaf). Having departed Bamfurlong Sidings, Class '5' No.45290 approaches the A573 Warrington Road bridge with a mixed freight, and as there is a brakevan next the engine, this may well be a Bamfurlong-Halliwell working which will reverse at De Trafford Junction. 25th May 1968.
Dr.J.Gordon Blears.

Plate 235. A 'W.D'.2-8-0 is engaged on banking duty at Platt Bridge and is about to pass under Warrington Road (A573) assisting a heavy freight working Whelley to Standish Junction. These engines, built for service abroad during W.W.II., long outlasted their intended working life and being a utility design, all the more remarkable in doing so. Generally in unkempt appearance as seen here, many lasted until the final years of steam operation on Britain's railways.
Eddie Bellass.

Plate 237. The photographer does a quick an about turn for the going-away shot of 45290 heading towards Amberswood West Junction. Spring View cricket ground is right, and the Lancashire Union's route from Ince Moss to Amberswood runs across the picture.
Dr J. Gordon Blears.

Plate 238. Having worked south over the Whelley route, a BR Type '2' diesel No.5281, (no D prefix) passes Spring View with coal empties, probably from Lostock Hall on 24th September 1971.
Ian Isherwood.

Plate 239. A Down freight hauled by 'WD' No..90423 and banked by Hughes 'Crab' 2-6-0 No.42705 approaches Amberswood West Junction with another freight from Bamfurlong Sidings as an unidentified working heads towards Platt Bridge on the Up line on 2nd September 1964.
Jim Peden Collection, (B.Barlow.)

Plate 240. At Amberswood West Junction the Platt Bridge Junction Railway met the Lancashire Union Railway's metals. In this view on 24th April 1965, Stanier '8F' No.48494 is almost hidden by the shadow if its own towering exhaust working from Bamfurlong Sidings with a heavy van train. *Dr J.Gordon Blears.*

TIMED TRAINS FROM BAMFURLONG SIDINGS C1938

6.00a.m.	No.22 Trip to Balshaw Lane.
6.10a.m.	No.1 Trip to Golborne.
6.30a.m.	No.7 Trip to Bickershaw.
6.40a.m.	Bamfurlong to Southport.
6.45a.m.	Bamfurlong to Wigan L&Y. Wyre Dock engine.
7.00a.m.	Bamfurlong to L.N.E.R.
7.11a.m.	Bamfurlong to Astley Green.
8.00a.m.	No.16 Trip to Garswood.
8.40a.m.	No.38 Trip to Bolton L&Y. Salop engine.
9.00a.m.	No.32 to Springs Branch.
9.15a.m.	No.11 to Springs Branch.
9.30a.m.	Bamfurlong - Aintree.
9.40a.m.	Camden. Carnforth. Dallam. Edge Hill Tranship. Carlisle. No.1 Trip to Mains Colliery.
12.16p.m.	Bamfurlong - Crewe.
12.30p.m.	Green's Siding (Tyldesley). No.9 Trip to Bickershaw. No.26 Trip to Balshaw Lane. Carnforth. Warrington. No.1 Trip to Golborne. Bickershaw. Bullfield. Patricroft Engine. No.33 Trip to Wigan L&Y. No.36 Trip to Springs Branch. No.9 Trip Bickershaw to Springs Branch. No.34 Trip North End to Springs Branch.
7.10p.m.	Dallam. Southport. Warrington. No.2 Trip to Long Lane Colliery. No.37 to Springs Branch. Bury. Crewe engine to shed. No.3 Trip to Long Lane. Accrington engine to shed. Wigan L&Y. Clock Face,(St.Helens)
10.10p.m.	Engine to shed. Crewe.
11.50p.m.	Preston. Engine to shed.
1.30a.m.	Bamfurlong to Colne. Bamfurlong to Bolton.
2.25a.m.	Birkenhead. Carlisle.
2.35a.m.	Blackburn.
3.00a.m.	No.11 Trip Bamfurlong to Springs Branch. No. 7a Wigan L&Y. No.34 Wigan N.W. Carnforth. Crewe. Farrington. Crewe.
4.10a.m.	Bamfurlong- Salop.
5.00a.m.	Bamfurlong - Wigan.
5.05a.m.	Bamfurlong - Aintree. Bickershaw. Preston.
5.30a.m.	Bamfurlong - Birkenhead.
5.50a.m.	Bamfurlong - Carlisle.
6.00a.m.	Bamfurlong - Edge Hill. Carlisle. No.34 Trip to Ince Moss.

Workings between North End - South End, trip engines to/from Springs Branch or other light engine movements are not shown.

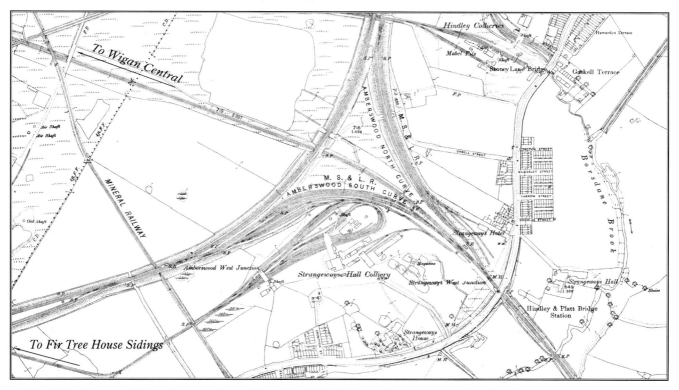

Fig 37. Amberswood Junctions are shown from the 1892 Ordnance Survey. Note that the Wigan Junction Railway passes beneath the Amberswood West - East Junction curve. The colliery line from Strangeways Hall continues out of survey, bottom left, to Fir Tree House Sidings; it was this route by which Henry Blundell, and later, Crompton & Shawcross were able to work their traffic to exit at Cromptons Sidings on the Tyldesley route near Manchester Lines Junction.

BIBILOGRAPHY

A Lancashire Triangle Part One. D.J.Sweeney. Triangle Publishing 1996
A Lancashire Triangle Part Two. D.J.Sweeney. Triangle Publishing 1997
Articles, Railway & Travel Monthly. S.M.Phillip. 1912.
Article, Crewe to Wigan. G.Hayes. Railway Magazine 1971.
British Locomotives of the 20th Century. O.S.Nock Guild Publishing 1985.
Crewe to Carlisle. Brian Reed. Ian Allan Publishing. 1969.
LMS Engine Sheds Vol 1. C.Hawkins & G.Reeves. Wild Swan Publishing 1981.
Railways of Great Britain & Ireland. Francis Whishaw. 1842.
The Industrial Railways of the Wigan Coalfield Part One.. C.H.A.Townley, F.D.Smith & J.A.Peden.
             Runpast Publishing 1991.
The Industrial Railways of the Wigan Coalfield Part Two. C.H.A.Townley, F.D.Smith & J.A.Peden.
             Runpast Publishing 1992.
Wigan Coal & Iron. D.Anderson & A.A.France. Smiths Books (Wigan) 1994.
W.T.T. information of colliery workings over Springs Branch supplied by the late Harry Townley

ABBREVIATIONS

A.R.P.	Air Raid Precaution
B.R.	British Railways
B.T.H.	British Thompson - Houston
C.WT.	Hundredweight
D.M.U.	Diesel Multiple Unit
E.W.S.	English Welsh & Scottish (Railways)
G.W.	Great Western (Railway)
L.M.S.	London, Midland & Scottish (Railway)
L.N.E.R.	London North Eastern Railway
L&N.W.	London & North Western (Railway)
LT&S	London Tilbury & Southend (Railway)
L&Y.	Lancashire & Yorkshire (Railway)
M.G.R.	Merry-Go-Round
M.R.	Midland Railway
M.o.S.	Ministry of Supply
M.S&L.	Manchester, Shefield & Lincolnshire (Railway)
N.C.B.	National Coal Board
P.B.J.R.	Platt Bridge Junction Railway
P.W.	Permanent Way
R.E.C.	Railway Executive Committee
R.O.F.	Royal Ordnance Factory
S.B.	Signal Box
S.LS.	Stephenson Locomotive Society
U.K.	United Kingdom
U.S.	United States
W.C.M.L.	West Coast Main Line
W.D.	War Department
W.T.T.	Working Time Table

Imperial to Metric conversion

1in (inch) = 25.4mm.
1ft (foot) = 304.8mm.
1yd (yard) = .944metres. (22yds = 1 chain).
1statute mile = 1.6093 kilometers.
1acre* (4,870 sq yds) = .4097 hectares.
20 cwt (hundredweight) = 1ton = 1.016 tonnes.

*English land measure was standardized in the reign of Edward I 1272-1307, although local variations occurred in Ireland, Scotland and some English counties, as in the Cheshire Acre at 10,240 sq yds. See page 126.